GEORGE BERNARD SHAW

The Devil's Disciple

Major Barbara

Saint Joan

DENT: LONDON
EVERYMAN'S LIBRARY
DUTTON: NEW YORK

All rights reserved
Made in Great Britain
at the
Aldine Press · Letchworth · Herts
for
J. M. DENT & SONS LTD
Aldine House · Bedford Street · London
First included in Everyman's Library 1966

NO. *109*

PRINCIPAL PLAYS OF BERNARD SHAW
(Dates are those of first performances)

Widowers' Houses, 1892
Arms and the Man, 1894
Candida, 1895
The Man of Destiny, 1897
The Devil's Disciple, 1897
You never can tell, 1899
Caesar and Cleopatra, 1899
Captain Brassbound's Conversion, 1900
John Bull's Other Island, 1904
Man and Superman, 1905
Major Barbara, 1905
The Doctor's Dilemma, 1906
Androcles and the Lion, 1913
Pygmalion, 1913 (Berlin), 1914 (London)
Heartbreak House, 1921
Back to Methuselah, 1923
Saint Joan, 1923 (New York), 1924 (London)
The Apple Cart, 1929

CONTENTS

THE DEVIL'S DISCIPLE   1

MAJOR BARBARA   63

SAINT JOAN   143

THE DEVIL'S DISCIPLE

NOTE

There never was a play more certain to be written than *The Devil's Disciple* at the end of the nineteenth century. The age was visibly poignant with it.

The well-fed Englishman, though he lives and dies a schoolboy, cannot play. He cannot even play cricket or football: he has to work at them. . . . To him playing means playing the fool. He can hunt and shoot and travel and fight: he can, when special holiday festivity is suggested to him, eat and drink, dice and drab, smoke and lounge. But play he cannot. The moment you make his theatre a place of amusement instead of a place of edification, you make it, not a real playhouse, but a place of excitement for the sportsman and the sensualist.

Dick Dudgeon, the devil's disciple, is a Puritan of the Puritans. He is brought up in a household where the Puritan religion has died, and become, in its confusion, an excuse for his mother's master passion of hatred in all its phases of cruelty and envy. . . In such a home the young Puritan finds himself starved of religion, which is the most clamorous need of his nature. With all his mother's indomitable selfishness, but with Pity instead of Hatred as his master passion, he pities the devil; takes his side; and champions him, like a true Covenanter, against the world. He thus becomes, like all genuinely religious men, a reprobate and an outcast.

Not one of my critics but has seen a hundred times in his paper how some policeman or fireman or nursemaid has received a medal or the compliments of a magistrate, or perhaps a public funeral, for risking his or her life to save another's. Has he ever seen it added that the saved was the husband of the woman the saver loved, or was that woman herself, or was even known to the saver as much as by sight? Never. When we want to read of the deeds that are done for love, whither do we turn? To the murder column; and there we are rarely disappointed.

G. B. S.

THE DEVIL'S DISCIPLE

ACT I

At the most wretched hour between a black night and a wintry morning in the year 1777, Mrs Dudgeon, of New Hampshire, is sitting up in the kitchen and general dwelling room of her farm house on the outskirts of the town of Websterbridge. She is not a prepossessing woman. No woman looks her best after sitting up all night; and Mrs Dudgeon's face, even at its best, is grimly trenched by the channels into which the barren forms and observances of a dead Puritanism can pen a bitter temper and a fierce pride. She is an elderly matron who has worked hard and got nothing by it except dominion and detestation in her sordid home, and an unquestioned reputation for piety and respectability among her neighbors, to whom drink and debauchery are still so much more tempting than religion and rectitude, that they conceive goodness simply as self-denial. This conception is easily extended to others-denial, and finally generalized as covering anything disagreeable. So Mrs Dudgeon, being exceedingly disagreeable, is held to be exceedingly good. Short of flat felony, she enjoys complete licence except for amiable weakness of any sort, and is consequently, without knowing it, the most licentious woman in the parish on the strength of never having broken the seventh commandment or missed a Sunday at the Presbyterian church.

The year 1777 is the one in which the passions roused by the breaking-off of the American colonies from England, more by their own weight than by their own will, boiled up to shooting point, the shooting being idealized to the English mind as suppression of rebellion and maintenance of British dominion, and to the American as defence of liberty, resistance to tyranny, and self-sacrifice on the altar of the Rights of Man. Into the merits of these idealizations it is not here necessary to inquire; suffice it to say, without prejudice, that they have convinced both Americans and English that the most highminded course for them to pursue is to kill as many of one another as possible, and that military operations to that end are in full swing, morally supported by confident requests from the clergy of both sides for the blessing of God on their arms.

Under such circumstances many other women besides this disagreeable Mrs Dudgeon find themselves sitting up all night waiting for news. Like her, too, they fall asleep towards morning at the risk of nodding themselves into the kitchen fire. Mrs Dudgeon sleeps with a shawl over her head, and her feet on a broad fender of iron laths, the step of the domestic altar of the fireplace, with its huge hobs and boiler, and its hinged arm above the smoky mantelshelf for roasting. The plain kitchen table is opposite the fire, at her elbow, with a candle on it in a tin sconce. Her chair, like all the others in the room, is uncushioned and unpainted; but as it has a round railed back and a seat conventionally moulded to the sitter's curves, it is comparatively a chair of state. The room has three doors, one on the same side as the fireplace, near the corner, leading to the best bedroom; one, at the opposite end of the opposite wall, leading to the scullery and wash-house; and the housedoor, with its latch, heavy lock, and clumsy wooden bar, in the front wall, between the window in its middle and the corner next the bedroom door. Between the door and the window a rack of pegs suggests to the deductive observer that the men of the house are all away, as there are no coats or hats on them. On the other side of the window the clock hangs on a nail, with its white wooden dial, black iron weights, and brass pendulum. Between the clock and the corner, a big cupboard, locked, stands on a dwarf dresser full of common crockery.

On the side opposite the fireplace, between the door and the corner, a shame-lessly ugly black horsehair sofa stands against the wall. An inspection of its stridulous surface shews that Mrs Dudgeon is not alone. A girl of sixteen or seventeen has fallen asleep on it. She is a wild, timid looking creature with black hair and tanned skin. Her frock, a scanty garment, is rent, weather-stained, berrystained, and by no means scrupulously clean. It hangs on her with a freedom which, taken with her brown legs and bare feet, suggests no great stock of underclothing.

Suddenly there comes a tapping at the door, not loud enough to wake the sleepers. Then knocking, which disturbs Mrs Dudgeon a little. Finally the latch is tried, whereupon she springs up at once.

MRS DUDGEON. [*Threateningly.*] Well, why dont you open the door? [*She sees that the girl is asleep, and immediately raises a clamor of heartfelt vexation.*] Well, dear, dear me! Now this is—— [*Shaking her.*] Wake up, wake up: do you hear?

THE GIRL. [*Sitting up.*] What is it?

MRS DUDGEON. Wake up; and be ashamed of yourself, you unfeeling sinful girl, falling asleep like that, and your father hardly cold in his grave.

THE GIRL. [*Half asleep still.*] I didnt mean to. I dropped off——

MRS DUDGEON. [*Cutting her short.*] Oh yes, youve plenty of excuses, I daresay. Dropped off! [*Fiercely, as the knocking recommences.*] Why dont you get up and let your uncle in—after me waiting up all night for him! [*She pushes her rudely off the sofa.*] There: I'll open the door: much good you are to wait up. Go and mend that fire a bit.

[*The girl, cowed and wretched, goes to the fire and puts a log on. Mrs Dudgeon unbars the door and opens it, letting into the stuffy kitchen a little of the freshness and a great deal of the chill of the dawn, also her second son Christy, a fattish, stupid, fair-haired roundfaced man of about twenty-two, muffled in a plaid shawl and grey overcoat. He hurries, shivering, to the fire, leaving Mrs Dudgeon to shut the door.*

CHRISTY. [*At the fire.*] F—f—f! But it is cold. [*Seeing the girl, and staring lumpishly at her.*] Why, who are you?

THE GIRL. [*Shyly.*] Essie.

MRS DUDGEON. Oh, you may well ask. [*To Essie.*] Go to your room, child, and lie down, since you havnt feeling enough to keep you awake. Your history isnt fit for your own ears to hear.

ESSIE. I——

MRS DUDGEON. [*Peremptorily.*] Dont answer me, Miss; but shew your obedience by doing what I tell you. [*Essie, almost in tears, crosses the room to the door near the sofa.*] And dont forget your prayers. [*Essie goes out.*] She'd have gone to bed last night just as if nothing had happened if I'd let her.

CHRISTY. [*Phlegmatically.*] Well, she cant be expected to feel Uncle Peter's death like one of the family.

MRS DUDGEON. What are you talking about, child? Isnt she his daughter—the punishment of his wickedness and shame?

[*She assaults her chair by sitting down.*

CHRISTY. [*Staring.*] Uncle Peter's daughter!

MRS DUDGEON. Why else should she be here? D' ye think Ive not had enough trouble and care put upon me bringing up my own girls, let alone you and your good-for-nothing brother, without having your uncle's bastards——

CHRISTY. [*Interrupting her with an apprehensive glance at the door by which Essie went out.*] Sh! She may hear you.

MRS DUDGEON. [*Raising her voice.*] Let her hear me. People who fear God dont fear to give the devil's work its right name. [*Christy, soullessly indifferent to the strife of Good and Evil, stares at the fire, warming himself.*] Well, how long are you going to stare there like a stuck pig? What news have you for me?

CHRISTY. [*Taking off his hat and shawl and going to the rack to hang them up.*] The minister is to break the news to you. He'll be here presently.

MRS DUDGEON. Break what news?

CHRISTY. [*Standing on tiptoe, from boyish habit, to hang his hat up, though he is quite tall enough to reach the peg, and speaking with callous placidity, considering the nature of the announcement.*] Father's dead too.

MRS DUDGEON. [*Stupent.*] Your father!

CHRISTY. [*Sulkily, coming back to the fire and warming himself again, attending much more to the fire than to his mother.*] Well, it's not my fault. When we got to Nevinstown we found him ill in bed. He didnt know us at first. The minister sat up with him and sent me away. He died in the night.

MRS DUDGEON. [*Bursting into dry angry tears.*] Well, I do think this is hard on me—very hard on me. His brother, that was a disgrace to us all his life, gets hanged on the public gallows as a rebel; and your father, instead of staying at home where his duty was, with his own family, goes after him and dies, leaving everything on my shoulders. After sending this girl to me to take care of, too! [*She plucks her shawl vexedly over her ears.*] It's sinful so it is: downright sinful.

CHRISTY. [*With a slow, bovine cheerfulness, after a pause.*] I think it's going to be a fine morning, after all.

MRS DUDGEON. [*Railing at him.*] A fine morning! And your father newly dead! Wheres your feelings, child?

CHRISTY. [*Obstinately.*] Well, I didnt mean any harm. I suppose a man may make a remark about the weather even if his father's dead.

MRS DUDGEON. [*Bitterly.*] A nice comfort my children are to me! One son a fool, and the other a lost sinner thats left his home to live with smugglers and gypsies and villains, the scum of the earth!   [*Someone knocks.*

CHRISTY. [*Without moving.*] Thats the minister.

MRS DUDGEON. [*Sharply.*] Well, arnt you going to let Mr Anderson in?

[*Christy goes sheepishly to the door. Mrs Dudgeon buries her face in her hands, as it is her duty as a widow to be overcome with grief. Christy opens the door, and admits the minister, Anthony Anderson, a shrewd, genial, ready Presbyterian divine of about fifty, with something of the authority of his profession in his bearing. But it is an altogether secular authority, sweetened by a conciliatory, sensible manner not at all suggestive of a quite thorough-going other-worldliness. He is a strong, healthy man too, with a thick sanguine neck; and his keen, cheerful mouth cuts into somewhat fleshy corners. No doubt an excellent parson, but still a man capable of making the most of this world, and perhaps a little apologetically conscious of getting on better with it than a sound Presbyterian ought.*]

ANDERSON. [*To Christy, at the door, looking at Mrs Dudgeon whilst he takes off his cloak.*] Have you told her?

CHRISTY. She made me.

[*He shuts the door; yawns; and loafs across to the sofa, where he sits down and presently drops off to sleep*

Anderson looks compassionately at Mrs Dudgeon. Then he hangs his cloak and hat on the rack. Mrs Dudgeon dries her eyes and looks up at him.

ANDERSON. Sister: the Lord has laid his hand very heavily upon you.

MRS DUDGEON. [*With intensely recalcitrant resignation.*] It's His will, I suppose; and I must bow to it. But I do think it hard. What call had Timothy to go to Springtown, and remind everybody that he belonged to a man that was being hanged? And [*spitefully*] that deserved it, if ever a man did.

ANDERSON. [*Gently.*] They were brothers, Mrs Dudgeon.

MRS DUDGEON. Timothy never acknowledged him as his brother after we were married: he had too much respect for me to insult me with such a brother. Would such a selfish wretch as Peter have come thirty miles to see Timothy hanged, do you think? Not thirty yards, not he. However, I must bear my cross as best I may: least said is soonest mended.

ANDERSON. [*Very grave, coming down to the fire to stand with his back to it.*] Your eldest son was present at the execution, Mrs Dudgeon.

MRS DUDGEON. [*Disagreeably surprised.*] Richard?

ANDERSON. [*Nodding.*] Yes.

MRS DUDGEON. [*Vindictively.*] Let it be a warning to him. He may end that way himself, the wicked, dissolute, godless . . . [*She suddenly stops; her voice fails; and she asks, with evident dread*] Did Timothy see him?

ANDERSON. Yes.

MRS DUDGEON. [*Holding her breath.*] Well?

ANDERSON. He only saw him in the crowd: they did not speak. [*Mrs Dudgeon, greatly relieved, exhales the pent up breath and sits at her ease again.*] Your husband was greatly touched and impressed by his brother's awful death. [*Mrs Dudgeon sneers. Anderson breaks off to demand with some indignation.*] Well, wasnt it only natural, Mrs Dudgeon? He softened towards his prodigal son in that moment. He sent for him to come to see him.

MRS DUDGEON. [*Her alarm renewed.*] Sent for Richard!

ANDERSON. Yes; but Richard would not come. He sent his father a message; but I'm sorry to say it was a wicked message—an awful message.

MRS DUDGEON. What was it?

ANDERSON. That he would stand by his wicked uncle and stand against his good parents, in this world and the next.

MRS DUDGEON. [*Implacably.*] He will be punished for it. He will be punished for it—in both worlds.

ANDERSON. That is not in our hands, Mrs Dudgeon.

MRS DUDGEON. Did I say it was, Mr Anderson? We are told that the wicked shall be punished. Why should we do our duty and keep God's law if there is to be no difference made between us and those who follow their own likings and dislikings, and make a jest of us and of their Maker's word?

ANDERSON. Well, Richard's earthly father has been merciful to him; and his heavenly judge is the father of us all.

MRS DUDGEON. [*Forgetting herself.*] Richard's earthly father was a softheaded——

ANDERSON. [*Shocked.*] Oh!

MRS DUDGEON. [*With a touch of shame.*] Well, I am Richard's mother. If I am against him who has any right to be for him? [*Trying to conciliate him.*] Wont you sit down, Mr Anderson? I should have asked you before; but I'm so troubled.

ANDERSON. Thank you. [*He takes a chair from beside the fireplace, and turns it so that he can sit comfortably at the fire. When he is seated he adds, in the tone of a man who knows that he is opening a difficult subject*] Has Christy told you about the new will?

MRS DUDGEON. [*All her fears returning.*] The new will! Did Timothy——?

[*She breaks off, gasping, unable to complete the question.*

ANDERSON. Yes. In his last hours he changed his mind.

MRS DUDGEON. [*White with intense rage.*] And you let him rob me?

ANDERSON. I had no power to prevent him giving what was his to his own son.

MRS DUDGEON. He had nothing of his own. His money was the money I brought him as my marriage portion. It was for me to deal with my own money and my own son. He dare not have done it if I had been with him; and well he knew it. That was why he stole away like a thief to take advantage of the law to rob me by making a new will behind my back. The more shame on you, Mr Anderson—you, a minister of the gospel—to act as his accomplice in such a crime.

ANDERSON. [*Rising.*] I will take no offence at what you say in the first bitterness of your grief.

MRS DUDGEON. [*Contemptuously.*] Grief!

ANDERSON. Well, of your disappointment, if you can find it in your heart to think that the better word.

MRS DUDGEON. My heart! My heart! And since when, pray, have you begun to hold up our hearts as trustworthy guides for us?

ANDERSON. [*Rather guiltily.*] I—er——

MRS DUDGEON. [*Vehemently.*] Dont lie, Mr Anderson. We are told that the heart of man is deceitful above all things, and desperately wicked. My heart belonged, not to Timothy, but to that poor wretched brother of his that has just ended his days with a rope round his neck—aye, to Peter Dudgeon. You know it: old Eli Hawkins, the man to whose pulpit you succeeded, though you are not worthy to loose his shoe latchet, told it you when he gave over our souls into your charge. He warned me and strengthened me against my heart, and made me marry a Godfearing man—as

he thought. What else but that discipline has made me the woman
I am? And you, you, who followed your heart in your marriage,
you talk to me of what I find in my heart. Go home to your pretty
wife, man; and leave me to my prayers.

[*She turns from him and leans with her elbows on the table, brooding
over her wrongs and taking no further notice of him.*

ANDERSON. [*Willing enough to escape.*] The Lord forbid that I should
come between you and the source of all comfort!

[*He goes to the rack for his coat and hat.*

MRS DUDGEON. [*Without looking at him.*] The Lord will know what
to forbid and what to allow without your help.

ANDERSON. And whom to forgive, I hope—Eli Hawkins and
myself, if we have ever set up our preaching against His law. [*He
fastens his cloak, and is now ready to go.*] Just one word—on necessary business, Mrs Dudgeon. There is the reading of the will to be
gone through; and Richard has a right to be present. He is in the
town; but he has the grace to say that he does not want to force
himself in here.

MRS DUDGEON. He shall come here. Does he expect us to leave
his father's house for his convenience? Let them all come, and
come quickly, and go quickly. They shall not make the will an
excuse to shirk half their day's work. I shall be ready, never
fear.

ANDERSON. [*Coming back a step or two.*] Mrs Dudgeon: I used to
have some little influence with you. When did I lose it?

MRS DUDGEON. [*Still without turning to him.*] When you married for
love. Now youre answered.

ANDERSON. Yes: I am answered.   [*He goes out, musing.*

MRS DUDGEON. [*To herself, thinking of her husband.*] Thief! Thief!
[*She shakes herself angrily out of her chair; throws back the shawl
from her head; and sets to work to prepare the room for the reading of
the will, beginning by replacing Anderson's chair against the wall, and
pushing back her own to the window. Then she calls, in her hard, driving,
wrathful way.*] Christy! [*No answer: he is fast asleep.*] Christy!
[*She shakes him roughly.*] Get up out of that; and be ashamed of
yourself—sleeping, and your father dead!

[*She returns to the table; puts the candle on the mantelshelf; and takes
from the table drawer a red table cloth which she spreads.*

CHRISTY. [*Rising reluctantly.*] Well, do you suppose we are never
going to sleep until we are out of mourning?

MRS DUDGEON. I want none of your sulks. Here: help me to set
this table. [*They place the table in the middle of the room, with Christy's
end towards the fireplace and Mrs Dudgeon's towards the sofa. Christy
drops the table as soon as possible, and goes to the fire, leaving his mother
to make the final adjustments of its position.*] We shall have the

minister back here with the lawyer and all the family to read the will before you have done toasting yourself. Go and wake that girl; and then light the stove in the shed: you cant have your breakfast here. And mind you wash yourself, and make yourself fit to receive the company. [*She punctuates these orders by going to the cupboard; unlocking it; and producing a decanter of wine, which has no doubts stood there untouched since the last state occasion in the family, and some glasses, which she sets on the table. Also two green ware plates, on one of which she puts a barnbrack with a knife beside it. On the other she shakes some biscuits out of a tin, putting back one or two, and counting the rest.*] Now mind: there are ten biscuits there: let there be ten there when I come back after dressing myself. And keep your fingers off the raisins in that cake. And tell Essie the same. I suppose I can trust you to bring in the case of stuffed birds without breaking the glass?

[*She replaces the tin in the cupboard, which she locks, pocketing the key carefully.*

CHRISTY. [*Lingering at the fire.*] Youd better put the inkstand instead, for the lawyer.

MRS DUDGEON. Thats no answer to make to me, sir. Go and do as youre told. [*Christy turns sullenly to obey.*] Stop: take down that shutter before you go, and let the daylight in: you cant expect me to do all the heavy work of the house with a great lout like you idling about.

[*Christy takes the window bar out of its clamps, and puts it aside; then opens the shutter, shewing the grey morning. Mrs Dudgeon takes the sconce from the mantelshelf; blows out the candle; extinguishes the snuff by pinching it with her fingers, first licking them for the purpose; and replaces the sconce on the shelf.*

CHRISTY. [*Looking through the window.*] Here's the minister's wife.

MRS DUDGEON. [*Displeased.*] What! Is she coming here?

CHRISTY. Yes.

MRS DUDGEON. What does she want troubling me at this hour, before I am properly dressed to receive people?

CHRISTY. Youd better ask her.

MRS DUDGEON. [*Threateningly.*] Youd better keep a civil tongue in your head. [*He goes sulkily towards the door. She comes after him, plying him with instructions.*] Tell that girl to come to me as soon as she's had her breakfast. And tell her to make herself fit to be seen before the people. [*Christy goes out and slams the door in her face.*] Nice manners, that! [*Someone knocks at the house door; she turns and cries inhospitably.*] Come in. [*Judith Anderson, the minister's wife, comes in. Judith is more than twenty years younger than her husband, though she will never be as young as he in vitality. She is pretty and proper and ladylike, and has been admired and petted into an opinion of herself sufficiently favorable to give her a self-assurance which serves her instead of strength. She has a pretty taste in dress, and in her face the pretty lines of a sentimental character formed by dreams. Even her little self-complacency is pretty, like a child's vanity. Rather a pathetic creature to any sympathetic observer who knows how rough a place the world is. One feels, on the whole, that Anderson might have chosen worse, and that she, needing protection, could not have chosen better.*] Oh, it's you, is it, Mrs Anderson?

JUDITH. [*Very politely—almost patronizingly.*] Yes. Can I do anything for you, Mrs Dudgeon? Can I help to get the place ready before they come to read the will?

MRS DUDGEON. [*Stiffly.*] Thank you, Mrs Anderson, my house is always ready for anyone to come into.

MRS ANDERSON. [*With complacent amiability.*] Yes, indeed it is. Perhaps you had rather I did not intrude on you just now.

MRS DUDGEON. Oh, one more or less will make no difference this morning, Mrs Anderson. Now that youre here, youd better stay. If you wouldnt mind shutting the door! [*Judith smiles, implying 'How stupid of me!' and shuts it with an exasperating air of doing something pretty and becoming.*] Thats better. I must go and tidy myself a bit. I suppose you dont mind stopping here to receive anyone that comes until I'm ready.

JUDITH. [*Graciously giving her leave.*] Oh yes, certainly. Leave that to me, Mrs Dudgeon; and take your time.

[*She hangs her cloak and bonnet on the rack.*

MRS DUDGEON. [*Half sneering.*] I thought that would be more in your way than getting the house ready. [*Essie comes back.*] Oh, here you are! [*Severely.*] Come here: let me see you. [*Essie timidly goes to her. Mrs Dudgeon takes her roughly by the arm and pulls her round to inspect the results of her attempt to clean and tidy herself results which shew little practice and less conviction.*] Mm! That's what you call doing your hair properly, I suppose. It's easy to see what you are, and how you were brought up. [*She throws her arm away and goes on, peremptorily.*] Now you listen to me and do as youre told. You sit down there in the corner by the fire; and when the company comes dont dare to speak until youre spoken to. [*Essie creeps away to the fireplace.*] Your father's people had better see you and know youre there: theyre as much bound to keep you from starvation as I am. At any rate they might help. But let me have no chattering and making free with them, as if you were their equal. Do you hear?

ESSIE. Yes.

MRS DUDGEON. Well, then go and do as youre told. [*Essie sits down miserably on the corner of the fender farthest from the door.*] Never mind her, Mrs Anderson: you know who she is and what she is.

If she gives you any trouble, just tell me; and I'll settle accounts with her.

> [*Mrs Dudgeon goes into the bedroom, shutting the door sharply behind her as if even it had to be made do its duty with a ruthless hand.*

JUDITH. [*Patronizing Essie, and arranging the cake and wine on the table more becomingly.*] You must not mind if your aunt is strict with you. She is a very good woman, and desires your good too.

ESSIE. [*In listless misery.*] Yes.

JUDITH. [*Annoyed with Essie for her failure to be consoled and edified, and to appreciate the kindly condescension of the remark.*] You are not going to be sullen, I hope, Essie.

ESSIE. No.

JUDITH. Thats a good girl! [*She places a couple of chairs at the table with their backs to the window, with a pleasant sense of being a more thoughtful housekeeper than Mrs Dudgeon.*] Do you know any of your father's relatives?

ESSIE. No. They wouldnt have anything to do with him: they were too religious. Father used to talk about Dick Dudgeon; but I never saw him.

JUDITH. [*Ostentatiously shocked.*] Dick Dudgeon! Essie: do you wish to be a really respectable and grateful girl, and to make a place for yourself here by steady good conduct?

ESSIE. [*Very half-heartedly.*] Yes.

JUDITH. Then you must never mention the name of Richard Dudgeon—never think even about him. He is a bad man.

ESSIE. What has he done?

JUDITH. You must not ask questions about him, Essie. You are too young to know what it is to be a bad man. But he is a smuggler; and he lives with gypsies; and he has no love for his mother and his family; and he wrestles and plays games on Sundays instead of going to church. Never let him into your presence, if you can help it, Essie; and try to keep yourself and all womanhood unspotted by contact with such men.

ESSIE. Yes.

JUDITH. [*Again displeased.*] I am afraid you say Yes and No without thinking very deeply.

ESSIE. Yes. At least I mean——

JUDITH. [*Severely.*] What do you mean?

ESSIE. [*Almost crying.*] Only—my father was a smuggler; and——

> [*Someone knocks.*

JUDITH. They are beginning to come. Now remember your aunt's directions, Essie; and be a good girl. [*Christy comes back with the stand of stuffed birds under a glass case, and an inkstand, which he places on the table.*] Good morning, Mr Dudgeon. Will you open the door, please: the people have come.

CHRISTY. Good morning.   [*He opens the house door.*

> [*The morning is now fairly bright and warm; and Anderson, who is the first to enter, has left his cloak at home. He is accompanied by Lawyer Hawkins, a brisk, middle-aged man in brown riding-gaiters and yellow breeches, looking as much squire as solicitor. He ana Anderson are allowed precedence as representing the learned professions. After them comes the family, headed by the senior uncle, William Dudgeon, a large, shapeless man, bottle-nosed and evidently no ascetic at table. His clothes are not the clothes, nor his anxious wife the wife, of a prosperous man. The junior uncle, Titus Dudgeon, is a wiry little terrier of a man, with an immense and visibly purse-proud wife, both free from the cares of the William household.*
>
> *Hawkins at once goes briskly to the table and takes the chair nearest the sofa, Christy having left the inkstand there. He puts his hat on the floor beside him, and produces the will. Uncle William comes to the fire and stands on the hearth warming his coat tails, leaving Mrs Wil iam derelict near the door. Uncle Titus, who is the lady's man of the family, rescues her by giving her his disengaged arm and bringing her to the sofa, where he sits down warmly between his own lady and his brother's. Anderson hangs up his hat and waits for a word with Judith.*

JUDITH. She will be here in a moment. Ask them to wait.

> [*She taps at the bedroom door. Receiving an answer from within, she opens it and passes through.*

ANDERSON. [*Taking his place at the table at the opposite end to Hawkins.*] Our poor afflicted sister will be with us in a moment. Are we all here?

CHRISTY. [*At the house door, which he has just shut.*] All except Dick.

> [*The callousness with which Christy names the reprobate jars on the moral sense of the family. Uncle William shakes his head slowly and repeatedly. Mrs Titus catches her breath convulsively through her nose. Her husband speaks.*

UNCLE TITUS. Well, I hope he will have the grace not to come. I hope so.

> [*The Dudgeons all murmur assent, except Christy, who goes to the window and posts himself there, looking out. Hawkins smiles secretively as if he knew something that would change their tune if they knew it. Anderson is uneasy: the love of solemn family councils, especially funeral ones, is not in his nature. Judith appears at the bedroom door.*

JUDITH. [*With gentle impressiveness.*] Friends, Mrs Dudgeon.

> [*She takes the chair from beside the fireplace; and places it for Mrs Dudgeon, who comes from the bedroom in black, with a clean handkerchief to her eyes. All rise, except Essie. Mrs Titus and*

Mrs William produce equally clean handkerchiefs and weep. It is an affecting moment.

UNCLE WILLIAM. Would it comfort you, sister, if we were to offer up a prayer?

UNCLE TITUS. Or sing a hymn?

ANDERSON. [*Rather hastily.*] I have been with our sister this morning already, friends. In our hearts we ask a blessing.

ALL. [*Except Essie.*] Amen.

[*They all sit down, except Judith, who stands behind Mrs Dudgeon's chair.*]

JUDITH. [*To Essie.*] Essie: did you say Amen?

ESSIE. [*Scaredly.*] No.

JUDITH. Then say it, like a good girl.

ESSIE. Amen.

UNCLE WILLIAM. [*Encouragingly.*] Thats right: thats right. We know who you are; but we are willing to be kind to you if you are a good girl and deserve it. We are all equal before the Throne.

[*This republican sentiment does not please the women, who are convinced that the Throne is precisely the place where their superiority, often questioned in this world, will be recognized and rewarded.*]

CHRISTY. [*At the window.*] Heres Dick.

[*Anderson and Hawkins look round sociably. Essie, with a gleam of interest breaking through her misery, looks up. Christy grins and gapes expectantly at the door. The rest are petrified with the intensity of their sense of Virtue menaced with outrage by the approach of flaunting Vice. The reprobate appears in the doorway, graced beyond his alleged merits by the morning sunlight. He is certainly the best-looking member of the family; but his expression is reckless and sardonic, his manner defiant and satirical, his dress picturesquely careless. Only, his forehead and mouth betray an extraordinary steadfastness; and his eyes are the eyes of a fanatic.*]

RICHARD. [*On the threshold, taking off his hat.*] Ladies and gentlemen: your servant, your very humble servant. [*With this comprehensive insult, he throws his hat to Christy with a suddenness that makes him jump like a negligent wicket-keeper, and comes into the middle of the room, where he turns and deliberately surveys the company.*] How happy you all look! How glad to see me! [*He turns towards Mrs Dudgeon's chair; and his lip rolls up horribly from his dog tooth as he meets her look of undisguised hatred.*] Well, mother: keeping up appearances as usual? Thats right, thats right. [*Judith pointedly moves away from his neighbourhood to the other side of the kitchen, holding her skirt instinctively as if to save it from contamination. Uncle Titus promptly marks his approval of her action by rising from the sofa and placing a chair for her to sit down upon.*] What! Uncle William! I havnt seen you since you gave up drinking. [*Poor Uncle William,*] *shamed, would protest; but Richard claps him heartily on his shoulder, adding*] You have given it up, havnt you? [*Releasing him with a playful push.*] Of course you have: quite right too: you overdid it. [*He turns away from Uncle William and makes for the sofa.*] And now, where is that upright horsedealer Uncle Titus? Uncle Titus: come forth. [*He comes upon him holding the chair as Judith sits down.*] As usual, looking after the ladies!

UNCLE TITUS. [*Indignantly.*] Be ashamed of yourself, sir——

RICHARD. [*Interrupting him and shaking his hand in spite of him.*] I am: I am; but I am proud of my uncle—proud of all my relatives —[*again surveying them*] who could look at them and not be proud and joyful? [*Uncle Titus, overborne, resumes his seat on the sofa. Richard turns to the table.*] Ah, Mr Anderson, still at the good work, still shepherding them? Keep them up to the mark, minister, keep them up to the mark. Come! [*With a spring he seats himself on the table and takes up the decanter.*] Clink a glass with me, Pastor, for the sake of old times.

ANDERSON. You know, I think, Mr Dudgeon, that I do not drink before dinner.

RICHARD. You will, some day, Pastor: Uncle William used to drink before breakfast. Come: it will give your sermons unction. [*He smells the wine and makes a wry face.*] But do not begin on my mother's company sherry. I stole some when I was six years old; and I have been a temperate man ever since. [*He puts the decanter down and changes the subject.*] So I hear you are married, Pastor, and that your wife has a most ungodly allowance of good looks.

ANDERSON. [*Quietly indicating Judith.*] Sir: you are in the presence of my wife.   [*Judith rises and stands with stony propriety.*

RICHARD. [*Quickly slipping down from the table with instinctive good manners.*] Your servant, madam: no offence. [*He looks at her earnestly.*] You deserve your reputation; but I'm sorry to see by your expression that youre a good woman. [*She looks shocked, and sits down amid a murmur of indignant sympathy from his relatives. Anderson, sensible enough to know that these demonstrations can only gratify and encourage a man who is deliberately trying to provoke them, remains perfectly goodhumored.*] All the same, Pastor, I respect you more than I did before. By the way, did I hear, or did I not, that our late lamented Uncle Peter, though unmarried, was a father?

UNCLE TITUS. He had only one irregular child, sir.

RICHARD. Only one! He thinks one a mere trifle! I blush for you, Uncle Titus.

ANDERSON. Mr Dudgeon: you are in the presence of your mother and her grief.

RICHARD. It touches me profoundly, Pastor. By the way, what has become of the irregular child?

ANDERSON. [*Pointing to Essie.*] There, sir, listening to you.

RICHARD. [*Shocked into sincerity.*] What! Why the devil didnt you tell me that before? Children suffer enough in this house without—— [*He hurries remorsefully to Essie.*] Come, little cousin! Never mind me: it was not meant to hurt you. [*She looks up gratefully at him. Her tearstained face affects him violently; and he bursts out, in a transport of wrath.*] Who has been making her cry? Who has been ill-treating her? By God——

MRS DUDGEON. [*Rising and confronting him.*] Silence your blasphemous tongue. I will bear no more of this. Leave my house.

RICHARD. How do you know it's your house until the will is read? [*They look at one another for a moment with intense hatred; and then she sinks, checkmated, into her chair. Richard goes boldly up past Anderson to the window, where he takes the railed chair in his hand.*] Ladies and gentlemen: as the eldest son of my late father, and the unworthy head of this household, I bid you welcome. By your leave, Minister Anderson: by your leave, Lawyer Hawkins. The head of the table for the head of the family. [*He places the chair at the table between the minister and the attorney; sits down between them; and addresses the assembly with a presidential air.*] We meet on a melancholy occasion: a father dead, an uncle actually hanged, and probably damned. [*He shakes his head deploringly. The relatives freeze with horror.*] Thats right: pull your longest faces [*his voice suddenly sweetens gravely as his glance lights on Essie*] provided only there is hope in the eyes of the child. [*Briskly.*] Now then, Lawyer Hawkins; business, business. Get on with the will, man.

TITUS. Do not let yourself be ordered or hurried, Mr Hawkins.

HAWKINS. [*Very politely and willingly.*] Mr Dudgeon means no offence, I feel sure. I will not keep you one second, Mr Dudgeon. Just while I get my glasses——

[*He fumbles for them. The Dudgeons look at one another with misgivings.*

RICHARD. Aha! They notice your civility, Mr Hawkins. They are prepared for the worst. A glass of wine to clear your voice before you begin.

[*He pours out one for him and hands it; then pours one for himself.*

HAWKINS. Thank you, Mr Dudgeon, Your good health, sir.

RICHARD. Yours, sir. [*With the glass half way to his lips, he checks himself, giving a dubious glance at the wine, and adds, with quaint intensity.*] Will anyone oblige me with a glass of water?

Essie, who has been hanging on his every word and movement, rises stealthily and slips out behind Mrs Dudgeon through the bedroom door, returning presently with a jug and going out of the house as quietly as possible.

HAWKINS. The will is not exactly in proper legal phraseology.

RICHARD. No: my father died without the consolations of the law.

HAWKINS. Good again, Mr Dudgeon, good again. [*Preparing to read.*] Are you ready, sir?

RICHARD. Ready, aye ready. For what we are about to receive, may the Lord make us truly thankful. Go ahead.

HAWKINS. [*Reading.*] 'This is the last will and testament of me Timothy Dudgeon on my deathbed at Nevinstown on the road from Springtown to Websterbridge on this twenty-fourth day of September, one thousand seven hundred and seventy seven. I hereby revoke all former wills made by me and declare that I am of sound mind and know well what I am doing and that this is my real will according to my own wish and affections.'

RICHARD. [*Glancing at his mother.*] Aha!

HAWKINS. [*Shaking his head.*] Bad phraseology, sir, wrong phraseology. 'I give and bequeath a hundred pounds to my younger son Christopher Dudgeon, fifty pounds to be paid to him on the day of his marriage to Sarah Wilkins if she will have him, and ten pounds on the birth of each of his children up to the number of five.'

RICHARD. How if she wont have him?

CHRISTY. She will if I have fifty pounds.

RICHARD. Good, my brother. Proceed.

HAWKINS. 'I give and bequeath to my wife Annie Dudgeon, born Annie Primrose'—you see he did not know the law, Mr Dudgeon: your mother was not born Annie: she was christened so—'an annuity of fifty-two pounds a year for life [*Mrs Dudgeon, with all eyes on her, holds herself convulsively rigid*] to be paid out of the interest on her own money'—theres a way to put it, Mr Dudgeon! Her own money!

MRS DUDGEON. A very good way to put God's truth. It was every penny my own. Fifty-two pounds a year!

HAWKINS. 'And I recommend her for her goodness and piety to the forgiving care of her children, having stood between them and her as far as I could to the best of my ability.'

MRS DUDGEON. And this is my reward! [*Raging inwardly.*] You know what I think, Mr Anderson: you know the word I gave to it.

ANDERSON. It cannot be helped, Mrs Dudgeon. We must take what comes to us. [*To Hawkins.*] Go on, sir.

HAWKINS. 'I give and bequeath my house at Websterbridge with the land belonging to it and all the rest of my property soever to my eldest son and heir, Richard Dudgeon.'

RICHARD. Oho! The fatted calf, Minister, the fatted calf.

HAWKINS. 'On these conditions——'

RICHARD. The devil! Are there conditions?

HAWKINS. 'To wit: first, that he shall not let my brother Peter's natural child starve or be driven by want to an evil life.'

RICHARD. [*Emphatically, striking his fist on the table.*] Agreed.

Mrs Dudgeon, turning to look malignantly at Essie, misses her and looks quickly round to see where she has moved to; then, seeing that she has left the room without leave, closes her lips vengefully.

HAWKINS. 'Second, that he shall be a good friend to my old horse Jim'—[*Again shaking his head.*] He should have written James, sir.

RICHARD. James shall live in clover. Go on.

HAWKINS. —'and keep my deaf farm labourer Prodger Feston in his service.'

RICHARD. Prodger Feston shall get drunk every Saturday.

HAWKINS. 'Third, that he make Christy a present on his marriage out of the ornaments in the best room.'

RICHARD. [*Holding up the stuffed birds.*] Here you are, Christy.

CHRISTY. [*Disappointed.*] I'd rather have the china peacocks.

RICHARD. You shall have both. [*Christy is greatly pleased.*] Go on.

HAWKINS. 'Fourthly and lastly, that he try to live at peace with his mother as far as she will consent to it.'

RICHARD. [*Dubiously.*] Hm! Anything more, Mr Hawkins?

HAWKINS. [*Solemnly.*] 'Finally I give and bequeath my soul into my Maker's hands, humbly asking forgiveness for all my sins and mistakes, and hoping that He will so guide my son that it may not be said that I have done wrong in trusting to him rather than to others in the perplexity of my last hour in this strange place.'

ANDERSON. Amen.

THE UNCLES AND AUNTS. Amen.

RICHARD. My mother does not say Amen.

MRS DUDGEON. [*Rising, unable to give up her property without a struggle.*] Mr Hawkins: is that a proper will? Remember, I have his rightful, legal will, drawn up by yourself, leaving all to me.

HAWKINS. This is a very wrongly and irregularly worded will, Mrs Dudgeon: though [*turning politely to Richard*] it contains in my judgment an excellent disposal of his property.

ANDERSON. [*Interposing before Mrs Dudgeon can retort.*] That is not what you are asked, Mr Hawkins. Is it a legal will?

HAWKINS. The courts will sustain it against the other.

ANDERSON. But why, if the other is more lawfully worded?

HAWKINS. Because, sir, the courts will sustain the claim of a man— and that man the eldest son—against any woman, if they can. I warned you, Mrs Dudgeon, when you got me to draw that other will, that it was not a wise will, and that though you might make him sign it, he would never be easy until he revoked it. But you wouldnt take advice; and now Mr Richard is cock of the walk.

[*He takes his hat from the floor; and begins pocketing his papers and spectacles.*

This is the signal for the breaking up of the party. Anderson takes his hat from the rack and joins Uncle William at the fire. Titus fetches Judith her things from the rack. The three on the sofa rise and chat with Hawkins. Mrs Dudgeon, now an intruder in her own house, stands inert, crushed by the weight of the law on women, accepting it, as she has been trained to accept all monstrous calamities, as proofs of the greatness of the power that inflicts them, and of her own worm-like insignificance. For at this time, remember, Mary Wollstonecraft is as yet only a girl of eighteen, and her Vindication of the Rights of Women is still fourteen years off. Mrs Dudgeon is rescued from her apathy by Essie, who comes back with the jug full of water. She is taking it to Richard when Mrs Dudgeon stops her.

MRS DUDGEON. [*Threatening her.*] Where have you been? [*Essie, appalled, tries to answer, but cannot.*] How dare you go out by yourself after the orders I gave you?

ESSIE. He asked for a drink——

[*She stops, her tongue cleaving to her palate with terror.*

JUDITH. [*With gentler severity.*] Who asked for a drink?

[*Essie, speechless, points to Richard.*

RICHARD. What! I!

JUDITH. [*Shocked.*] Oh Essie, Essie!

RICHARD. I believe I did. [*He takes a glass and holds it to Essie to be filled. Her hand shakes.*] What! Afraid of me?

ESSIE. [*Quickly.*] No. I—— [*She pours out the water.*

RICHARD. [*Tasting it.*] Ah, youve been up the street to the market gate spring to get that. [*He takes a draught.*] Delicious! Thank you. [*Unfortunately, at this moment he chances to catch sight of Judith's face, which expresses the most prudish disapproval of his evident attraction for Essie, who is devouring him with her grateful eyes. His mocking expression returns instantly. He puts down the glass, deliberately winds his arm round Essie's shoulders, and brings her into the middle of the company. Mrs Dudgeon being in Essie's way as they come past the table, he says*] By your leave, mother. [*and compels her to make way for them.*] What do they call you? Bessie?

ESSIE. Essie.

RICHARD. Essie, to be sure. Are you a good girl, Essie?

ESSIE. [*Greatly disappointed that he, of all people, should begin at her in this way.*] Yes. [*She looks doubtfully at Judith.*] I think so. I mean I—I hope so.

RICHARD. Essie, did you ever hear of a person called the devil?

ANDERSON. [*Revolted.*] Shame on you, sir, with a mere child——

RICHARD. By your leave, Minister: I do not interfere with your

sermons: do not you interrupt mine. [*To Essie.*] Do you know
what they call me, Essie?

ESSIE. Dick.

RICHARD. [*Amused: patting her on the shoulder.*] Yes, Dick; but
something else too. They call me the Devil's Disciple.

ESSIE. Why do you let them?

RICHARD. [*Seriously.*] Because it's true. I was brought up in the
other service; but I knew from the first that the Devil was my
natural master and captain and friend. I saw that he was in the
right, and that the world cringed to his conqueror only through
fear. I prayed secretly to him: and he comforted me, and saved
me from having my spirit broken in this house of children's tears.
I promised him my soul, and swore an oath that I would stand up
for him in this world and stand by him in the next. [*Solemnly.*]
That promise and that oath made a man of me. From this day this
house is his home; and no child shall cry in it: this hearth is his
altar; and no soul shall ever cower over it in the dark evenings
and be afraid. Now [*turning forcibly on the rest*] which of you good
men will take this child and rescue her from the house of the
devil?

JUDITH. [*Coming to Essie and throwing a protecting arm about her.*] I
will. You should be burnt alive.

ESSIE. But I dont want to.

> [*She shrinks back, leaving Richard and Judith face to face.*

RICHARD. [*To Judith.*] Actually doesnt want to, most virtuous lady!

UNCLE TITUS. Have a care, Richard Dudgeon. The law——

RICHARD. [*Turning threateningly on him.*] Have a care, you. In an
hour from this there will be no law here but martial law. I passed
the soldiers within six miles on my way here: before noon Major
Swindon's gallows for rebels will be up in the market place.

ANDERSON. [*Calmly.*] What have we to fear from that, sir?

RICHARD. More than you think. He hanged the wrong man at
Springtown: he thought Uncle Peter was respectable, because
the Dudgeons had a good name. But his next example will be the
best man in the town to whom he can bring home a rebellious
word. Well, we're all rebels; and you know it.

ALL THE MEN. [*Except Anderson.*] No, no, no!

RICHARD. Yes, you are. You havnt damned King George up hill
and down dale as I have; but youve prayed for his defeat; and
you, Anthony Anderson, have conducted the service, and sold
your family Bible to buy a pair of pistols. They maynt hang me,
perhaps; because the moral effect of the Devil's Disciple dancing
on nothing wouldnt help them. But a minister! [*Judith, dismayed,
clings to Anderson.*] Or a lawyer! [*Hawkins smiles like a man able to
take care of himself.*] Or an upright horsedealer! [*Uncle Titus*

snarls at him in rage and terror.] Or a reformed drunkard! [*Uncle William, utterly unnerved, moans and wobbles with fear.*] Eh? Would that shew that King George meant business—ha?

ANDERSON. [*Perfectly self-possessed.*] Come, my dear: he is only trying to frighten you. There is no danger.

[*He takes her out of the house. The rest crowd to the door to follow him, except Essie, who remains near Richard.*

RICHARD. [*Boisterously derisive.*] Now then: how many of you will stay with me; run up the American flag on the devil's house; and make a fight for freedom? [*They scramble out, Christy among them, hustling one another in their haste.*] Ha ha! Long live the devil! [*To Mrs Dudgeon, who is following them.*] What, mother! Are you off too?

MRS DUDGEON. [*Deadly pale, with her hand on her heart as if she had received a death blow.*] My curse on you! My dying curse!

[*She goes out.*

RICHARD. [*Calling after her.*] It will bring me luck. Ha ha ha!

ESSIE. [*Anxiously.*] Maynt I stay?

RICHARD. [*Turning to her.*] What! Have they forgotten to save your soul in their anxiety about their own bodies? Oh yes: you may stay. [*He turns excitedly away again and shakes his fist after them. His left fist, also clenched, hangs down. Essie seizes it and kisses it, her tears falling on it. He starts and looks at it.*] Tears! The devil's baptism! [*She falls on her knees, sobbing. He stoops goodnaturedly to raise her, saying.*] Oh yes, you may cry that way, Essie, if you like.

Minister Anderson's house is in the main street of Websterbridge, not far from the town hall. To the eye of the eighteenth-century New Englander, it is much grander than the plain farmhouse of the Dudgeons; but it is so plain itself that a modern house agent would let both at about the same rent. The chief dwelling-room has the same sort of kitchen fireplace, with boiler, toaster hanging on the bars, movable iron griddle socketed to the hob, hook above for roasting, and broad fender, on which stand a kettle and a plate of buttered toast. The door, between the fireplace and the corner, has neither panels, fingerplates nor handles: it is made of plain boards, and fastens with a latch. The table is a kitchen table, with a treacle-colored cover of American cloth, chapped at the corners by draping. The tea service on it consists of two thick cups and saucers of the plainest ware, with milk jug and bowl to match, each large enough to contain nearly a quart, on a black japanned tray, and, in the middle of the table, a wooden trencher with a big loaf upon it, and a square half-pound block of butter in a crock. The big oak press facing the fire from the opposite side of the room is for use and storage, not for ornament; and the minister's house coat hangs on a peg from its door, shewing that he is out; for when he is in, it is his best coat that hangs there. His big riding-boots stand beside the press, evidently in their usual place, and rather proud of themselves. In fact, the evolution of the minister's kitchen, dining-room and drawing-room into three separate apartments has not yet taken place; and so, from the point of view of our pampered period, he is no better off than the Dudgeons.

But there is a difference, for all that. To begin with, Mrs Anderson is a pleasanter person to live with than Mrs Dudgeon. To which Mrs Dudgeon would at once reply, with reason, that Mrs Anderson has no children to look after; no poultry, pigs nor cattle; a steady and sufficient income not directly dependent on harvests and prices at fairs; an affectionate husband who is a tower of strength to her: in short, that life is as easy at the minister's house as it is hard at the farm. This is true; but to explain a fact is not to alter it; and however little credit Mrs Anderson may deserve for making her home happier, she has certainly succeeded in doing it. The outward and visible signs of her superior social pretensions are a drugget on the floor, a plaster ceiling between the timbers, and chairs which, though not upholstered, are stained and polished. The fine arts are represented by a mezzotint portrait of some Presbyterian divine, a copperplate of Raphael's St Paul preaching at Athens, a rococo presentation clock on the mantelshelf, flanked by a couple of miniatures, a pair of crockery dogs with baskets in their mouths, and, at the corners, two large cowrie shells. A pretty feature of the room is the low wide latticed window, nearly its whole width, with little red curtains running on a rod half way up it to serve as a blind. There is no sofa; but one of the seats, standing near the press, has a railed back and is long enough to accommodate two people easily. On the whole, it is rather the sort of room that the nineteenth century has ended in struggling to get back to under the leadership of Mr Philip Webb and his disciples in domestic architecture, though no genteel clergyman would have tolerated it fifty years ago.

The evening has closed in; and the room is dark except for the cosy firelight and the dim oil lamps seen through the window in the wet street where there is a quiet, steady, warm, windless downpour of rain. As the town clock strikes the quarter, Judith comes in with a couple of candles in earthenware candlesticks, and sets them on the table. Her self-conscious airs of the morning are gone: she is anxious and frightened. She goes to the window and peers into the street. The first thing she sees there is her husband, hurrying home through the rain. She gives a little gasp of relief, not very far removed from a sob, and turns to the door. Anderson comes in, wrapped in a very wet cloak.

JUDITH. [*Running to him.*] Oh, here you are at last, at last!
[*She attempts to embrace him.*

ANDERSON. [*Keeping her off.*] Take care, my love: I'm wet. Wait till I get my cloak off. [*He places a chair with its back to the fire; hangs his cloak on it to dry; shakes the rain from his hat and puts it on the fender; and at last turns with his hands outstretched to Judith.*] Now! [*She flies into his arms.*] I am not late, am I? The town clock struck the quarter as I came in at the front door. And the town clock is always fast.

JUDITH. I'm sure it's slow this evening. I'm so glad youre back.

ANDERSON. [*Taking her more closely in his arms.*] Anxious, my dear?

JUDITH. A little.

ANDERSON. Why, youve been crying.

JUDITH. Only a little. Never mind: it's all over now. [*A bugle call is heard in the distance. She starts in terror and retreats to the long seat, listening.*] Whats that?

ANDERSON. [*Following her tenderly to the seat and making her sit down with him.*] Only King George, my dear. He's returning to barracks, or having his roll called, or getting ready for tea, or booting or saddling or something. Soldiers dont ring the bell or call over the banisters when they want anything: they send a boy out with a bugle to disturb the whole town.

JUDITH. Do you think there is really any danger?

ANDERSON. Not the least in the world.

JUDITH. You say that to comfort me, not because you believe it.

ANDERSON. My dear: in this world there is always danger for those who are afraid of it. Theres a danger that the house will catch fire in the night; but we shant sleep any the less soundly for that.

JUDITH. Yes, I know what you always say; and youre quite right. Oh, quite right: I know it. But—I suppose I'm not brave: thats all. My heart shrinks every time I think of the soldiers.

ANDERSON. Never mind that, dear: bravery is none the worse for costing a little pain.

JUDITH. Yes, I suppose so. [*Embracing him again.*] Oh, how brave you are, my dear! [*With tears in her eyes.*] Well, I'll be brave too: you shant be ashamed of your wife.

ANDERSON. Thats right. Now you make me happy. Well, well! [*He rises and goes cheerily to the fire to dry his shoes.*] I called on Richard Dudgeon on my way back; but he wasnt in.

JUDITH. [*Rising in consternation.*] You called on that man!

ANDERSON. [*Reassuring her.*] Oh, nothing happened, dearie. He was out.

JUDITH. [*Almost in tears, as if the visit were a personal humiliation to her.*] But why did you go there?

ANDERSON. [*Gravely.*] Well, it is all the talk that Major Swindon is going to do what he did in Springtown—make an example of some notorious rebel, as he calls us. He pounced on Peter Dudgeon as the worst character there; and it is the general belief that he will pounce on Richard as the worst here.

JUDITH. But Richard said——

ANDERSON. [*Goodhumoredly cutting her short.*] Pooh! Richard said! He said what he thought would frighten you and frighten me, my dear. He said what perhaps (God forgive him!) he would like to believe. It's a terrible thing to think of what death must mean for a man like that. I felt that I must warn him. I left a message for him.

JUDITH. [*Querulously.*] What message?

ANDERSON. Only that I should be glad to see him for a moment on a matter of importance to himself, and that if he would look in here when he was passing he would be welcome.

JUDITH. [*Aghast.*] You asked that man to come here!

ANDERSON. I did.

JUDITH. [*Sinking on the seat and clasping her hands.*] I hope he wont come! Oh, I pray that he may not come!

ANDERSON. Why? Dont you want him to be warned?

JUDITH. He must know his danger. Oh, Tony, is it wrong to hate a blasphemer and a villain? I do hate him. I cant get him out of my mind: I know he will bring harm with him. He insulted you: he insulted me: he insulted his mother.

ANDERSON. [*Quaintly.*] Well, dear, lets forgive him; and then it
wont matter.

JUDITH. Oh, I know it's wrong to hate anybody; but——

ANDERSON. [*Going over to her with humorous tenderness.*] Come, dear,
youre not so wicked as you think. The worst sin towards our
fellow creatures is not to hate them, but to be indifferent to
them; thats the essence of inhumanity. After all, my dear, if you
watch people carefully, youll be surprised to find how like hate
is to love. [*She starts, strangely touched—even appalled. He is amused
at her.*] Yes: I'm quite in earnest. Think of how some of our
married friends worry one another, tax one another, are jealous
of one another, cant bear to let one another out of sight for a
day, are more like jailers and slave-owners than lovers. Think
of those very same people with their enemies, scrupulous, lofty,
self-respecting, determined to be independent of one another,
careful of how they speak of one another—pooh! havnt you
often thought that if they only knew it, they were better friends
to their enemies than to their own husbands and wives? Come:
depend on it, my dear, you are really fonder of Richard than you
are of me, if you only knew it, Eh?

JUDITH. Oh, dont say that: dont say that, Tony, even in jest. You
dont know what a horrible feeling it gives me.

ANDERSON. [*Laughing.*] Well, well: never mind, pet. He's a bad
man; and you hate him as he deserves. And youre going to make
the tea, arnt you?

JUDITH. [*Remorsefully.*] Oh yes, I forgot. Ive been keeping you
waiting all this time.   [*She goes to the fire and puts on the kettle.*

ANDERSON. [*Going to the press and taking his coat off.*] Have you
stitched up the shoulder of my old coat?

JUDITH. Yes, dear.

[*She goes to the table, and sets about putting the tea into the teapot
from the caddy.*

ANDERSON. [*As he changes his coat for the older one hanging on the press,
and replaces it by the one he has just taken off.*] Did anyone call when I
was out?

JUDITH. No, only—— [*Someone knocks at the door. With a start
which betrays her intense nervousness, she retreats to the farther end of the
table with the tea caddy and spoon in her hands exclaiming*] Who's that?

ANDERSON. [*Going to her and patting her encouragingly on the shoulder.*]
All right, pet, all right. He wont eat you, whoever he is. [*She tries
to smile, and nearly makes herself cry. He goes to the door and opens it.
Richard is there, without overcoat or cloak.*] You might have raised
the latch and come in, Mr Dudgeon. Nobody stands on much
ceremony with us. [*Hospitably.*] Come in. [*Richard comes in carelessly and stands at the table, looking round the room with a slight pucker*

of his nose at the mezzotinted divine on the wall. Judith keeps her eyes on the tea caddy.] Is it still raining?   [*He shuts the door.*

RICHARD. Raining like the very—— [*His eye catches Judith's as she looks quickly and haughtily up.*]—I beg your pardon; but [*shewing that his coat is wet*] you see!

ANDERSON. Take it off, sir; and let it hang before the fire a while: my wife will excuse your shirtsleeves. Judith: put in another spoonful of tea for Mr Dudgeon.

RICHARD. [*Eyeing him cynically.*] The magic of property, Pastor! Are even you civil to me now that I have succeeded to my father's estate?

[*Judith throws down the spoon indignantly.*

ANDERSON. [*Quite unruffled, and helping Richard off with his coat.*] I think, sir, that since you accept my hospitality, you cannot have so bad an opinion of it. Sit down.

[*With the coat in his hand, he points to the railed seat. Richard, in his shirtsleeves, looks at him half quarrelsomely for a moment; then, with a nod, acknowledges that the minister has got the better of him, and sits down on the seat. Anderson pushes his cloak into a heap on the seat of the chair at the fire, and hangs Richard's coat on the back in its place.*

RICHARD. I come, sir, on your own invitation. You left word you had something important to tell me.

ANDERSON. I have a warning which it is my duty to give you.

RICHARD. [*Quickly rising.*] You want to preach to me. Excuse me: I prefer a walk in the rain.   [*He makes for his coat.*

ANDERSON. [*Stopping him.*] Dont be alarmed, sir: I am no great preacher. You are quite safe. [*Richard smiles in spite of himself. His glance softens: he even makes a gesture of excuse. Anderson, seeing that he has tamed him, now addresses him earnestly.*] Mr Dudgeon: you are in danger in this town.

RICHARD. What danger?

ANDERSON. Your uncle's danger. Major Swindon's gallows.

RICHARD. It is you who are in danger. I warned you——

ANDERSON. [*Interrupting him goodhumoredly but authoritatively.*] Yes, yes, Mr Dudgeon; but they do not think so in the town. And even if I were in danger, I have duties here which I must not forsake. But you are a free man. Why should you run any risk?

RICHARD. Do you think I should be any great loss, Minister?

ANDERSON. I think that a man's life is worth saving, whoever it belongs to. [*Richard makes him an ironical bow. Anderson returns the bow humorously.*] Come: youll have a cup of tea, to prevent you catching cold?

RICHARD. I observe that Mrs Anderson is not quite so pressing as you are, Pastor.

JUDITH. [*Almost stifled with resentment, which she has been expecting her husband to share and express for her at every insult of Richard's.*] You are welcome for my husband's sake.

[*She brings the teapot to the fireplace and sets it on the hob.*

RICHARD. I know I am not welcome for my own, madam. [*He rises.*] But I think I will not break bread here, Minister.

ANDERSON. [*Cheerily.*] Give me a good reason for that.

RICHARD. Because there is something in you that I respect, and that makes me desire to have you for my enemy.

ANDERSON. Thats well said. On these terms, sir, I will accept your enmity or any man's. Judith: Mr Dudgeon will stay to tea. Sit down: it will take a few minutes to draw by the fire. [*Richard glances at him with a troubled face; then sits down with his head bent, to hide a convulsive swelling of his throat.*] I was just saying to my wife, Mr Dudgeon, that enmity—— [*She grasps his hand and looks imploringly at him, doing both with an intensity that checks him at once.*] Well, well, I mustnt tell you, I see; but it was nothing that need leave us worse friend—enemies, I mean. Judith is a great enemy of yours.

RICHARD. If all my enemies were like Mrs Anderson, I should be the best Christian in America.

ANDERSON. [*Gratified, patting her hand.*] You hear that, Judith? Mr Dudgeon knows how to turn a compliment.

[*The latch is lifted from without.*

JUDITH. [*Staring.*] Who is that?

[*Christy comes in.*

CHRISTY. [*Stopping and staring at Richard.*] Oh, are you here?

RICHARD. Yes. Begone, you fool: Mrs Anderson doesnt want the whole family to tea at once.

CHRISTY. [*Coming farther in.*] Mother's very ill.

RICHARD. Well, does she want to see me?

CHRISTY. No.

RICHARD. I thought not.

CHRISTY. She wants to see the minister—at once.

JUDITH. [*To Anderson.*] Oh, not before youve had some tea.

ANDERSON. I shall enjoy it more when I come back, dear.

[*He is about to take up his cloak.*

CHRISTY. The rain's over.

ANDERSON. [*Dropping the cloak and picking up his hat from the fender.*] Where is your mother, Christy?

CHRISTY. At Uncle Titus's.

ANDERSON. Have you fetched the doctor?

CHRISTY. No: she didnt tell me to.

ANDERSON. Go on there at once: I'll overtake you on his doorstep.

[*Christy turns to go.*] Wait a moment. Your brother must be anxious to know the particulars.

RICHARD. Psha! Not I: he doesn't know; and I dont care. [*Violently.*] Be off, you oaf. [*Christy runs out. Richard adds, a little shamefacedly*] We shall know soon enough.

ANDERSON. Well, perhaps you will let me bring you the news myself. Judith: will you give Mr Dudgeon his tea, and keep him here until I return.

JUDITH. [*White and trembling.*] Must I——

ANDERSON. [*Taking her hands and interrupting her to cover her agitation.*] My dear: I can depend on you?

JUDITH. [*With a piteous effort to be worthy of his trust.*] Yes.

ANDERSON. [*Pressing her hand against his cheek.*] You will not mind two old people like us, Mr Dudgeon. [*Going.*] I shall not say good evening: you will be here when I come back.

[*He goes out.*

[*They watch him pass the window, and then look at each other dumbly, quite disconcerted. Richard, noting the quiver of her lips, is the first to pull himself together.*

RICHARD. Mrs Anderson: I am perfectly aware of the nature of your sentiments towards me. I shall not intrude on you. Good evening. [*Again he starts for the fireplace to get his coat.*

JUDITH. [*Getting between him and the coat.*] No, no. Dont go: please dont go.

RICHARD. [*Roughly.*] Why? You dont want me here.

JUDITH. Yes, I—— [*Wringing her hands in despair.*] Oh, if I tell you the truth, you will use it to torment me.

RICHARD. [*Indignantly.*] Torment! What right have you to say that? Do you expect me to stay after that?

JUDITH. I want you to stay; but [*suddenly raging at him like an angry child*] it is not because I like you.

RICHARD. Indeed!

JUDITH. Yes: I had rather you did go than mistake me about that. I hate and dread you; and my husband knows it. If you are not here when he comes back, he will believe that I disobeyed him and drove you away.

RICHARD. [*Ironically.*] Whereas, of course, you have really been so kind and hospitable and charming to me that I only want to go away out of mere contrariness, eh?

[*Judith, unable to bear it, sinks on the chair and bursts into tears.*

RICHARD. Stop, stop, stop, I tell you. Dont do that. [*Putting his hand to his breast as if to a wound.*] He wrung my heart by being a man. Need you tear it by being a woman? Has he not raised you above my insults, like himself? [*She stops crying, and recovers herself somewhat, looking at him with a scared curiosity.*] There: thats right. [*Sympathetically.*] Youre better now, arnt you? [*He puts his hand encouragingly on her shoulder. She instantly rises haughtily, and stares at him defiantly. He at once drops into his usual sardonic tone.*] Ah, thats better. You are yourself again: so is Richard. Well, shall we go to tea like a quiet respectable couple, and wait for your husband's return?

JUDITH. [*Rather ashamed of herself.*] If you please. I—I am sorry to have been so foolish.

          [*She stoops to take up the plate of toast from the fender.*

RICHARD. I am sorry, for your sake, that I am—what I am. Allow me.   [*He takes the plate from her and goes with it to the table.*

JUDITH. [*Following with the teapot.*] Will you sit down? [*He sits down at the end of the tadle nearest the press. There is a plate and knife laid there. The other plate is laid near it: but Judith stays at the opposite end of the table, next theifire, and takes her place there, drawing the tray towards her.*] Do you take sugar?

RICHARD. No: but plenty of milk. Let me give you some toast.

    [*He puts some on the second plate, and hands it to her, with the knife. The action shews quickly how well he knows that she has avoided her usual place so as to be as far from him as possible.*

JUDITH. [*Consciously.*] Thanks. [*She gives him his tea.*] Wont you help yourself?

RICHARD. Thanks.

    [*He puts a piece of toast on his own plate; and she pours out tea for herself.*

JUDITH. [*Observing that he tastes nothing.*] Dont you like it? You are not eating anything.

RICHARD. Neither are you.

JUDITH. [*Nervously.*] I never care much for my tea. Please dont mind me.

RICHARD. [*Looking dreamily round.*] I am thinking. It is all so strange to me. I can see the beauty and peace of this home: I think I have never been more at rest in my life than at this moment; and yet I know quite well I could never live here. It's not in my nature, I suppose, to be domesticated. But it's very beautiful: it's almost holy.   [*He muses a moment, and then laughs softly.*

JUDITH. [*Quickly.*] Why do you laugh?

RICHARD. I was thinking that if any stranger came in here now, he would take us for man and wife.

JUDITH. [*Taking offence.*] You mean, I suppose, that you are more my age than he is.

RICHARD. [*Staring at this unexpected turn.*] I never thought of such a thing. [*Sardonic again.*] I see there is another side to domestic joy.

JUDITH. [*Angrily.*] I would rather have a husband whom everybody respects than—than——

RICHARD. Than the devil's disciple. You are right; but I daresay
your love helps him to be a good man, just as your hate helps me
to be a bad one.

JUDITH. My husband has been very good to you. He has forgiven
you for insulting him, and is trying to save you. Can you not
forgive him for being so much better than you are? How dare
you belittle him by putting yourself in his place?

RICHARD. Did I?

JUDITH. Yes, you did. You said that if anybody came in they
would take us for man and—— [*She stops, terror stricken, as a
squad of soldiers tramps past the window.*] The English soldiers! Oh,
what do they——

RICHARD. [*Listening.*] Sh!

A VOICE. [*Outside.*] Halt! Four outside: two in with me.

[*Judith half rises, listening and looking with dilated eyes at Richard,
who takes up his cup prosaically, and is drinking his tea when the
latch goes up with a sharp click, and an English sergeant walks into
the room with two privates, who post themselves at the door. He
comes promptly to the table between them.*]

THE SERGEANT. Sorry to disturb you, mum. Duty! Anthony
Anderson: I arrest you in King George's name as a rebel.

JUDITH. [*Pointing at Richard.*] But that is not——

[*He looks up quickly at her, with a face of iron. She stops her mouth
hastily with the hand she has raised to indicate him, and stands
staring affrightedly.*]

THE SERGEANT. Come, parson: put your coat on and come along.

RICHARD. Yes: I'll come. [*He rises and takes a step towards his own
coat; then recollects himself, and, with his back to the sergeant, moves his
gaze slowly round the room without turning his head until he sees Anderson's black coat hanging up on the press. He goes composedly to it; takes
it down; and puts it on. The idea of himself as a parson tickles him: he
looks down at the black sleeve on his arm, and then smiles slyly at
Judith, whose white face shews him that what she is painfully struggling
to grasp is not the humor of the situation but its horror. He turns to the
sergeant, who is approaching him with a pair of handcuffs hidden behind
him, and says lightly*] Did you ever arrest a man of my cloth before,
Sergeant?

THE SERGEANT. [*Instinctively respectful, half to the black coat, and half
to Richard's good breeding.*] Well, no, sir. At least, only an army
chaplain. [*Shewing the handcuffs.*] I'm sorry sir; but duty——

RICHARD. Just so, Sergeant. Well, I'm not ashamed of them:
thank you kindly for the apology.   [*He holds out his hands.*

SERGEANT. [*Not availing himself of the offer.*] One gentleman to
another, sir. Wouldnt you like to say a word to your missis, sir,
before you go?

RICHARD. [*Smiling.*] Oh, we shall meet again before—eh?
[*Meaning 'before you hang me'.*]
SERGEANT. [*Loudly, with ostentatious cheerfulness.*] Oh, of course, of course. No call for the lady to distress herself. Still— [*in a lower voice, intended for Richard alone*] your last chance, sir.

[*They look at one another significantly for a moment. Then Richard exhales a deep breath and turns towards Judith.*
RICHARD. [*Very distinctly.*] My love. [*She looks at him, pitiably pale, and tries to answer, but cannot—tries also to come to him, but cannot trust herself to stand without the support of the table.*] This gallant gentleman is good enough to allow us a moment of leavetaking. [*The sergeant retires delicately and joins his men near the door.*] He is trying to spare you the truth; but you had better know it. Are you listening to me? [*She signifies assent.*] Do you understand that I am going to my death? [*She signifies that she understands.*] Remember, you must find our friend who was with us just now. Do you understand? [*She signifies yes.*] See that you get him safely out of harm's way. Dont for your life let him know of my danger; but if he finds it out, tell him that he cannot save me: they would hang him; and they would not spare me. And tell him that I am steadfast in my religion as he is in his, and that he may depend on me to the death. [*He turns to go, and meets the eyes of the sergeant, who looks a little suspicious. He considers a moment, and then, turning roguishly to Judith with something of a smile breaking through his earnestness, says*] And now, my dear, I am afraid the sergeant will not believe that you love me like a wife unless you give one kiss before I go.

[*He approaches her and holds out his arms. She quits the table and almost falls into them.*
JUDITH. [*The words choking her.*] I ought to—it's murder——
RICHARD. No: only a kiss [*softly to her*] for his sake.
JUDITH. I cant. You must——
RICHARD. [*Folding her in his arms with an impulse of compassion for her distress.*] My poor girl!

[*Judith, with a sudden effort, throws her arms round him; kisses him; and swoons away, dropping from his arms to the ground as if the kiss had killed her.*
RICHARD. [*Going quickly to the sergeant.*] Now, Sergeant: quick, before she comes to. The handcuffs. [*He puts out his hands.*
SERGEANT. [*Pocketing them.*] Never mind, sir: I'll trust you. Youre a game one. You ought to a bin a soldier, sir. Between them two, please.

[*The soldiers place themselves one before Richard and one behind him. The sergeant opens the door.*

RICHARD. [*Taking a last look round him.*] Goodbye, wife: goodbye, home. Muffle the drums, and quick march!

> [*The sergeant signs to the leading soldier to march. They file out quickly.*
>
> [*When Anderson returns from Mrs Dudgeon's, he is astonished to find the room apparently empty and almost in darkness except for the glow from the fire; for one of the candles has burnt out, and the other is at its last flicker.*

ANDERSON. Why, what on earth——? [*Calling.*] Judith, Judith! [*He listens: there is no answer.*] Hm! [*He goes to the cupboard; takes a candle from the drawer; lights it at the flicker of the expiring one on the table; and looks wonderingly at the untasted meal by its light. Then he sticks it in the candlestick; takes off his hat; and scratches his head, much puzzled. This action causes him to look at the floor for the first time; and there he sees Judith lying motionless with her eyes closed. He runs to her and stoops beside her, lifting her head.*] Judith.

JUDITH. [*Waking; for her swoon has passed into the sleep of exhaustion after suffering.*] Yes. Did you call? Whats the matter?

ANDERSON. Ive just come in and found you lying here with the candles burnt out and the tea poured out and cold. What has happened?

JUDITH. [*Still astray.*] I dont know. Have I been asleep? I suppose—— [*She stops blankly.*] I dont know.

ANDERSON. [*Groaning.*] Heaven forgive me, I left you alone with that scoundrel. [*Judith remembers. With an agonized cry, she clutches his shoulders and drags herself to her feet as he rises with her. He clasps her tenderly in his arms.*] My poor pet!

JUDITH. [*Frantically clinging to him.*] What shall I do? Oh my God, what shall I do?

ANDERSON. Never mind, never mind, my dearest dear: it was my fault. Come: youre safe now; and youre not hurt, are you? [*He takes his arms from her to see whether she can stand.*] There: thats right, thats right. If only you are not hurt, nothing else matters.

JUDITH. No, no, no: I'm not hurt.

ANDERSON. Thank Heaven for that! Come now. [*Leading her to the railed seat and making her sit down beside him.*] Sit down and rest: you can tell me about it tomorrow. Or [*misunderstanding her distress*] you shall not tell me at all if it worries you. There, there! [*Cheerfully.*] I'll make you some fresh tea: that will set you up again. [*He goes to the table, and empties the teapot into the slop bowl.*

JUDITH. [*In a strained tone.*] Tony.

ANDERSON. Yes, dear?

JUDITH. Do you think we are only in a dream now?

ANDERSON. [*Glancing round at her for a moment with a pang of anxiety, though he goes on steadily and cheerfully putting fresh tea into the pot.*]

Perhaps so, pet. But you may as well dream a cup of tea when youre about it.

JUDITH. Oh stop, stop. You dont know——

[*Distracted, she buries her face in her knotted hands.*

ANDERSON. [*Breaking down and coming to her.*] My dear, what is it? I cant bear it any longer: you must tell me. It was all my fault: I was mad to trust him.

JUDITH. No: dont say that. You mustnt say that. He—oh no, no: I cant. Tony: dont speak to me. Take my hands—both my hands. [*He takes them, wondering.*] Make me think of you, not of him. Theres danger, frightful danger; but it is your danger; and I cant keep thinking of it: I cant, I cant: my mind goes back to his danger. He must be saved—no: you must be saved: you, you, you. [*She springs up as if to do something or go somewhere, exclaiming*] Oh, Heaven help me!

ANDERSON. [*Keeping his seat and holding her hands with resolute composure.*] Calmly, calmly, my pet. Youre quite distracted.

JUDITH. I may well be. I dont know what to do. I dont know what to do. [*Tearing her hands away.*] I must save him. [*Anderson rises in alarm as she runs wildly to the door. It is opened in her face by Essie, who hurries in full of anxiety. The surprise is so disagreeable to Judith that it brings her to her senses. Her tone is sharp and angry as she demands.*] What do you want?

ESSIE. I was to come to you.

ANDERSON. Who told you to?

ESSIE. [*Staring at him, as if his presence astonished her.*] Are you here?

JUDITH. Of course. Dont be foolish, child.

ANDERSON. Gently, dearest: youll frighten her. [*Going between them.*] Come here, Essie. [*She comes to him.*] Who sent you?

ESSIE. Dick. He sent me word by a soldier. I was to come here at once do whatever Mrs Anderson told me.

ANDERSON. [*Enlightened.*] A soldier! Ah, I see it all now! They have arrested Richard.   [*Judith makes a gesture of despair.*

ESSIE. No. I asked the soldier. Dick's safe. But the soldier said you had been taken.

ANDERSON. I!   [*Bewildered, he turns to Judith for an explanation.*

JUDITH. [*Coaxingly.*] All right, dear: I understand. [*To Essie.*] Thank you, Essie, for coming: but I dont need you now. You may go home.

ESSIE. [*Suspicious.*] Are you sure Dick has not been touched? Perhaps he told the soldier to say it was the minister. [*Anxiously.*] Mrs Anderson: do you think it can have been that?

ANDERSON. Tell her the truth if it is so, Judith. She will learn it from the first neighbor she meets in the street.

[*Judith turns away and covers her eyes with her hands.*

ESSIE. [*Wailing.*] But what will they do to him? Oh, what will they do to him? Will they hang him?

> [*Judith shudders convulsively, and throws herself into the chair in which Richard sat at the tea table.*

ANDERSON. [*Patting Essie's shoulder and trying to comfort her.*] I hope not. I hope not. Perhaps if youre very quiet and patient, we may be able to help him in some way.

ESSIE. Yes—help him—yes, yes, yes. I'll be good.

ANDERSON. I must go to him at once, Judith.

JUDITH. [*Springing up.*] Oh no. You must go away—far away, to some place of safety.

ANDERSON. Pooh!

JUDITH. [*Passionately.*] Do you want to kill me? Do you think I can bear to live for days and days with every knock at the door—every footstep—giving me a spasm of terror? to lie awake for nights and nights in an agony of dread, listening for them to come and arrest you?

ANDERSON. Do you think it would be better to know that I had run away from my post at the first sign of danger?

JUDITH. [*Bitterly.*] Oh, you wont go. I know it. Youll stay; and I shall go mad.

ANDERSON. My dear, your duty——

JUDITH. [*Fiercely.*] What do I care about my duty?

ANDERSON. [*Shocked.*] Judith!

JUDITH. I am doing my duty. I am clinging to my duty. My duty is to get away, to save you, to leave him to his fate. [*Essie utters a cry of distress and sinks on the chair at the fire, sobbing silently.*] My instinct is the same as hers—to save him above all things, though it would be so much better for him to die! so much greater! But I know you will take your own way as he took it. I have no power. [*She sits down sullenly on the railed seat.*] I'm only a woman; I can do nothing but sit here and suffer. Only, tell him I tried to save you—that I did my best to save you.

ANDERSON. My dear, I am afraid he will be thinking more of his own danger than of mine.

JUDITH. Stop; or I shall hate you.

ANDERSON. [*Remonstrating.*] Come, come, come! How am I to leave you if you talk like this? You are quite out of your senses. [*He turns to Essie.*] Essie.

ESSIE. [*Eagerly rising and drying her eyes.*] Yes?

ANDERSON. Just wait outside a moment, like a good girl; Mrs Anderson is not well. [*Essie looks doubtful.*] Never fear; I'll come to you presently; and I'll go to Dick.

ESSIE. You are sure you will go to him? [*Whispering.*] You wont let her prevent you?

ANDERSON. [*Smiling.*] No, no; it's all right. All right. [*She goes.*]
Thats a good girl.   [*He closes the door, and returns to Judith.*

JUDITH. [*Seated—rigid.*] You are going to your death.

ANDERSON. [*Quaintly.*] Then I shall go in my best coat, dear. [*He
turns to the press, beginning to take off his coat.*] Where——? [*He
stares at the empty nail for a moment; then looks quickly round to the
fire; strides across to it; and lifts Richard's coat.*] Why, my dear, it
seems that he has gone in my best coat.

JUDITH. [*Still motionless.*] Yes.

ANDERSON. Did the soldiers make a mistake?

JUDITH. Yes: they made a mistake.

ANDERSON. He might have told them. Poor fellow, he was too
upset, I suppose.

JUDITH. Yes: he might have told them. So might I.

ANDERSON. Well, it's all very puzzling—almost funny. It's curious
how these little things strike us even in the most—— [*He breaks
off and begins putting on Richard's coat.*] I'd better take him his
own coat. I know what he'll say—— [*Imitating Richard's sardonic
manner.*] 'Anxious about my soul, Pastor, and also about your
best coat.' Eh?

JUDITH. Yes, that is just what he will say to you. [*Vacantly.*] It
doesnt matter: I shall never see either of you again.

ANDERSON. [*Rallying her.*] Oh pooh, pooh, pooh! [*He sits down
beside her.*] Is this how you keep your promise that I shant be
ashamed of my brave wife?

JUDITH. No: this is how I break it. I cannot keep my promises to
him: why should I keep my promises to you?

ANDERSON. Dont speak so strangely, my love. It sounds insincere
to me. [*She looks unutterable reproach at him.*] Yes, dear, nonsense
is always insincere; and my dearest is talking nonsense. Just
nonsense. [*Her face darkens into dumb obstinacy. She stares straight
before her, and does not look at him again, absorbed in Richard's fate.
He scans her face; sees that his rallying has produced no effect; and gives
it up, making no further effort to conceal his anxiety.*] I wish I knew
what has frightened you so. Was there a struggle? Did he fight?

JUDITH. No. He smiled.

ANDERSON. Did he realize his danger, do you think?

JUDITH. He realized yours.

ANDERSON. Mine!

JUDITH. [*Monotonously.*] He said 'See that you get him safely out
of harm's way.' I promised: I cant keep my promise. He said,
'Dont for your life let him know of my danger.' Ive told you of
it. He said that if you found it out, you could not save him—that
they will hang him and not spare you.

ANDERSON. [*Rising in generous indignation.*] And you think that I will let a man with that much good in him die like a dog, when a few words might make him die like a Christian? I'm ashamed of you, Judith.

JUDITH. He will be steadfast in his religion as you are in yours; and you may depend on him to the death. He said so.

ANDERSON. God forgive him! What else did he say?

JUDITH. He said goodbye.

ANDERSON. [*Fidgeting nervously to and fro in great concern.*] Poor fellow, poor fellow! You said goodbye to him in all kindness and charity, Judith, I hope.

JUDITH. I kissed him.

ANDERSON. What! Judith!

JUDITH. Are you angry?

ANDERSON. No, no. You were right: you were right. Poor fellow, poor fellow! [*Greatly distressed.*] To be hanged like that at his age! And then did they take him away?

JUDITH. [*Wearily.*] Then you were here: thats the next thing I remember. I suppose I fainted. Now bid me goodbye, Tony. Perhaps I shall faint again. I wish I could die.

ANDERSON. No, no, my dear: you must pull yourself together and be sensible. I am in no danger—not the least in the world.

JUDITH. [*Solemnly.*] You are going to your death, Tony—your sure death, if God will let innocent men be murdered. They will not let you see him: they will arrest you the moment you give your name. It was for you the soldiers came.

ANDERSON. [*Thunderstruck.*] For me!!!

[*His fists clinch; his neck thickens; his face reddens; the fleshy purses under his eyes become injected with hot blood; the man of peace vanishes, transfigured into a choleric and formidable man of war. Still, she does not come out of her absorption to look at him: her eyes are steadfast with a mechanical reflection of Richard's steadfastness.*]

JUDITH. He took your place: he is dying to save you. That is why he went in your coat. That is why I kissed him.

ANDERSON. [*Exploding.*] Blood an' owns! [*His voice is rough and dominant, his gesture full of brute energy.*] Here! Essie, Essie!

ESSIE. [*Running in.*] Yes.

ANDERSON. [*Impetuously.*] Off with you as hard as you can run, to the inn. Tell them to saddle the fastest and strongest horse they have—[*Judith rises breathless, and stares at him incredulously.*]—the chestnut mare, if she's fresh—without a moment's delay. Go into the stable yard and tell the black man there that I'll give him a silver dollar if the horse is waiting for me when I come, and that I am close on your heels. Away with you.

[*His energy sends Essie flying from the room. He pounces on his riding-boots; rushes with them to the chair at the fire; and begins pulling them on.*

JUDITH. [*Unable to believe such a thing of him.*] You are not going to him!

ANDERSON. [*Busy with the boots.*] Going to him! What good would that do? [*Growling to himself as he gets the first boot on with a wrench.*] I'll go to them, so I will. [*To Judith peremptorily.*] Get me the pistols: I want them. And money, money: I want money—all the money in the house. [*He stoops over the other boot, grumbling.*] A great satisfaction it would be to him to have my company on the gallows.   [*He pulls on the boot.*

JUDITH. You are deserting him, then?

ANDERSON. Hold your tongue, woman; and get me the pistols. [*She goes to the press and takes from it a leather belt with two pistols, a powder horn, and a bag of bullets attached to it. She throws it on the table. Then she unlocks a drawer in the press and takes out a purse. Anderson grabs the belt and buckles it on, saying*] If they took him for me in my coat, perhaps theyll take me for him in his. [*Hitching the belt into its place.*] Do I look like him?

JUDITH. [*Turning with the purse in her hand.*] Horribly unlike him.

ANDERSON. [*Snatching the purse from her and emptying it on the table.*] Hm! We shall see.

JUDITH. [*Sitting down helplessly.*] Is it of any use to pray, do you think, Tony?

ANDERSON. [*Counting the money.*] Pray! Can we pray Swindon's rope off Richard's neck?

JUDITH. God may soften Major Swindon's heart.

ANDERSON. [*Contemptuously—pocketing a handful of money.*] Let him, then. I am not God; and I must go to work another way. [*Judith gasps at the blasphemy. He throws the purse on the table.*] Keep that. Ive taken twenty-five dollars.

JUDITH. Have you forgotten even that you are a minister?

ANDERSON. Minister be—faugh! My hat: wheres my hat? [*He snatches up hat and cloak, and puts both on in hot haste.*] Now listen, you. If you can get a word with him by pretending youre his wife, tell him to hold his tongue until morning: that will give me all the start I need.

JUDITH. [*Solemnly.*] You may depend on him to the death.

ANDERSON. Youre a fool, a fool, Judith. [*For a moment checking the torrent of his haste, and speaking with something of his old quiet and impressive conviction.*] You dont know the man youre married to. [*Essie returns. He swoops at her at once.*] Well: is the horse ready?

ESSIE. [*Breathless.*] It will be ready when you come.

ANDERSON. Good.   [*He makes for the door.*

JUDITH. [*Rising and stretching out her arms after him involuntarily.*]
Wont you say goodbye?

ANDERSON. And waste another half minute! Psha!

[*He rushes out like an avalanche.*

ESSIE. [*Hurrying to Judith.*] He has gone to save Richard, hasnt he?

JUDITH. To save Richard! No: Richard has saved him. He has
gone to save himself. Richard must die.

*Essie screams with terror and falls on her knees, hiding her face.
Judith, without heeding her, looks rigidly straight in front of her, at
the vision of Richard, dying.*

ACT III

Early next morning the sergeant, at the British headquarters in the Town Hall, unlocks the door of a little empty panelled waiting room, and invites Judith to enter. She has had a bad night, probably a rather delirious one; for even in the reality of the raw morning, her fixed gaze comes back at moments when her attention is not strongly held.

The sergeant considers that her feelings do her credit, and is sympathetic in an encouraging military way. Being a fine figure of a man, vain of his uniform and of his rank, he feels specially qualified, in a respectful way, to console her.

SERGEANT. You can have a quiet word with him here, mum.

JUDITH. Shall I have long to wait?

SERGEANT. No, mum, not a minute. We kep him in the Bridewell for the night; and he's just been brought over here for the court martial. Dont fret, mum: he slep like a child, and has made a rare good breakfast.

JUDITH. [*Incredulously.*] He is in good spirits!

SERGEANT. Tip top, mum. The chaplain looked in to see him last night; and he won seventeen shillings off him at spoil five. He spent it among us like the gentleman he is. Duty's duty, mum, of course; but youre among friends here. [*The tramp of a couple of soldiers is heard approaching.*] There: I think he's coming. [*Richard comes in, without a sign of care or captivity in his bearing. The sergeant nods to the two soldiers, and shows them the key of the room in his hand. They withdraw.*] Your good lady, sir.

RICHARD. [*Going to her.*] What! My wife. My adored one. [*He takes her hand and kisses it with a perverse, raffish gallantry.*] How long do you allow a brokenhearted husband for leave-taking, Sergeant?

SERGEANT. As long as we can, sir. We shall not disturb you till the court sits.

RICHARD. But it has struck the hour.

SERGEANT. So it has, sir; but theres a delay. General Burgoyne's just arrived—Gentlemanly Johnny we call him, sir—and he wont have done finding fault with everything this side of half past. I know him, sir: I served with him in Portugal. You may count on twenty minutes, sir; and by your leave I wont waste any more of them.

[*He goes out, locking the door. Richard immediately drops his raffish manner and turns to Judith with considerate sincerity.*

RICHARD. Mrs Anderson: this visit is very kind of you. And how are you after last night? I had to leave you before you recovered; but I sent word to Essie to go and look after you. Did she understand the message?

JUDITH. [*Breathless and urgent.*] Oh, dont think of me: I havnt come here to talk about myself. Are they going to—to——? [*Meaning ' to hang you'.*]

RICHARD. [*Whimsically.*] At noon, punctually. At least, that was when they disposed of Uncle Peter. [*She shudders.*] Is your husband safe? Is he on the wing?

JUDITH. He is no longer my husband.

RICHARD. [*Opening his eyes wide.*] Eh?

JUDITH. I disobeyed you. I told him everything. I expected him to come here and save you. I wanted him to come here and save you. He ran away instead.

RICHARD. Well, thats what I meant him to do. What good would his staying have done? Theyd only have hanged us both.

JUDITH. [*With reproachful earnestness.*] Richard Dudgeon: on your honour, what would you have done in his place?

RICHARD. Exactly what he has done, of course.

JUDITH. Oh, why will you not be simple with me—honest and straightforward? If you are so selfish as that, why did you let them take you last night?

RICHARD. [*Gaily.*] Upon my life, Mrs Anderson, I dont know. Ive been asking myself that question ever since; and I can find no manner of reason for acting as I did.

JUDITH. You know you did it for his sake, believing he was a more worthy man than yourself.

RICHARD. [*Laughing.*] Oho! No: thats a very pretty reason, I must say; but I'm not so modest as that. No: It wasnt for his sake.

JUDITH. [*After a pause, during which she looks shamefacedly at him, blushing painfully.*] Was it for my sake?

RICHARD. [*Gallantly.*] Well, you had a hand in it. It must have been a little for your sake. You let them take me, at all events.

JUDITH. Oh, do you think I have not been telling myself that all night? Your death will be at my door. [*Impulsively, she gives him her hand, and adds, with intense earnestness*] If I could save you as you saved him, I would do it, no matter how cruel the death was.

RICHARD. [*Holding her hand and smiling, but keeping her almost at arm's length.*] I am very sure I shouldnt let you.

JUDITH. Dont you see that I can save you?

RICHARD. How? By changing clothes with me, eh?

JUDITH. [*Disengaging her hand to touch his lips with it.*] Dont. [*Meaning ' Dont jest'.*] No: by telling the court who you really are.

RICHARD. [*Frowning.*] No use: they wouldnt spare me; and it would spoil half his chance of escaping. They are determined to cow us by making an example of somebody on that gallows today. Well, let us cow them by showing that we can stand by one another to the death. That is the only force that can send Burgoyne back across the Atlantic and make America a nation.

JUDITH. [*Impatiently.*] Oh, what does all that matter?

RICHARD. [*Laughing.*] True: what does it matter? What does anything matter? You see, men have these strange notions, Mrs Anderson; and women see the folly of them.

JUDITH. Women have to lose those they love through them.

RICHARD. They can easily get fresh lovers.

JUDITH. [*Revolted.*] Oh! [*Vehemently.*] Do you realize that you are going to kill yourself?

RICHARD. The only man I have any right to kill, Mrs Anderson. Dont be concerned: no woman will lose her lover through my death. [*Smiling.*] Bless you, nobody cares for me. Have you heard that my mother is dead?

JUDITH. Dead!

RICHARD. Of heart disease—in the night. Her last word to me was her curse: I dont think I could have borne her blessing. My other relatives will not grieve much on my account. Essie will cry for a day or two; but I have provided for her: I made my own will last night.

JUDITH. [*Stonily, after a moment's silence.*] And I!

RICHARD. [*Surprised.*] You?

JUDITH. Yes, I. Am I not to care at all?

RICHARD. [*Gaily and bluntly.*] Not a scrap. Oh, you expressed your feelings towards me very frankly yesterday. What happened may have softened you for the moment; but believe me, Mrs Anderson, you dont like a bone in my skin or a hair on my head. I shall be as good a riddance at twelve today as I should have been at twelve yesterday.

JUDITH. [*Her voice trembling.*] What can I do to shew you that you are mistaken?

RICHARD. Dont trouble. I'll give you credit for liking me a little better than you did. All I say is that my death will not break your heart.

JUDITH. [*Almost in a whisper.*] How do you know?

[*She puts her hands on his shoulders and looks intently at him.*]

RICHARD. [*Amazed—divining the truth.*] Mrs Anderson! [*The bell of the town clock strikes the quarter. He collects himself, and removes her hands, saying rather coldly*] Excuse me: they will be here for me presently. It is too late.

JUDITH. It is not too late. Call me as witness: they will never kill you when they know how heroically you have acted.

RICHARD. [*With some scorn.*] Indeed! But if I dont go through with it, where will the heroism be? I shall simply have tricked them; and theyll hang me for that like a dog. Serve me right too!

JUDITH. [*Wildly.*] Oh, I believe you want to die.

RICHARD. [*Obstinately.*] No, I dont.

JUDITH. Then why not try to save yourself? I implore you—listen. You said just now that you saved him for my sake—yes [*clutching him as he recoils with a gesture of denial*] a little for my sake. Well, save yourself for my sake. And I will go with you to the end of the world.

RICHARD. [*Taking her by the wrists and holding her a little way from him, looking steadily at her.*] Judith.

JUDITH. [*Breathless—delighted at the name.*] Yes.

RICHARD. If I said—to please you—that I did what I did ever so little for your sake, I lied as men always lie to women. You know how much I have lived with worthless men—aye, and worthless women too. Well, they could all rise to some sort of goodness and kindness when they were in love. [*The word love comes from him with true Puritan scorn.*] That has taught me to set very little store by the goodness that only comes out red hot. What I did last night, I did in cold blood, caring not half so much for your husband, or [*ruthlessly*] for you [*she droops, stricken*] as I do for myself. I had no motive and no interest: all I can tell you is that when it came to the point whether I would take my neck out of the noose and put another man's into it, I would not do it. I dont know why not: I see myself as a fool for my pains; but I could not and I cannot. I have been brought up standing by the law of my own nature; and I may not go against it, gallows or no gallows. [*She has slowly raised her head and is now looking full at him.*] I should have done the same for any other man in the town, or any other man's wife. [*Releasing her.*] Do you understand that?

JUDITH. Yes: you mean that you do not love me.

RICHARD. [*Revolted—with fierce contempt.*] Is that all it means to you?

JUDITH. What more—what worse—can it mean to me? [*The sergeant knocks. The blow on the door jars on her heart.*] Oh, one moment more. [*She throws herself on her knees.*] I pray to you——

RICHARD. Hush! [*Calling.*] Come in.

[*The sergeant unlocks the door and opens it. The guard is with him.*

SERGEANT. [*Coming in.*] Time's up, sir.

RICHARD. Quite ready, Sergeant. Now, my dear.

[*He attempts to raise her.*

JUDITH. [*Clinging to him.*] Only one thing more—I entreat, I implore you. Let me be present in the court. I have seen Major Swindon: he said I should be allowed if you asked it. You will ask it. It is my last request: I shall never ask you anything again. [*She clasps his knee.*] I beg and pray it of you.

RICHARD. If I do, will you be silent?

JUDITH. Yes.

RICHARD. You will keep faith?

JUDITH. I will keep——   [*She breaks down, sobbing.*

RICHARD. [*Taking her arm to lift her.*] Just—her other arm, Sergeant.

[*They go out, she sobbing convulsively, supported by the two men. Meanwhile, the Council Chamber is ready for the court martial. It is a large, lofty room, with a chair of state in the middle under a tall canopy with a gilt crown, and maroon curtains with the royal monogram G.R. In front of the chair is a table, also draped in maroon, with a bell, a heavy inkstand, and writing materials on it. Several chairs are set at the table. The door is at the right hand of the occupant of the chair of state when it has an occupant: at present it is empty. Major Swindon, a pale, sandy-haired, very conscientious-looking man of about forty-five, sits at the end of the table with his back to the door, writing. He is alone until the sergeant announces the General in a subdued manner which suggests that Gentlemanly Johnny has been making his presence felt rather heavily.*

SERGEANT. The General, sir.

[*Swindon rises hastily. The general comes in: the sergeant goes out. General Burgoyne is fifty-five, and very well preserved. He is a man of fashion, gallant enough to have made a distinguished marriage by an elopement, witty enough to write successful comedies, aristocratically-connected enough to have had opportunities of high military distinction. His eyes, large, brilliant, apprehensive, and intelligent, are his most remarkable feature: without them his fine nose and small mouth would suggest rather more fastidiousness and less force than go to the making of a first-rate general. Just now the eyes are angry and tragic, and the mouth and the nostrils tense.*

BURGOYNE. Major Swindon, I presume.

SWINDON. Yes. General Burgoyne, if I mistake not. [*They bow to one another ceremoniously.*] I am glad to have the support of your presence this morning. It is not particularly lively business, hanging this poor devil of a minister.

BURGOYNE. [*Throwing himself into Swindon's chair.*] No, sir, it is not. It is making too much of the fellow to execute him: what more could you have done if he had been a member of the Church of England? Martyrdom, sir, is what these people like: it is the only way in which a man can become famous without ability. However, you have committed us to hanging him; and the sooner he is hanged the better.

SWINDON. We have arranged it for twelve o'clock. Nothing remains to be done except to try him.

BURGOYNE. [*Looking at him with suppressed anger.*] Nothing—except
to save your own necks, perhaps. Have you heard the news
from Springtown?

SWINDON. Nothing special. The latest reports are satisfactory.

BURGOYNE. [*Rising in amazement.*] Satisfactory, sir! Satisfactory!!
[*He stares at him for a moment, and then adds, with grim intensity.*] I
am glad you take that view of them.

SWINDON. [*Puzzled.*] Do I understand that in your opinion——

BURGOYNE. I do not express my opinion. I never stoop to that
habit of profane language which unfortunately coarsens our
profession. If I did, sir, perhaps I should be able to express my
opinion of the news from Springtown—the news which you
[*severely*] have apparently not heard. How soon do you get news
from your supports here?—in the course of a month, eh?

SWINDON. [*Turning sulky.*] I suppose the reports have been taken
to you, sir, instead of to me. Is there anything serious?

BURGOYNE. [*Taking a report from his pocket and holding it up.*] Springtown's in the hands of the rebels.

[*He throws the report on the table.*

SWINDON. [*Aghast.*] Since yesterday!

BURGOYNE. Since two o'clock this morning. Perhaps we shall be
in their hands before two o'clock tomorrow morning. Have you
thought of that?

SWINDON. [*Confidently.*] As to that, General, the British soldier will
give a good account of himself.

BURGOYNE. [*Bitterly.*] And therefore, I suppose, sir, the British
officer need not know his business: the British soldier will get
him out of all his blunders with the bayonet. In future, sir, I
must ask you to be a little less generous with the blood of your
men, and a little more generous with your own brains.

SWINDON. I am sorry I cannot pretend to your intellectual eminence, sir. I can only do my best, and rely on the devotion of
my countrymen.

BURGOYNE. [*Suddenly becoming suavely sarcastic.*] May I ask are you
writing a melodrama, Major Swindon?

SWINDON. [*Flushing.*] No, sir.

BURGOYNE. What a pity! What a pity! [*Dropping his sarcastic tone
and facing him suddenly and seriously.*] Do you at all realize, sir,
that we have nothing standing between us and destruction but
our own bluff and the sheepishness of these colonists? They are
men of the same English stock as ourselves: six to one of us
[*repeating it emphatically*] six to one, sir; and nearly half our troops
are Hessians, Brunswickers, German dragoons, and Indians with
scalping knives. These are the countrymen on whose devotion
you rely! Suppose the colonists find a leader! Suppose the news

from Springtown should turn out to mean that they have already found a leader! What shall we do then? Eh?

SWINDON. [*Sullenly.*] Our duty, sir, I presume.

BURGOYNE. [*Again sarcastic—giving him up as a fool.*] Quite so, quite so. Thank you, Major Swindon, thank you. Now youve settled the question, sir—thrown a flood of light on the situation. What a comfort to me to feel that I have at my side so devoted and able an officer to support me in this emergency! I think, sir, it will probably relieve both our feelings if we proceed to hang this dissenter without further delay [*he strikes the bell*] especially as I am debarred by my principles from the customary military vent for my feelings. [*The sergeant appears.*] Bring your man in.

SERGEANT. Yes, sir.

BURGOYNE. And mention to any officer you may meet that the court cannot wait any longer for him.

SWINDON. [*Keeping his temper with difficulty.*] The staff is perfectly ready, sir. They have been waiting your convenience for fully half an hour. Perfectly ready, sir.

BURGOYNE. [*Blandly.*] So am I. [*Several officers come in and take their seats. One of them sits at the end of the table farthest from the door, and acts throughout as clerk of the court, making notes of the proceedings. The uniforms are those of the 9th, 20th, 21st, 24th, 47th, 53rd, and 62nd British Infantry. One officer is a Major General of the Royal Artillery. There are also German officers of the Hessian Rifles, and of German dragoon and Brunswicker regiments.*] Oh, good morning, gentlemen. Sorry to disturb you, I am sure. Very good of you to spare us a few moments.

SWINDON. Will you preside, sir?

BURGOYNE. [*Becoming additionally polished, lofty, sarcastic, and urbane now that he is in public.*] No, sir: I feel my own deficiencies too keenly to presume so far. If you will kindly allow me, I will sit at the feet of Gamaliel.

[*He takes the chair at the end of the table next the door, and motions Swindon to the chair of state, waiting for him to be seated before sitting down himself.*]

SWINDON. [*Greatly annoyed.*] As you please, sir. I am only trying to do my duty under excessively trying circumstances.

[*He takes his place in the chair of state.*]

[*Burgoyne, relaxing his studied demeanor for the moment, sits down and begins to read the report with knitted brows and careworn looks, reflecting on his desperate situation and Swindon's uselessness. Richard is brought in. Judith walks beside him. Two soldiers precede and two follow him, with the sergeant in command. They cross the room to the wall opposite the door; but when Richard has just passed before the chair of state the sergeant stops him with a touch*]

*on the arm, and posts himself behind him, at his elbow. Judith
stands timidly at the wall. The four soldiers place themselves in a
squad near her.*

BURGOYNE. [*Looking up and seeing Judith.*] Who is that woman?

SERGEANT. Prisoner's wife, sir.

SWINDON. [*Nervously.*] She begged me to allow her to be present;
and I thought——

BURGOYNE. [*Completing the sentence for him ironically.*] You thought it
would be a pleasure for her. Quite so, quite so. [*Blandly.*] Give
the lady a chair; and make her thoroughly comfortable.

[*The sergeant fetches a chair and places it near Richard.*

JUDITH. Thank you, sir.

[*She sits down after an awestricken curtsy to Burgoyne, which he
acknowledges by a dignified bend of his head.*

SWINDON. [*To Richard, sharply.*] Your name, sir?

RICHARD. [*Affable, but obstinate.*] Come: you dont mean to say that
youve brought me here without knowing who I am?

SWINDON. As a matter of form, sir, give your name.

RICHARD. As a matter of form then, my name is Anthony Anderson,
Presbyterian minister in this town.

BURGOYNE. [*Interested.*] Indeed! Pray, Mr Anderson, what do you
gentlemen believe?

RICHARD. I shall be happy to explain if time is allowed me. I
cannot undertake to complete your conversion in less than a
fortnight.

SWINDON. [*Snubbing him.*] We are not here to discuss your views.

BURGOYNE. [*With an elaborate bow to the unfortunate Swindon.*] I
stand rebuked.

SWINDON. [*Embarrassed.*] Oh, not you, I as——

BURGOYNE. Dont mention it. [*To Richard, very politely.*] Any political
views, Mr Anderson?

RICHARD. I understand that that is just what we are here to find out.

SWINDON. [*Severely.*] Do you mean to deny that you are a rebel?

RICHARD. I am an American, sir.

SWINDON. What do you expect me to think of that speech, Mr
Anderson?

RICHARD. I never expect a soldier to think, sir.

[*Burgoyne is boundlessly delighted by this retort, which almost reconciles
him to the loss of America.*

SWINDON. [*Whitening with anger.*] I advise you not to be insolent,
prisoner.

RICHARD. You cant help yourself, General. When you make up
your mind to hang a man, you put yourself at a disadvantage
with him. Why should I be civil to you? I may as well be hanged
for a sheep as a lamb.

SWINDON. You have no right to assume that the court has made up its mind without a fair trial. And you will please not address me as General. I am Major Swindon.

RICHARD. A thousand pardons. I thought I had the honor of addressing Gentlemanly Johnny.

[*Sensation among the officers. The sergeant has a narrow escape from a guffaw.*

BURGOYNE. [*With extreme suavity.*] I believe I am Gentlemanly Johnny, sir, at your service. My more intimate friends call me General Burgoyne. [*Richard bows with perfect politeness.*] You will understand, sir, I hope, since you seem to be a gentleman and a man of some spirit in spite of your calling, that if we should have the misfortune to hang you, we shall do so as a mere matter of political necessity and military duty, without any personal ill-feeling.

RICHARD. Oh, quite so. That makes all the difference in the world, of course.

[*They all smile in spite of themselves; and some of the younger officers burst out laughing.*

JUDITH. [*Her dread and horror deepening at every one of these jests and compliments.*] How can you?

RICHARD. You promised to be silent.

BURGOYNE. [*To Judith, with studied courtesy.*] Believe me, Madam, your husband is placing us under the greatest obligation by taking this very disagreeable business so thoroughly in the spirit of a gentleman. Sergeant: give Mr Anderson a chair. [*The sergeant does so. Richard sits down.*] Now, Major Swindon: we are waiting for you.

SWINDON. You are aware, I presume, Mr Anderson, of your obligations as a subject of His Majesty King George the Third.

RICHARD. I am aware, sir, that His Majesty King George the Third is about to hang me because I object to Lord North's robbing me.

SWINDON. That is a treasonable speech, sir.

RICHARD. [*Briefly.*] Yes. I meant it to be.

BURGOYNE. [*Strongly deprecating this line of defence, but still polite.*] Dont you think, Mr Anderson, that this is rather—if you will excuse the word—a vulgar line to take? Why should you cry out robbery because of a stamp duty and a tea duty and so forth? After all, it is the essence of your position as a gentleman that you pay with a good grace.

RICHARD. It is not the money, General. But to be swindled by a pig-headed lunatic like King George——

SWINDON. [*Scandalized.*] Chut, sir—silence!

SERGEANT. [*In stentorian tones, greatly shocked.*] Silence!

BURGOYNE. [*Unruffled.*] Ah, this is another point of view. My
position does not allow of my going into that, except in private.
But [*shrugging his shoulders*] of course, Mr Anderson, if you are
determined to be hanged [*Judith flinches*] there's nothing more to
be said. An unusual taste! However [*with a final shrug*]——!

SWINDON. [*To Burgoyne.*] Shall we call witnesses?

RICHARD. What need is there of witnesses? If the townspeople
here had listened to me, you would have found the streets barri-
caded, the houses loopholed, and the people in arms to hold the
town against you to the last man. But you arrived, unfortunately,
before we had got out of the talking stage; and then it was too
late.

SWINDON. [*Severely.*] Well, sir, we shall teach you and your townspeople a lesson they will not forget. Have you anything more
to say?

RICHARD. I think you might have the decency to treat me as a
prisoner of war, and shoot me like a man instead of hanging me
like a dog.

BURGOYNE. [*Sympathetically.*] Now there, Mr Anderson, you talk
like a civilian, if you will excuse my saying so. Have you any idea
of the average marksmanship of the army of His Majesty King
George the Third? If we make you up a firing party, what will
happen? Half of them will miss you: the rest will make a mess of
the business and leave you to the provo-marshal's pistol. Whereas
we can hang you in a perfectly workmanlike and agreeable way.
[*Kindly.*] Let me persuade you to be hanged, Mr Anderson?

JUDITH. [*Sick with horror.*] My God!

RICHARD. [*To Judith.*] Your promise! [*To Burgoyne.*] Thank you,
General: that view of the case did not occur to me before. To
oblige you, I withdraw my objection to the rope. Hang me, by
all means.

BURGOYNE. [*Smoothly.*] Will twelve o'clock suit you, Mr Anderson?

RICHARD. I shall be at your disposal then, General.

BURGOYNE. [*Rising.*] Nothing more to be said, gentlemen.

[*They all rise.*

JUDITH. [*Rushing to the table.*] Oh, you are not going to murder a
man like that, without a proper trial—without thinking of what
you are doing—without—— [*She cannot find words.*

RICHARD. Is this how you keep your promise?

JUDITH. If I am not to speak, you must. Defend yourself: save
yourself: tell them the truth.

RICHARD. [*Worriedly.*] I have told them truth enough to hang me
ten times over. If you say another word you will risk other lives;
but you will not save mine.

BURGOYNE. My good lady, our only desire is to save unpleasantness.

What satisfaction would it give you to have a solemn fuss made, with my friend Swindon in a black cap and so forth? I am sure we are greatly indebted to the admirable tact and gentlemanly feeling shewn by your husband.

JUDITH. [*Throwing the words in his face.*] Oh, you are mad. Is it nothing to you what wicked thing you do if only you do it like a gentleman? Is it nothing to you whether you are a murderer or not, if only you murder in a red coat? [*Desperately.*] You shall not hang him: that man is not my husband.

[*The officers look at one another, and whisper: some of the Germans asking their neighbors to explain what the woman had said. Burgoyne, who has been visibly shaken by Judith's reproach, recovers himself promptly at this new development. Richard meanwhile raises his voice above the buzz.*

RICHARD. I appeal to you, gentlemen, to put an end to this. She will not believe that she cannot save me. Break up the court.

BURGOYNE. [*In a voice so quiet and firm that it restores silence at once.*] One moment, Mr Anderson. One moment, gentlemen. [*He resumes his seat. Swindon and the officers follow his example.*] Let me understand you clearly, madam. Do you mean that this gentleman is not your husband, or merely—I wish to put this with all delicacy—that you are not his wife?

JUDITH. I dont know what you mean. I say that he is not my husband—that my husband has escaped. This man took his place to save him. Ask anyone in the town—send out into the street for the first person you find there, and bring him in as a witness. He will tell you that the prisoner is not Anthony Anderson.

BURGOYNE. [*Quietly, as before.*] Sergeant.

SERGEANT. Yes, sir.

BURGOYNE. Go out into the street and bring in the first townsman you see there.

SERGEANT. [*Making for the door.*] Yes, sir.

BURGOYNE. [*As the sergeant passes.*] The first clean, sober townsman you see.

SERGEANT. Yes, sir.   [*He goes out.*

BURGOYNE. Sit down, Mr Anderson—if I may call you so for the present. [*Richard sits down.*] Sit down, madam, whilst we wait. Give the lady a newspaper.

RICHARD. [*Indignantly.*] Shame!

BURGOYNE. [*Keenly, with a half smile.*] If you are not her husband, sir, the case is not a serious one—for her.

[*Richard bites his lip, silenced.*

JUDITH. [*To Richard, as she returns to her seat.*] I couldnt help it.

[*He shakes his head. She sits down.*

BURGOYNE. You will understand of course, Mr Anderson, that

you must not build on this little incident. We are bound to make an example of somebody.

RICHARD. I quite understand. I suppose theres no use in my explaining.

BURGOYNE. I think we should prefer independent testimony, if you dont mind.

[*The sergeant, with a packet of papers in his hand, returns conducting Christy, who is much scared.*

SERGEANT. [*Giving Burgoyne the packet.*] Dispatches, sir. Delivered by a corporal of the 33rd. Dead beat with hard riding, sir.

[*Burgoyne opens the dispatches, and presently becomes absorbed in them. They are so serious as to take his attention completely from the court martial.*

THE SERGEANT. [*To Christy.*] Now then. Attention; and take your hat off.

[*He posts himself in charge of Christy, who stands on Burgoyne's side of the court.*

RICHARD. [*In his usual bullying tone to Christy.*] Dont be frightened, you fool: youre only wanted as a witness. Theyre not going to hang you.

SWINDON. Whats your name?

CHRISTY. Christy.

RICHARD. [*Impatiently.*] Christopher Dudgeon, you blatant idiot. Give your full name.

SWINDON. Be silent, prisoner. You must not prompt the witness.

RICHARD. Very well. But I warn you youll get nothing out of him unless you shake it out of him. He has been too well brought up by a pious mother to have any sense or manhood left in him.

BURGOYNE. [*Springing up and speaking to the sergeant in a startling voice.*] Where is the man who brought these?

SERGEANT. In the guard-room, sir.

[*Burgoyne goes out with a haste that sets the officers exchanging looks.*

SWINDON. [*To Christy.*] Do you know Anthony Anderson, the Presbyterian minister?

CHRISTY. Of course I do.

[*Implying that Swindon must be an ass not to know it.*

SWINDON. Is he here?

CHRISTY. [*Staring round.*] I dont know.

SWINDON. Do you see him?

CHRISTY. No.

SWINDON. You seem to know the prisoner?

CHRISTY. Do you mean Dick?

SWINDON. Which is Dick?

CHRISTY. [*Pointing to Richard.*] Him.

SWINDON. What is his name?

CHRISTY. Dick.

RICHARD. Answer properly, you jumping jackass. What do they know about Dick?

CHRISTY. Well, you are Dick, aint you? What am I to say?

SWINDON. Address me, sir; and do you, prisoner, be silent. Tell us who the prisoner is.

CHRISTY. He's my brother Dick—Richard—Richard Dudgeon.

SWINDON. Your brother!

CHRISTY. Yes.

SWINDON. You are sure he is not Anderson.

CHRISTY. Who?

RICHARD. [*Exasperatedly.*] Me, me, me, you——

SWINDON. Silence, sir.

SERGEANT. [*Shouting.*] Silence.

RICHARD. [*Impatiently.*] Yah! [*To Christy.*] He wants to know am I Minister Anderson. Tell him, and stop grinning like a zany.

CHRISTY. [*Grinning more than ever.*] You Pastor Anderson! [*To Swindon.*] Why, Mr Anderson's a minister—a very good man; and Dick's a bad character: the respectable people wont speak to him. He's the bad brother: I'm the good one.

> [*The officers laugh outright. The soldiers grin.*

SWINDON. Who arrested this man?

SERGEANT. I did, sir. I found him in the minister's house, sitting at tea with the lady with his coat off, quite at home. If he isnt married to her, he ought to be.

SWINDON. Did he answer to the minister's name?

SERGEANT. Yes, sir, but not to a minister's nature. You ask the chaplain, sir.

SWINDON. [*To Richard, threateningly.*] So, sir, you have attempted to cheat us. And your name is Richard Dudgeon?

RICHARD. Youve found it out at last, have you?

SWINDON. Dudgeon is a name well known to us, eh?

RICHARD. Yes: Peter Dudgeon, whom you murdered, was my uncle.

SWINDON. Hm!

> [*He compresses his lips, and looks at Richard with vindictive gravity.*

CHRISTY. Are they going to hang you, Dick?

RICHARD. Yes. Get out: theyve done with you.

CHRISTY. And I may keep the china peacocks?

RICHARD. [*Jumping up.*] Get out. Get out, you blithering baboon, you.

> [*Christy flies, panic-stricken.*

SWINDON. [*Rising—all rise.*] Since you have taken the minister's place, Richard Dudgeon, you shall go through with it. The execution will take place at twelve o'clock as arranged; and unless

Anderson surrenders before then, you shall take his place on the gallows. Sergeant: take your man out.

JUDITH. [*Distracted.*] No, no——

SWINDON. [*Fiercely, dreading a renewal of her entreaties.*] Take that woman away.

RICHARD. [*Springing across the table with a tiger-like bound, and seizing Swindon by the throat.*] You infernal scoundrel——

[*The sergeant rushes to the rescue from one side, the soldiers from the other. They seize Richard and drag him back to his place. Swindon, who has been thrown supine on the table, rises, arranging his stock. He is about to speak, when he is anticipated by Burgoyne, who has just appeared at the door with two papers in his hand: a white letter and a blue dispatch.*

BURGOYNE. [*Advancing to the table, elaborately cool.*] What is this? Whats happening? Mr Anderson: I'm astonished at you.

RICHARD. I am sorry I disturbed you, General. I merely wanted to strangle your understrapper there. [*Breaking out violently at Swindon.*] Why do you raise the devil in me by bullying the woman like that? You oatmeal-faced dog, I'd twist your cursed head off with the greatest satisfaction. [*He puts out his hands to the sergeant.*] Here: handcuff me, will you; or I'll not undertake to keep my fingers off him.

[*The sergeant takes out a pair of handcuffs and looks at Burgoyne for instructions.*

BURGOYNE. Have you addressed profane language to the lady, Major Swindon?

SWINDON. [*Very angry.*] No, sir, certainly not. That question should not have been put to me. I ordered the woman to be removed, as she was disorderly; and the fellow sprang at me. Put away those handcuffs. I am perfectly able to take care of myself.

RICHARD. Now you talk like a man, I have no quarrel with you.

BURGOYNE. Mr Anderson——

SWINDON. His name is Dudgeon, sir, Richard Dudgeon. He is an impostor.

BURGOYNE. [*Brusquely.*] Nonsense, sir: you hanged Dudgeon at Springtown.

RICHARD. It was my uncle, General.

BURGOYNE. Oh, your uncle. [*To Swindon, handsomely.*] I beg your pardon, Major Swindon. [*Swindon acknowledges the apology stiffly. Burgoyne turns to Richard.*] We are somewhat unfortunate in our relations with your family. Well, Mr Dudgeon, what I wanted to ask you is this. Who is [*reading the name from the letter*] William Maindeck Parshotter?

RICHARD. He is the Mayor of Springtown.

BURGOYNE. Is William—Maindeck and so on—a man of his word?

RICHARD. Is he selling you anything?

BURGOYNE. No.

RICHARD. Then you may depend on him.

BURGOYNE. Thank you, Mr—'m Dudgeon. By the way, since you are not Mr Anderson, do we still—eh, Major Swindon?

> [*Meaning 'do we still hang him?'*]

RICHARD. The arrangements are unaltered, General.

BURGOYNE. Ah, indeed. I am sorry. Good morning, Mr Dudgeon. Good morning, madam.

RICHARD. [*Interrupting Judith almost fiercely as she is about to make some wild appeal, and taking her arm resolutely.*] Not one word more. Come.

> [*She looks imploringly at him, but is overborne by his determination. They are marched out by the four soldiers: the sergeant very sulky, walking between Swindon and Richard, whom he watches as if he were a dangerous animal.*

BURGOYNE. Gentlemen: we need not detain you. Major Swindon: a word with you. [*The officers go out. Burgoyne waits with unruffled serenity until the last of them disappears. Then he becomes very grave, and addresses Swindon for the first time without his title.*] Swindon: do you know what this is? [*Shewing him the letter.*

SWINDON. What?

BURGOYNE. A demand for a safe-conduct for an officer of their militia to come here and arrange terms with us.

SWINDON. Oh, they are giving in.

BURGOYNE. They add that they are sending the man who raised Springtown last night and drove us out; so that we may know that we are dealing with an officer of importance.

SWINDON. Pooh!

BURGOYNE. He will be fully empowered to arrange the terms of—guess what.

SWINDON. The surrender, I hope.

BURGOYNE. No: our evacuation of the town. They offer us just six hours to clear out.

SWINDON. What monstrous impudence!

BURGOYNE. What shall we do, eh?

SWINDON. March on Springtown and strike a decisive blow at once.

BURGOYNE. [*Quietly.*] Hm! [*Turning to the door.*] Come to the adjutant's office.

SWINDON. What for?

BURGOYNE. To write out that safe-conduct.

> [*He puts his hand to the door knob to open it.*

SWINDON. [*Who has not budged.*] General Burgoyne.

BURGOYNE. [*Returning.*] Sir?

SWINDON. It is my duty to tell you, sir, that I do not consider the
threats of a mob of rebellious tradesmen a sufficient reason for
our giving way.

BURGOYNE. [*Imperturbable.*] Suppose I resign my command to you,
what will you do?

SWINDON. I will undertake to do what we have marched south
from Quebec to do, and what General Howe has marched north
from New York to do: effect a junction at Albany and wipe out
the rebel army with our united forces.

BURGOYNE. [*Enigmatically.*] And will you wipe out our enemies in
London, too?

SWINDON. In London! What enemies?

BURGOYNE. [*Forcibly.*] Jobbery and snobbery, incompetence and
Red Tape. [*He holds up the dispatch and adds, with despair in his face
and voice.*] I have just learnt, sir, that General Howe is still in
New York.

SWINDON. [*Thunderstruck.*] Good God! He has disobeyed orders!

BURGOYNE. [*With sardonic calm.*] He has received no orders, sir.
Some gentleman in London forgot to dispatch them: he was
leaving town for his holiday, I believe. To avoid upsetting his
arrangements, England will lose her American colonies; and in
a few days you and I will be at Saratoga with five thousand men
to face eighteen thousand rebels in an impregnable position.

SWINDON. [*Appalled.*] Impossible?

BURGOYNE. [*Coldly.*] I beg your pardon?

SWINDON. I cant believe it! What will History say?

BURGOYNE. History, sir, will tell lies, as usual. Come: we must
send the safe-conduct.   [*He goes out.*

SWINDON. [*Following distractedly.*] My God, my God! We shall be
wiped out.

[*As noon approaches there is excitement in the market place. The
gallows which hang there permanently for the terror of evildoers,
with such minor advertizers and examples of crime as the pillory,
the whipping post, and the stocks, has a new rope attached, with the
noose hitched up to one of the uprights, out of reach of the boys. Its
ladder, too, has been brought out and placed in position by the town
beadle, who stands by to guard it from unauthorized climbing. The
Websterbridge townsfolk are present in force, and in high spirits;
for the news has spread that it is the devil's disciple and not the
minister that King George and his terrible general are about to
hang; consequently the execution can be enjoyed without any misgiving
as to its righteousness, or to the cowardice of allowing it to take
place without a struggle. There is even some fear of a disappointment
as midday approaches and the arrival of the beadle with the ladder*

remains the only sign of preparation. But at last reassuring shouts
of Here they come: Here they are, are heard; and a company of
soldiers with fixed bayonets, half British infantry, half Hessians,
tramp quickly into the middle of the market place, driving the
crowd to the sides.

THE SERGEANT. Halt, Front. Dress. [*The soldiers change their column*
into a square enclosing the gallows, their petty officers, energetically led
by the sergeant, hustling the persons who find themselves inside the square
out at the corners.] Now then! Out of it with you: out of it. Some
o youll get strung up yourselves presently. Form that square
there, will you, you damned Hoosians. No use talkin German to
them: talk to their toes with the butt ends of your muskets: theyll
understand that. Get out of it, will you. [*He comes upon Judith,*
standing near the gallows.] Now then: youve no call here.

JUDITH. May I not stay? What harm am I doing?

SERGEANT. I want none of your argufying. You ought to be
ashamed of yourself, running to see a man hanged thats not your
husband. And he's no better than yourself. I told my major he
was a gentleman; and then he goes and tries to strangle him, and
calls his blessed Majesty a lunatic. So out of it with you, double
quick.

JUDITH. Will you take these two silver dollars and let me stay?

[*The sergeant, without an instant's hesitation, looks quickly and*
furtively round as he shoots the money dexterously into his pocket.
Then he raises his voice in virtuous indignation.]

THE SERGEANT. Me take money in the execution of my duty!
Certainly not. Now I'll tell you what I'll do, to teach you to
corrupt the King's officer. I'll put you under arrest until the
execution's over. You just stand there; and dont let me see you as
much as move from that spot until youre let. [*With a swift wink at*
her he points to the corner of the square behind the gallows on his right,
and turns noisily away, shouting.] Now then, dress up and keep em
back, will you.

[*Cries of 'Hush' and 'Silence' are heard among the townsfolk; and the*
sound of a military band, playing the Dead March from 'Saul', is
heard. The crowd becomes quiet at once; and the sergeant and petty
officers, hurrying to the back of the square, with a few whispered
orders and some stealthy hustling cause it to open and admit the
funeral procession, which is protected from the crowd by a double file
of soldiers. First come Burgoyne and Swindon, who, on entering the
square, glance with distaste at the gallows, and avoid passing under it
by wheeling a little to the right and stationing themselves on that side.
Then Mr Brudenell, the chaplain, in his surplice, with his prayer
book open in his hand, walking beside Richard, who is moody and
disorderly. He walks doggedly through the gallows framework, and

posts himself a little in front of it. Behind him comes the executioner, a stalwart soldier in his shirtsleeves. Following him, two soldiers haul a light military wagon. Finally comes the band, which posts itself at the back of the square, and finishes the Dead March. Judith, watching Richard, painfully steals down to the gallows, and stands leaning against its right post. During the conversation which follows, the two soldiers place the cart under the gallows, and stand by the shafts, which point backwards. The executioner takes a set of steps from the cart and places it ready for the prisoner to mount. Then he climbs the tall ladder which stands against the gallows, and cuts the string by which the rope is hitched up; so that the noose drops dangling over the cart, into which he steps as he descends.

RICHARD. [*With suppressed impatience, to Brudenell.*] Look here, sir: this is no place for a man of your profession. Hadnt you better go away?

SWINDON. I appeal to you, prisoner, if you have any sense of decency left, to listen to the ministrations of the chaplain, and pay due heed to the solemnity of the occasion.

THE CHAPLAIN. [*Gently reproving Richard.*] Try to control yourself, and submit to the divine will.

[*He lifts his book to proceed with the service.*

RICHARD. Answer for your own will, sir, and those of your accomplices here. [*Indicating Burgoyne and Swindon.*] I see little divinity about them or you. You talk to me of Christianity when you are in the act of hanging your enemies. Was there ever such blasphemous nonsense! [*To Swindon, more rudely.*] Youve got up the solemnity of the occasion, as you call it, to impress the people with your own dignity—Handel's music and a clergyman to make murder look like piety! Do you suppose *I* am going to help you? Youve asked me to choose the rope because you dont know your own trade well enough to shoot me properly. Well, hang away and have done with it.

SWINDON. [*To the chaplain.*] Can you do nothing with him, Mr Brudenell?

CHAPLAIN. I will try, sir. [*Beginning to read.*] 'Man that is born of woman hath——'

RICHARD. [*Fixing his eyes on him.*] 'Thou shalt not kill.'

[*The book drops in Brudenell's hands.*

CHAPLAIN. [*Confessing his embarrassment.*] What am I to say, Mr Dudgeon?

RICHARD. Let me alone, cant you?

BURGOYNE. [*With extreme urbanity.*] I think, Mr Brudenell, that as the usual professional observations seem to strike Mr Dudgeon as incongruous under the circumstances, you had better omit

them until—er—until Mr Dudgeon can no longer be incon-
venienced by them. [*Brudenell, with a shrug, shuts his book and retires
behind the gallows.*] You seem in a hurry, Mr Dudgeon.

RICHARD. [*With the horror of death upon him.*] Do you think this is
a pleasant sort of thing to be kept waiting for? Youve made up
your mind to commit murder: well, do it and have done with it.

BURGOYNE. Mr Dudgeon: we are only doing this——

RICHARD. Because youre paid to do it.

SWINDON. You insolent——   [*He swallows his rage.*

BURGOYNE. [*With much charm of manner.*] Ah, I am really sorry that
you should think that, Mr Dudgeon. If you knew what my
commission cost me, and what my pay is, you would think
better of me. I should be glad to part from you on friendly
terms.

RICHARD. Hark ye, General Burgoyne. If you think that I like
being hanged, youre mistaken. I dont like it; and I dont mean to
pretend that I do. And if you think I'm obliged to you for hanging me in a gentlemanly way, youre wrong there too. I take the
whole business in devilish bad part; and the only satisfaction I
have in it is that youll feel a good deal meaner than I'll look when
it's over. [*He turns away, and is striding to the cart when Judith
advances and interposes with her arms stretched out to him. Richard,
feeling that a very little will upset his self-possession, shrinks from her,
crying*] What are you doing here? This is no place for you. [*She
makes a gesture as if to touch him. He recoils impatiently.*] No: go
away, go away: youll unnerve me. Take her away, will you.

JUDITH. Wont you bid me goodbye?

RICHARD. [*Allowing her to take his hand.*] Oh goodbye, goodbye.
Now go—go—quickly.

  [*She clings to his hand—will not be put off with so cold a last farewell
  —at last, as he tries to disengage himself, throws herself on his
  breast in agony.*

SWINDON. [*Angrily to the sergeant, who, alarmed at Judith's movement,
has come from the back of the square to pull her back, and stopped
irresolutely on finding that he is too late.*] How is this? Why is she
inside the lines?

SERGEANT. [*Guiltily.*] I dunno, sir. She's that artful—cant keep
her away.

BURGOYNE. You were bribed.

SERGEANT. [*Protesting.*] No, sir——

SWINDON. [*Severely.*] Fall back.   [*He obeys.*

RICHARD. [*Imploringly to those around him, and finally to Burgoyne, as
the least stolid of them.*] Take her away. Do you think I want a
woman near me now?

BURGOYNE. [*Going to Judith and taking her hand.*] Here, madam: you

had better keep inside the lines; but stand here behind us; and
dont look.

> [*Richard, with a great sobbing sigh of relief as she releases him and
> turns to Burgoyne, flies for refuge to the cart and mounts into it. The
> executioner takes off his coat and pinions him.*

JUDITH. [*Resisting Burgoyne quietly and drawing her hand away.*] No:
I must stay. I wont look.

> [*She goes to the right of the gallows. She tries to look at Richard, but
> turns away with a frightful shudder, and falls on her knees in prayer.
> Brudenell comes towards her from the back of the square.*

BURGOYNE. [*Nodding approvingly as she kneels.*] Ah, quite so. Do not
disturb her, Mr Brudenell: that will do very nicely. [*Brudenell
nods also, and withdraws a little, watching her sympathetically. Burgoyne
resumes his former position and takes out a handsome gold chronometer.*]
Now then, are those preparations made? We must not detain
Mr Dudgeon.

> [*By this time Richard's hands are bound behind him; and the noose
> is round his neck. The two soldiers take the shafts of the wagon,
> ready to pull it away. The executioner, standing in the cart behind
> Richard, makes a sign to the sergeant.*

SERGEANT. [*To Burgoyne.*] Ready, sir.

BURGOYNE. Have you anything more to say, Mr Dudgeon? It
wants two minutes of twelve still.

RICHARD. [*In a strong voice of a man who has conquered the bitterness
of death.*] Your watch is two minutes slow by the town clock,
which I can see from here, General. [*The town clock strikes the
first stroke of twelve, Involuntarily the people flinch at the sound, and a
subdued groan breaks from them.*] Amen! My life for the world's
future!

ANDERSON. [*Shouting as he rushes into the market place.*] Amen; and
stop the execution. [*He bursts through the line of soldiers opposite
Burgoyne, and rushes, panting, to the gallows.*] I am Anthony Anderson,
the man you want.

> [*The crowd, intensely excited, listens with all its ears. Judith, half
> rising, stares at him; then lifts her hands like one whose dearest
> prayer has been granted.*

SWINDON. Indeed. Then you are just in time to take your place
on the gallows. Arrest him.

> [*At a sign from the sergeant, two soldiers come forward to seize
> Anderson.*

ANDERSON. [*Thrusting a paper under Swindon's nose.*] Theres my
safe-conduct, sir.

SWINDON. [*Taken aback.*] Safe-conduct! Are you——!

ANDERSON. [*Emphatically.*] I am. [*The two soldiers take him by the
elbows.*] Tell these men to take their hands off me.

SWINDON. [*To the men.*] Let him go.

SERGEANT. Fall back.

> [*The two men return to their places. The townsfolk raise a cheer; and begin to exchange exultant looks, with a presentiment of triumph as they see their Pastor speaking with their enemies in the gate.*

ANDERSON. [*Exhaling a deep breath of relief, and dabbing his perspiring brow with his handkerchief.*] Thank God I was in time!

BURGOYNE. [*Calm as ever, and still watch in hand.*] Ample time, sir. Plenty of time. I should never dream of hanging any gentleman by an American clock.   [*He puts up his watch.*

ANDERSON. Yes: we are some minutes ahead of you already, General. Now tell them to take the rope from the neck of that American citizen.

BURGOYNE. [*To the executioner in the cart—very politely.*] Kindly undo Mr Dudgeon.

> [*The executioner takes the rope from Richard's neck, unties his hands and helps him on with his coat.*

JUDITH. [*Stealing timidly to Anderson.*] Tony.

ANDERSON. [*Putting his arm round her shoulders and bantering her affectionately.*] Well, what do you think of your husband now, eh?—eh??—eh???

JUDITH. I am ashamed—   [*She hides her face against his breast.*

BURGOYNE. [*To Swindon.*] You look disappointed, Major Swindon.

SWINDON. You look defeated, General Burgoyne.

BURGOYNE. I am, sir; and I am humane enough to be glad of it. [*Richard jumps down from the cart, Brudenell offering his hand to help him, and runs to Anderson, whose left hand he shakes heartily, the right being occupied by Judith.*] By the way, Mr Anderson, I do not quite understand. The safe-conduct was for a commander of the militia. I understand you are a —[*He looks as pointedly as his good manners permit at the riding boots, the pistols and Richard's coat, and adds*]— a clergyman.

ANDERSON. [*Between Judith and Richard.*] Sir; it is in the hour of trial that a man finds his true profession. This foolish young man [*placing his hand on Richard's shoulder*] boasted himself the Devil's Disciple; but when the hour of trial came to him, he found that it was his destiny to suffer and be faithful to the death. I thought myself a decent minister of the gospel of peace; but when the hour of trial came to me, I found that it was my destiny to be a man of action, and that my place was amid the thunder of the captains and the shouting. So I am starting life at fifty as Captain Anthony Anderson of the Springtown militia; and the Devil's Disciple here will start presently as the Reverend Richard Dudgeon, and wag his pow in my old pulpit, and give good advice to this silly sentimental little wife of mine. [*Putting his other hand on her shoulder. She steals a glance at Richard to see how the prospect pleases him.*] Your mother told me, Richard, that I should never have chosen Judith if I'd been born for the ministry. I am afraid she was right; so, by your leave, you may keep my coat and I'll keep yours.

RICHARD. Minister—I should say Captain. I have behaved like a fool.

JUDITH. Like a hero.

RICHARD. Much the same thing, perhaps. [*With some bitterness towards himself.*] But no: if I had been any good, I should have done for you what you did for me, instead of making a vain sacrifice.

ANDERSON. Not vain, my boy. It makes all sorts to make a world —saints as well as soldiers. [*Turning to Burgoyne.*] And now, General, time presses; and America is in a hurry. Have you realized that though you may occupy towns and win battles, you cannot conquer a nation?

BURGOYNE. My good sir, without a Conquest you cannot have an aristocracy. Come and settle the matter at my quarters.

ANDERSON. At your service, sir. [*To Richard.*] See Judith home for me, will you, my boy. [*He hands her over to him.*] Now, General.

[*He goes busily up the market place towards the Town Hall, leaving Judith and Richard together. Burgoyne follows him a step or two; then checks himself and turns to Richard.*

BURGOYNE. Oh, by the way, Mr Dudgeon, I shall be glad to see you at lunch at half-past one. [*He pauses a moment and adds, with politely veiled slyness.*] Bring Mrs Anderson, if she will be so good. [*To Swindon, who is fuming.*] Take it quietly, Major Swindon: your friend the British soldier can stand up to anything except the British War Office.   [*He follows Anderson.*

SERGEANT. [*To Swindon.*] What orders, sir?

SWINDON. [*Savagely.*] Orders! What use are orders now! Theres no army. Back to quarters; and be d——

[*He turns on his heel and goes.*

SERGEANT. [*Pugnacious and patriotic, repudiating the idea of defeat.*] 'Tention. Now then: cock up your chins, and shew em you dont care a damn for em. Slope arms! Fours! Wheel! Quick march!

[*The drums mark time with a tremendous bang; the band strikes up 'British Grenadiers'; and the Sergeant, Brudenell and the English troops march off defiantly to their quarters. The townsfolk press in behind, and follow them up the market, jeering at them; and the town band, a very primitive affair, brings up the rear, playing 'Yankee Doodle'. Essie, who comes in with them, runs to Richard.*

ESSIE. Oh, Dick!

RICHARD. [*Good-humoredly, but wilfully.*] Now, now: come, come! I dont mind being hanged: but I will not be cried over.

ESSIE. No, I promise. I'll be good. [*She tries to restrain her tears, but cannot.*] I—I want to see where the soldiers are going to.

[*She goes a little way up the market, pretending to look after the crowd.*

JUDITH. Promise me you will never tell him.

RICHARD. Dont be afraid.

[*They shake hands on it.*

ESSIE. [*Calling to them.*] Theyre coming back. They want you.

[*Jubilation in the market. The townsfolk surge back again in wild enthusiasm with their band, and hoist Richard on their shoulders, cheering him.*

MAJOR BARBARA

NOTE

In the millionaire Undershaft I have represented a man who has become intellectually and spiritually as well as practically conscious of the irresistible natural truth which we all abhor and repudiate: to wit, that the greatest of our evils, and the worst of our crimes, is poverty, and that our first duty, to which every other consideration should be sacrificed, is not to be poor.

Undershaft, the hero of *Major Barbara*, is simply a man who, having grasped the fact that poverty is a crime, knows that when society offered him the alternative of poverty or a lucrative trade in death and destruction, it offered him, not a choice between opulent villainy and humble virtue but between energetic enterprise and cowardly infamy. His conduct stands the Kantian test, which Peter Shirley's does not. Peter Shirley is what we call the honest poor man. Undershaft is what we call the wicked rich one. . . . Well, the misery of the world is due to the fact that the great mass of men act and believe as Peter Shirley acts and believes. If they acted and believed as Undershaft acts and believes, the immediate result would be a revolution of incalculable beneficence.

If a man cannot look evil in the face without illusion, he will never know what it really is, or combat it effectually. The few men who have been able (relatively) to do this have been called cynics, and have sometimes had an abnormal share of evil in themselves, corresponding to the abnormal strength of their minds; but they have never done mischief unless they intended to do it. That is why great scoundrels have been beneficent rulers whilst amiable and privately harmless monarchs have ruined their countries by trusting to the hocus-pocus of innocence and guilt, reward and punishment, virtuous indignation and pardon, instead of standing up to the facts without either malice or mercy. Major Barbara stands up to Bill Walker in that way, with the result that the ruffian who cannot get hated has to hate himself.

G. B. S.

MAJOR BARBARA

It is after dinner in January 1906, in the library in Lady Britomart Undershaft's house in Wilton Crescent. A large and comfortable settee is in the middle of the room, upholstered in dark leather. A person sitting on it (it is vacant at present) would have, on his right, Lady Britomart's writing table, with the lady herself busy at it; a smaller writing table behind him on his left; the door behind him on Lady Britomart's side; and a window with a window seat directly on his left. Near the window is an armchair.

Lady Britomart is a woman of fifty or thereabouts, well dressed and yet careless of her dress, well bred and quite reckless of her breeding, well mannered and yet appallingly outspoken and indifferent to the opinion of her interlocutors, amiable and yet peremptory, arbitrary, and high-tempered to the last bearable degree, and withal a very typical managing matron of the upper class, treated as a naughty child until she grew into a scolding mother, and finally settling down with plenty of practical ability and worldly experience, limited in the oddest way with domestic and class limitations, conceiving the universe exactly as if it were a large house in Wilton Crescent, though handling her corner of it very effectively on that assumption, and being quite enlightened and liberal as to the books in the library, the pictures on the walls, the music in the portfolios and the articles in the papers.

Her son, Stephen, comes in. He is a gravely correct young man under twenty-five, taking himself very seriously, but still in some awe of his mother, from childish habit and bachelor shyness rather than from any weakness of character.

STEPHEN. Whats the matter?

LADY BRITOMART. Presently, Stephen.

> [*Stephen submissively walks to the settee and sits down. He takes up a Liberal weekly called 'The Speaker'.*]

LADY BRITOMART. Dont begin to read, Stephen. I shall require all your attention.

STEPHEN. It was only while I was waiting——

LADY BRITOMART. Dont make excuses, Stephen. [*He puts down 'The Speaker'.*] Now! [*She finishes her writing; rises; and comes to the settee.*] I have not kept you waiting very long, I think.

STEPHEN. Not at all, mother.

LADY BRITOMART. Bring me my cushion. [*He takes the cushion from the chair at the desk and arranges it for her as she sits down on the settee.*] Sit down. [*He sits down and fingers his tie nervously.*] Dont fiddle with your tie, Stephen: there is nothing the matter with it.

STEPHEN. I beg your pardon. [*He fiddles with his watch chain instead.*

LADY BRITOMART. Now are you attending to me, Stephen?

STEPHEN. Of course, mother.

LADY BRITOMART. No: it's not of course. I want something much more than your everyday matter-of-course attention. I am going to speak to you very seriously, Stephen. I wish you would let that chain alone.

STEPHEN. [*Hastily relinquishing the chain.*] Have I done anything to annoy you, mother? If so, it was quite unintentional.

LADY BRITOMART. [*Astonished.*] Nonsense! [*With some remorse.*] My poor boy, did you think I was angry with you?

STEPHEN. What is it, then, mother? You are making me very uneasy.

LADY BRITOMART. [*Squaring herself at him rather aggressively.*] Stephen: may I ask how soon you intend to realize that you are a grown-up man, and that I am only a woman?

STEPHEN. [*Amazed.*] Only a——

LADY BRITOMART. Dont repeat my words, please: it is a most aggravating habit. You must learn to face life seriously, Stephen. I really cannot bear the whole burden of our family affairs any longer. You must advise me: you must assume the responsibility.

STEPHEN. I!

LADY BRITOMART. Yes, you, of course. You were twenty-four last June. Youve been at Harrow and Cambridge. Youve been to India and Japan. You must know a lot of things, now; unless you have wasted your time most scandalously. Well, advise me.

STEPHEN. [*Much perplexed.*] You know I have never interfered in the household——

LADY BRITOMART. No: I should think not. I dont want you to order the dinner.

STEPHEN. I mean in our family affairs.

LADY BRITOMART. Well, you must interfere now; for they are getting quite beyond me.

STEPHEN. [*Troubled.*] I have thought sometimes that perhaps I ought; but really, mother, I know so little about them; and what I do know is so painful! It is so impossible to mention some things to you—— [*He stops, ashamed.*

LADY BRITOMART. I suppose you mean your father.

STEPHEN. [*Almost inaudibly.*] Yes.

LADY BRITOMART. My dear: we cant go on all our lives not mentioning him. Of course you were quite right not to open the subject
until I asked you to; but you are old enough now to be taken
into my confidence, and to help me to deal with him about the
girls.

STEPHEN. But the girls are all right. They are engaged.

LADY BRITOMART. [*Complacently.*] Yes: I have made a very good
match for Sarah. Charles Lomax will be a millionaire at thirty-
five. But that is ten years ahead; and in the meantime his trustees
cannot under the terms of his father's will allow him more than
£800 a year.

STEPHEN. But the will says also that if he increases his income by
his own exertions, they may double the increase.

LADY BRITOMART. Charles Lomax's exertions are much more
likely to decrease his income than to increase it. Sarah will have
to find at least another £800 a year for the next ten years; and
even then they will be as poor as church mice. And what about
Barbara? I thought Barbara was going to make the most brilliant
career of all of you. And what does she do? Joins the Salvation
Army; discharges her maid; lives on a pound a week; and walks
in one evening with a professor of Greek whom she has picked
up in the street, and who pretends to be a Salvationist, and
actually plays the big drum for her in public because he has
fallen head over ears in love with her.

STEPHEN. I was certainly rather taken aback when I heard they
were engaged. Cusins is a very nice fellow, certainly: nobody
would ever guess that he was born in Australia; but——

LADY BRITOMART. Oh, Adolphus Cusins will make a very good
husband. After all, nobody can say a word against Greek: it
stamps a man at once as an educated gentleman. And my family,
thank heaven, is not a pig-headed Tory one. We are Whigs, and
believe in liberty. Let snobbish people say what they please:
Barbara shall marry, not the man they like, but the man *I* like.

STEPHEN. Of course I was thinking only of his income. However,
he is not likely to be extravagant.

LADY BRITOMART. Dont be too sure of that, Stephen. I know your
quiet, simple, refined, poetic people like Adolphus: quite content
with the best of everything! They cost more than your extravagant people, who are always as mean as they are second rate. No:
Barbara will need at least £2000 a year. You see it means two
additional households. Besides, my dear, you must marry soon.
I dont approve of the present fashion of philandering bachelors
and late marriages; and I am trying to arrange something for you.

STEPHEN. It's very good of you, mother; but perhaps I had better
arrange that for myself.

LADY BRITOMART. Nonsense! You are much too young to begin matchmaking: you would be taken in by some pretty little nobody. Of course I dont mean that you are not to be consulted: you know that as well as I do. [*Stephen closes his lips and is silent.*] Now dont sulk, Stephen.

STEPHEN. I am not sulking, mother. What has all this got to do with—with—with my father?

LADY BRITOMART. My dear Stephen: where is the money to come from? It is easy enough for you and the other children to live on my income as long as we are in the same house; but I cant keep four families in four separate houses. You know how poor my father is: he has barely seven thousand a year now; and really, if he were not the Earl of Stevenage, he would have to give up society. He can do nothing for us. He says, naturally enough, that it is absurd that he should be asked to provide for the children of a man who is rolling in money. You see, Stephen, your father must be fabulously wealthy, because there is always a war going on somewhere.

STEPHEN. You need not remind me of that, mother. I have hardly ever opened a newspaper in my life without seeing our name in it. The Undershaft torpedo! The Undershaft quick firers! The Undershaft ten inch! the Undershaft disappearing rampart gun! the Undershaft submarine! and now the Undershaft aerial battleship! At Harrow they called me the Woolwich Infant. At Cambridge it was the same. A little brute at King's who was always trying to get up revivals, spoilt my Bible—your first birthday present to me—by writing under my name, 'Son and heir to Undershaft and Lazarus, Death and Destruction Dealers: address Christendom and Judea.' But that was not so bad as the way I was kowtowed to everywhere because my father was making millions by selling cannons.

LADY BRITOMART. It is not only the cannons, but the war loans that Lazarus arranges under cover of giving credit for the cannons. You know, Stephen, it's perfectly scandalous. Those two men, Andrew Undershaft and Lazarus, positively have Europe under their thumbs. That is why your father is able to behave as he does. He is above the law. Do you think Bismarck or Gladstone or Disraeli could have openly defied every social and moral obligation all their lives as your father has? They simply wouldnt have dared. I asked Gladstone to take it up. I asked *The Times* to take it up. I asked the Lord Chamberlain to take it up. But it was just like asking them to declare war on the Sultan. They wouldnt. They said they couldnt touch him. I believe they were afraid.

STEPHEN. What could they do? He does not actually break the law.

LADY BRITOMART. Not break the law! He is always breaking the law. He broke the law when he was born: his parents were not married.

STEPHEN. Mother! Is that true?

LADY BRITOMART. Of course it's true: that was why we separated.

STEPHEN. He married without letting you know this!

LADY BRITOMART. [*Rather taken aback by this inference.*] Oh no. To do Andrew justice, that was not the sort of thing he did. Besides, you know the Undershaft motto: Unashamed. Everybody knew.

STEPHEN. But you said that was why you separated.

LADY BRITOMART. Yes, because he was not content with being a foundling himself: he wanted to disinherit you for another foundling. That was what I couldnt stand.

STEPHEN. [*Ashamed.*] Do you mean for—for—for——

LADY BRITOMART. Dont stammer. Stephen. Speak distinctly.

STEPHEN. But this is so frightful to me, mother. To have to speak to you about such things!

LADY BRITOMART. It's not pleasant for me, either, especially if you are still so childish that you must make it worse by a display of embarrassment. It is only in the middle classes, Stephen, that people get into a state of dumb helpless horror when they find that there are wicked people in the world. In our class, we have to decide what is to be done with wicked people; and nothing should disturb our self-possession. Now ask your question properly.

STEPHEN. Mother: have you no consideration for me? For heaven's sake either treat me as a child, as you always do, and tell me nothing at all; or tell me everything and let me take it as best I can.

LADY BRITOMART. Treat you as a child! What do you mean? It is most unkind and ungrateful of you to say such a thing. You know I have never treated any of you as children. I have always made you my companions and friends, and allowed you perfect freedom to do and say whatever you liked, so long as you liked what I could approve of.

STEPHEN. [*Desperately.*] I daresay we have been the very imperfect children of a very perfect mother; but I do beg you to let me alone for once, and tell me about this horrible business of my father wanting to set me aside for another son.

LADY BRITOMART. [*Amazed.*] Another son! I never said anything of the kind. I never dreamt of such a thing. This is what comes of interrupting me.

STEPHEN. But you said——

LADY BRITOMART. [*Cutting him short.*] Now be a good boy, Stephen, and listen to me patiently. The Undershafts are descended from a foundling in the parish of St Andrew Undershaft in the city.

That was long ago, in the reign of James the First. Well, this foundling was adopted by an armorer and gun-maker. In the course of time the foundling succeeded to the business; and from some notion of gratitude, or some vow or something, he adopted another foundling, and left the business to him. And that foundling did the same. Ever since that, the cannon business has always been left to an adopted foundling named Andrew Undershaft.

STEPHEN. But did they never marry? Were there no legitimate sons?

LADY BRITOMART. Oh yes: they married just as your father did; and they were rich enough to buy land for their own children and leave them well provided for. But they always adopted and trained some foundling to succeed them in the business; and of course they always quarrelled with their wives furiously over it. Your father was adopted in that way; and he pretends to consider himself bound to keep up the tradition and adopt somebody to leave the business to. Of course I was not going to stand that. There may have been some reason for it when the Undershafts could only marry women in their own class, whose sons were not fit to govern great estates. But there could be no excuse for passing over my son.

STEPHEN. [*Dubiously.*] I am afraid I should make a poor hand of managing a cannon foundry.

LADY BRITOMART. Nonsense! You could easily get a manager and pay him a salary.

STEPHEN. My father evidently had no great opinion of my capacity.

LADY BRITOMART. Stuff, child! You were only a baby: it had nothing to do with your capacity. Andrew did it on principle, just as he did every perverse and wicked thing on principle. When my father remonstrated, Andrew actually told him to his face that history tells us of only two successful institutions: one the Undershaft firm, and the other the Roman Empire under the Antonines. That was because the Antonine emperors all adopted their successors. Such rubbish! The Stevenages are as good as the Antonines, I hope; and you are a Stevenage. But that was Andrew all over. There you have the man! Always clever and unanswerable when he was defending nonsense and wickedness: always awkward and sullen when he had to behave sensibly and decently!

STEPHEN. Then it was on my account that your home life was broken up, mother. I am sorry.

LADY BRITOMART. Well, dear, there were other differences. I really cannot bear an immoral man. I am not a Pharisee, I hope; and I should not have minded his merely doing wrong things: we are none of us perfect. But your father didnt exactly do wrong things: he said them and thought them: that was what was so dreadful. He really had a sort of religion of wrongness. Just as one doesnt

mind men practising immorality so long as they own that they
are in the wrong by preaching morality; so I couldnt forgive
Andrew for preaching immorality while he practised morality.
You would all have grown up without principles, without any
knowledge of right and wrong, if he had been in the house. You
know, my dear, your father was a very attractive man in some
ways. Children did not dislike him; and he took advantage of it
to put the wickedest ideas into their heads, and make them quite
unmanageable. I did not dislike him myself: very far from it;
but nothing can bridge over moral disagreement.

STEPHEN. All this simply bewilders me, mother. People may
differ about matters of opinion, or even about religion; but
how can they differ about right and wrong? Right is right;
and wrong is wrong; and if a man cannot distinguish them
properly, he is either a fool or a rascal: thats all.

LADY BRITOMART. [*Touched.*] Thats my own boy! [*She pats his
cheek.*] Your father never could answer that: he used to laugh
and get out of it under cover of some affectionate nonsense.
And now that you understand the situation, what do you advise
me to do?

STEPHEN. Well, what c a n you do?

LADY BRITOMART. I must get the money somehow.

STEPHEN. We cannot take money from him. I had rather go and
live in some cheap place like Bedford Square or even Hampstead
than take a farthing of his money.

LADY BRITOMART. But after all, Stephen, our present income comes
from Andrew.

STEPHEN. [*Shocked.*] I never knew that.

LADY BRITOMART. Well, you surely didnt suppose your grandfather
had anything to give me. The Stevenages could not do everything
for you. We gave you social position. Andrew had to contribute
something. He had a very good bargain, I think.

STEPHEN. [*Bitterly.*] We are utterly dependent on him and his
cannons, then?

LADY BRITOMART. Certainly not: the money is settled. But he
provided it. So you see it is not a question of taking money from
him or not: it is simply a question of how much. I dont want any
more for myself.

STEPHEN. Nor do I.

LADY BRITOMART. But Sarah does; and Barbara does. That is,
Charles Lomax and Adolphus Cusins will cost them more. So I
must put my pride in my pocket and ask for it, I suppose. That
is your advice, Stephen, is it not?

STEPHEN. No.

LADY BRITOMART. [*Sharply.*] Stephen!

STEPHEN. Of course if you are determined——

LADY BRITOMART. I am not determined: I ask your advice; and I am waiting for it. I will not have all the responsibility thrown on my shoulders.

STEPHEN. [*Obstinately.*] I would die sooner than ask him for another penny.

LADY BRITOMART. [*Resignedly.*] You mean that *I* must ask him. Very well, Stephen: it shall be as you wish. You will be glad to know that your grandfather concurs. But he thinks I ought to ask Andrew to come here and see the girls. After all, he must have some natural affection for them.

STEPHEN. Ask him here!!!

LADY BRITOMART. Do not repeat my words, Stephen. Where else can I ask him?

STEPHEN. I never expected you to ask him at all.

LADY BRITOMART. Now dont tease, Stephen. Come! You see that it is necessary that he should pay us a visit, dont you?

STEPHEN. [*Reluctantly.*] I suppose so, if the girls cannot do without his money.

LADY BRITOMART. Thank you, Stephen: I knew you would give me the right advice when it was properly explained to you. I have asked your father to come this evening. [*Stephen bounds from his seat.*] Dont jump, Stephen: it fidgets me.

STEPHEN. [*In utter consternation.*] Do you mean to say that my father is coming here tonight—that he may be here at any moment?

LADY BRITOMART. [*Looking at her watch.*] I said nine. [*He gasps. She rises.*] Ring the bell, please. [*Stephen goes to the smaller writing table; presses a button on it; and sits at it with his elbows on the table and his head in his hands, outwitted and overwhelmed.*] It is ten minutes to nine yet; and I have to prepare the girls. I asked Charles Lomax and Adolphus to dinner on purpose that they might be here. Andrew had better see them in case he should cherish any delusions as to their being capable of supporting their wives. [*The butler enters: Lady Britomart goes behind the settee to speak to him.*] Morrison: go up to the drawing-room and tell everybody to come down here at once. [*Morrison withdraws. Lady Britomart turns to Stephen.*] Now remember, Stephen: I shall need all your countenance and authority. [*He rises and tries to recover some vestige of these attributes.*] Give me a chair, dear. [*He pushes a chair forward from the wall to where she stands, near the smaller writing table. She sits down; and he goes to the armchair, into which he throws himself.*] I dont know how Barbara will take it. Ever since they made her a major in the Salvation Army she has developed a propensity to have her own way and order people about which quite cows me sometimes. It's not ladylike: I'm sure I dont know where she picked

it up. Anyhow, Barbara shant bully me; but still it's just as well
that your father should be here before she has time to refuse to
meet him or make a fuss. Dont look nervous, Stephen: it will
only encourage Barbara to make difficulties. *I* am nervous enough,
goodness knows; but I dont shew it.

[*Sarah and Barbara come in with their respective young men, Charles
Lomax and Adolphus Cusins. Sarah is slender, bored, and
mundane. Barbara is robuster, jollier, much more energetic. Sarah
is fashionably dressed: Barbara is in Salvation Army uniform.
Lomax, a young man about town, is like many other young men
about town. He is afflicted with a frivolous sense of humor which
plunges him at the most inopportune moments into paroxysms of
imperfectly suppressed laughter. Cusins is a spectacled student,
slight, thin haired and sweet voiced, with a more complex form of
Lomax's complaint. His sense of humor is intellectual and subtle,
and is complicated by an appalling temper. The lifelong struggle of a
benevolent temperament and a high conscience against impulses of
inhuman ridicule and fierce impatience has set up a chronic strain
which has visibly wrecked his constitution. He is a most implacable,
determined, tenacious, intolerant person who by mere force of character presents himself as—and indeed actually is—considerate,
gentle, explanatory, even mild and apologetic, capable possibly of
murder, but not of cruelty or coarseness. By the operation of some
instinct which is not merciful enough to blind him with the illusions
of love, he is obstinately bent on marrying Barbara. Lomax likes
Sarah and thinks it will be rather a lark to marry her. Consequently
he has not attempted to resist Lady Britomart's arrangements to
that end.*

*All four look as if they had been having a good deal of fun in the
drawing-room. The girls enter first, leaving the swains outside. Sarah
comes to the settee. Barbara comes in after her and stops at the door.*]

BARBARA. Are Cholly and Dolly to come in?

LADY BRITOMART. [*Forcibly.*] Barbara: I will not have Charles
called Cholly: the vulgarity of it positively makes me ill.

BARBARA. It's all right, mother: Cholly is quite correct nowadays.
Are they to come in?

LADY BRITOMART. Yes, if they will behave themselves.

BARBARA. [*Through the door.*] Come in, Dolly; and behave yourself.
[*Barbara comes to her mother's writing table. Cusins enters smiling,
and wanders towards Lady Britomart.*]

SARAH. [*Calling.*] Come in, Cholly.
[*Lomax enters, controlling his features very imperfectly, and places
himself vaguely between Sarah and Barbara.*]

LADY BRITOMART. [*Peremptorily.*] Sit down, all of you. [*They sit.
Cusins crosses to the window and seats himself there. Lomax takes a*

chair. Barbara sits at the writing table and Sarah on the settee.] I dont in the least know what you are laughing at, Adolphus. I am surprised at you, though I expected nothing better from Charles Lomax.

CUSINS. [*In a remarkably gentle voice.*] Barbara has been trying to teach me the West Ham Salvation March.

LADY BRITOMART. I see nothing to laugh at in that; nor should you if you are really converted.

CUSINS. [*Sweetly.*] You were not present. It was really funny, I believe.

LOMAX. Ripping.

LADY BRITOMART. Be quiet, Charles. Now listen to me, children. Your father is coming here this evening.

[*General stupefaction. Lomax, Sarah and Barbara rise; Sarah scared, and Barbara amused and expectant.*

LOMAX. [*Remonstrating.*] Oh I say!

LADY BRITOMART. You are not called on to say anything, Charles.

SARAH. Are you serious, mother?

LADY BRITOMART. Of course I am serious. It is on your account, Sarah, and also on Charles's. [*Silence. Sarah sits, with a shrug. Charles looks painfully unworthy.*] I hope you are not going to object, Barbara.

BARBARA. I! Why should I? My father has a soul to be saved like anybody else. He's quite welcome as far as I am concerned.

[*She sits on the table, and softly whistles 'Onward, Christian Soldiers'.*

LOMAX. [*Still remonstrant.*] But really, dont you know! Oh, I say!

LADY BRITOMART. [*Frigidly.*] What do you wish to convey, Charles?

LOMAX. Well, you must admit that this is a bit thick.

LADY BRITOMART. [*Turning with ominous suavity to Cusins.*] Adolphus: you are a professor of Greek. Can you translate Charles Lomax's remarks into reputable English for us?

CUSINS. [*Cautiously.*] If I may say so, Lady Brit, I think Charles has rather happily expressed what we all feel. Homer, speaking of Autolycus, uses the same phrase. πυκινὸν δόμον ἐλθεῖν means a bit thick.

LOMAX. [*Handsomely.*] Not that I mind, you know, if Sarah dont.

[*He sits.*

LADY BRITOMART. [*Crushingly.*] Thank you. Have I your permission, Adolphus, to invite my own husband to my own house?

CUSINS. [*Gallantly.*] You have my unhesitating support in everything you do.

LADY BRITOMART. Tush! Sarah: have you nothing to say?

SARAH. Do you mean that he is coming regularly to live here?

LADY BRITOMART. Certainly not. The spare room is ready for him if he likes to stay for a day or two and see a little more of you; but there are limits.

SARAH. Well, he cant eat us, I suppose. *I* dont mind.

LOMAX. [*Chuckling.*] I wonder how the old man will take it.

LADY BRITOMART. Much as the old woman will, no doubt, Charles.

LOMAX. [*Abashed.*] I didnt mean—at least——

LADY BRITOMART. You didnt think, Charles. You never do; and the result is, you never mean anything. And now please attend to me, children. Your father will be quite a stranger to us.

LOMAX. I suppose he hasnt seen Sarah since she was a little kid.

LADY BRITOMART. Not since she was a little kid, Charles, as you express it with that elegance of diction and refinement of thought that seem never to desert you. Accordingly—er—[*impatiently*] now I have forgotten what I was going to say. That comes of your provoking me to be sarcastic, Charles. Adolphus: will you kindly tell me where I was.

CUSINS. [*Sweetly.*] You were saying that as Mr Undershaft has not seen his children since they were babies, he will form his opinion of the way you have brought them up from their behaviour tonight, and that therefore you wish us all to be particularly careful to conduct ourselves well, especially Charles.

LADY BRITOMART. [*With emphatic approval.*] Precisely.

LOMAX. Look here, Dolly: Lady Brit didnt say that.

LADY BRITOMART. [*Vehemently.*] I did, Charles. Adolphus's recollection is perfectly correct. It is most important that you should be good; and I do beg you for once not to pair off into opposite corners and giggle and whisper while I am speaking to your father.

BARBARA. All right, mother. We'll do you credit.

[*She comes off the table, and sits in her chair with ladylike elegance.*

LADY BRITOMART. Remember, Charles, that Sarah will want to feel proud of you instead of ashamed of you.

LOMAX. Oh I say! theres nothing to be exactly proud of, dont you know.

LADY BRITOMART. Well, try and look as if there was.

[*Morrison, pale and dismayed, breaks into the room in unconcealed disorder.*

MORRISON. Might I speak a word to you, my lady?

LADY BRITOMART. Nonsense! Shew him up.

MORRISON. Yes, my lady. [*He goes.*]

LOMAX. Does Morrison know who it is?

LADY BRITOMART. Of course. Morrison has always been with us.

LOMAX. It must be a regular corker for him, dont you know.

LADY BRITOMART. Is this a moment to get on my nerves, Charles, with your outrageous expressions?

LOMAX. But this is something out of the ordinary, really——

MORRISON. [*At the door.*] The—er—Mr Undershaft.

[*He retreats in confusion.*

[*Andrew Undershaft comes in. All rise. Lady Britomart meets him in the middle of the room behind the settee.*

Andrew is, on the surface, a stoutish, easygoing elderly man, with kindly patient manners, and an engaging simplicity of character. But he has a watchful, deliberate, waiting, listening face, and formidable reserves of power, both bodily and mental, in his capacious chest and long head. His gentleness is partly that of a strong man who has learnt by experience that his natural grip hurts ordinary people unless he handles them very carefully, and partly the mellowness of age and success. He is also a little shy in his present very delicate situation.

LADY BRITOMART. Good evening, Andrew.

UNDERSHAFT. How d'ye do, my dear.

LADY BRITOMART. You look a good deal older.

UNDERSHAFT. [*Apologetically.*] I am somewhat older. [*Taking her hand with a touch of courtship.*] Time has stood still with you.

LADY BRITOMART. [*Throwing away his hand.*] Rubbish! This is your family.

UNDERSHAFT. [*Surprised.*] Is it so large? I am sorry to say my memory is failing very badly in some things.

[*He offers his hand with paternal kindness to Lomax.*

LOMAX. [*Jerkily shaking his hand.*] Ahdedoo.

UNDERSHAFT. I can see you are my eldest. I am very glad to meet you again, my boy.

LOMAX. [*Remonstrating.*] No, but look here, dont you know—— [*Overcome.*] Oh, I say!

LADY BRITOMART. [*Recovering from momentary speechlessness.*] Andrew: do you mean to say that you dont remember how many children you have?

UNDERSHAFT. Well, I am afraid I—— They have grown so much— er. Am I making any ridiculous mistake? I may as well confess: I recollect only one son. But so many things have happened since, of course—er——

LADY BRITOMART. [*Decisively.*] Andrew: you are talking nonsense. Of course you have only one son.

UNDERSHAFT. Perhaps you will be good enough to introduce me, my dear.

LADY BRITOMART. That is Charles Lomax, who is engaged to Sarah.

UNDERSHAFT. My dear sir, I beg your pardon.

LOMAX. Notatall. Delighted, I assure you.

LADY BRITOMART. This is Stephen.

UNDERSHAFT. [*Bowing.*] Happy to make your acquaintance, Mr Stephen. Then [*going to Cusins*] you must be my son. [*Taking*

Cusins' hands in his.] How are you, my young friend? [*To Lady Britomart.*] He is very like you, my love.

CUSINS. You flatter me, Mr Undershaft. My name is Cusins: engaged to Barbara. [*Very explicitly.*] That is Major Barbara Undershaft, of the Salvation Army. That is Sarah, your second daughter. This is Stephen Undershaft, your son.

UNDERSHAFT. My dear Stephen, I beg your pardon.

STEPHEN. Not at all.

UNDERSHAFT. Mr Cusins: I am much indebted to you for explaining so precisely. [*Turning to Sarah.*] Barbara, my dear——

SARAH. [*Prompting him.*] Sarah.

UNDERSHAFT. Sarah, of course. [*They shake hands. He goes over to Barbara.*] Barbara—I am right this time, I hope?

BARBARA. Quite right.   [*They shake hands.*

LADY BRITOMART. [*Resuming command.*] Sit down, all of you. Sit down, Andrew.

[*She comes forward and sits on the settee. Cusins also brings his chair forward on her left. Barbara and Stephen resume their seats. Lomax gives his chair to Sarah and goes for another.*

UNDERSHAFT. Thank you, my love.

LOMAX. [*Conversationally, as he brings a chair forward between the writing table and the settee, and offers it to Undershaft.*] Takes you some time to find out exactly where you are, dont it?

UNDERSHAFT. [*Accepting the chair, but remaining standing.*] That is not what embarrasses me, Mr Lomax. My difficulty is that if I play the part of a father, I shall produce the effect of an intrusive stranger; and if I play the part of a discreet stranger, I may appear a callous father.

LADY BRITOMART. There is no need for you to play any part at all, Andrew. You had much better be sincere and natural.

UNDERSHAFT. [*Submissively.*] Yes, my dear: I daresay that will be best. [*He sits down comfortably.*] Well, here I am. Now what can I do for you all?

LADY BRITOMART. You need not do anything, Andrew. You are one of the family. You can sit with us and enjoy yourself.

[*A painfully conscious pause. Barbara makes a face at Lomax, whose too long suppressed mirth immediately explodes in agonized neighings.*

LADY BRITOMART. [*Outraged.*] Charles Lomax: if you can behave yourself, behave yourself. If not, leave the room.

LOMAX. I'm awfully sorry, Lady Brit; but really you know, upon my soul!

[*He sits on the settee between Lady Britomart and Undershaft, quite overcome.*

BARBARA. Why dont you laugh if you want to, Cholly? It's good for your inside.

LADY BRITOMART. Barbara: you have had the education of a lady. Please let your father see that; and dont talk like a street girl.

UNDERSHAFT. Never mind me, my dear. As you know, I am not a gentleman; and I was never educated.

LOMAX. [*Encouragingly.*] Nobody'd know it, I assure you. You look all right, you know.

CUSINS. Let me advise you to study Greek, Mr Undershaft. Greek scholars are privileged men. Few of them know Greek; and none of them know anything else; but their position is unchallengeable. Other languages are the qualifications of waiters and commercial travellers: Greek is to a man of position what the hallmark is to silver.

BARBARA. Dolly: dont be insincere. Cholly: fetch your concertina and play something for us.

LOMAX. [*Jumps up eagerly, but checks himself to remark doubtfully to Undershaft.*] Perhaps that sort of thing isnt in your line, eh?

UNDERSHAFT. I am particulary fond of music.

LOMAX. [*Delighted.*] Are you? Then I'll get it.

[*He goes upstairs for the instrument.*

UNDERSHAFT. Do you play, Barbara?

BARBARA. Only the tambourine. But Cholly's teaching me the concertina.

UNDERSHAFT. Is Cholly also a member of the Salvation Army?

BARBARA. No: he says it's bad form to be a dissenter. But I dont despair of Cholly. I made him come yesterday to a meeting at the dock gates, and take the collection in his hat.

[*Undershaft looks whimsically at his wife.*

LADY BRITOMART. It is not my doing, Andrew. Barbara is old enough to take her own way. She has no father to advise her.

BARBARA. Oh yes, she has. There are no orphans in the Salvation Army.

UNDERSHAFT. Your father there has a great many children and plenty of experience, eh?

BARBARA. [*Looking at him with quick interest and nodding.*] Just so. How did you come to understand that?

[*Lomax is heard at the door trying the concertina.*

LADY BRITOMART. Come in, Charles. Play us something at once.

LOMAX. Righto! [*He sits down in his former place, and preludes.*

UNDERSHAFT. One moment, Mr Lomax. I am rather interested in the Salvation Army. Its motto might be my own: Blood and Fire.

LOMAX. [*Shocked.*] But not your sort of blood and fire, you know.

UNDERSHAFT. My sort of blood cleanses: my sort of fire purifies.

BARBARA. So do ours. Come down tomorrow to my shelter—the West Ham shelter—and see what we're doing. We're going to march to a great meeting in the Assembly Hall at Mile End. Come and see the shelter and then march with us: it will do you a lot of good. Can you play anything?

LISTED. UNDERSHAFT. In my youth I earned pennies, and even shillings occasionally, in the streets and in public house parlors by my natural talent for stepdancing. Later on, I became a member of the Undershaft orchestral society, and performed passably on the tenor trombone.

LOMAX. [*Scandalized—putting down the concertina.*] Oh, I say!

BARBARA. Many a sinner has played himself into heaven on the trombone, thanks to the Army.

LOMAX. [*To Barbara, still rather shocked.*] Yes; but what about the cannon business, dont you know? [*To Undershaft.*] Getting into heaven is not exactly in your line, is it?

LADY BRITOMART. Charles!!!

LOMAX. Well; but it stands to reason, dont it? The cannon business may be necessary and all that: we cant get on without cannons; but it isnt right, you know. On the other hand, there may be a certain amount of tosh about the Salvation Army—I belong to the Established Church myself—but still you cant deny that it's religion; and you cant go against religion, can you? At least unless youre downright immoral, dont you know.

UNDERSHAFT. You hardly appreciate my position, Mr Lomax——

LOMAX. [*Hastily.*] I'm not saying anything against you person-ally——

UNDERSHAFT. Quite so, quite so. But consider for a moment. Here I am, a profiteer in mutilation and murder. I find myself in a specially amiable humor just now because, this morning, down at the foundry, we blew twenty-seven dummy soldiers into fragments with a gun which formerly destroyed only thirteen.

LOMAX. [*Leniently.*] Well, the more destructive war becomes, the sooner it will be abolished, eh?

UNDERSHAFT. Not at all. The more destructive war becomes the more fascinating we find it. No, Mr Lomax: I am obliged to you for making the usual excuse for my trade; but I am not ashamed of it. I am not one of those men who keep their morals and their business in watertight compartments. All the spare money my trade rivals spend on hospitals, cathedrals and other receptacles for conscience money, I devote to experiments and researches in improved methods of destroying life and property. I have always done so; and I always shall. Therefore your Christmas card moralities of peace on earth and goodwill among men are of no use to me. Your Christianity, which enjoins you to resist not evil, and to turn the other cheek, would make me a bankrupt. My morality—my religion—must have a place for cannons and torpedoes in it.

STEPHEN. [*Coldly—almost sullenly.*] You speak as if there were half a dozen moralities and religions to choose from, instead of one true morality and one true religion.

UNDERSHAFT. For me there is only one true morality; but it might not fit you, as you do not manufacture aerial battleships. There is only one true morality for every man; but every man has not the same true morality.

LOMAX. [*Overtaxed.*] Would you mind saying that again? I didnt quite follow it.

CUSINS. It's quite simple. As Euripides says, one man's meat is another man's poison morally as well as physically.

UNDERSHAFT. Precisely.

LOMAX. Oh, that! Yes, yes, yes. True. True.

STEPHEN. In order words, some men are honest and some are scoundrels.

BARBARA. Bosh! There are no scoundrels.

UNDERSHIFT. Indeed? Are there any good men?

BARBARA. No. Not one. There are neither good men nor scoundrels: there are just children of one Father; and the sooner they stop calling one another names the better. You neednt talk to me: I know them. Ive had scores of them through my hands: scoundrels, criminals, infidels, philanthropists, missionaries, county councillors, all sorts. Theyre all just the same sort of sinner; and theres the same salvation ready for them all.

UNDERSHAFT. May I ask have you ever saved a maker of cannons?

BARBARA. No. Will you let me try?

UNDERSHAFT. Well, I will make a bargain with you. If I go to see you tomorrow in your Salvation Shelter, will you come the day after to see me in my cannon works?

BARBARA. Take care. It may end in your giving up the cannons for the sake of the Salvation Army.

UNDERSHAFT. Are you sure it will not end in your giving up the Salvation Army for the sake of the cannons?

BARBARA. I will take my chance of that.

UNDERSHAFT. And I will take my chance of the other. [*They shake hands on it.*] Where is your shelter?

BARBARA. In West Ham. At the sign of the cross. Ask anybody in Canning Town. Where are your works?

UNDERSHAFT. In Perivale St Andrews. At the sign of the sword. Ask anybody in Europe.

LOMAX. Hadnt I better play something?

BARBARA. Yes. Give us 'Onward, Christian Soldiers'.

LOMAX. Well, thats rather a strong order to begin with, dont you know. Suppose I sing 'Thourt passing hence, my brother'. It's much the same tune.

BARBARA. It's too melancholy. You get saved, Cholly; and youll pass hence, my brother, without making such a fuss about it.

LADY BRITOMART. Really, Barbara, you go on as if religion were a pleasant subject. Do have some sense of propriety.

UNDERSHAFT. I do not find it an unpleasant subject, my dear. It is the only one that capable people really care for.

LADY BRITOMART. [Looking at her watch.] Well, if you are determined to have it, I insist on having it in a proper and respectable way. Charles: ring for prayers.

[General amazement. Stephen rises in dismay.

LOMAX. [Rising.] Oh, I say!

UNDERSHAFT. [Rising.] I am afraid I must be going.

LADY BRITOMART. You cannot go now, Andrew: it would be most improper. Sit down. What will the servants think?

UNDERSHAFT. My dear: I have conscientious scruples. May I suggest a compromise? If Barbara will conduct a little service in the drawing-room, with Mr Lomax as organist, I will attend it willingly. I will even take part, if a trombone can be procured.

LADY BRITOMART. Dont mock, Andrew.

UNDERSHAFT. [Shocked—to Barbara.] You dont think I am mocking, my love, I hope.

BARBARA. No, of course not; and it wouldnt matter if you were: half the Army came to their first meeting for a lark. [Rising.] Come along. [She throws her arm round her father and sweeps him out, calling to the others from the threshold.] Come, Dolly. Come, Cholly.

[Cusins rises.

LADY BRITOMART. I will not be disobeyed by everybody. Adolphus: sit down. [He does not.] Charles: you may go. You are not fit for prayers: you cannot keep your countenance.

LOMAX. Oh I say!   [He goes out.

LADY BRITOMART. [Continuing.] But you, Adolphus, can behave yourself if you choose to. I insist on your staying.

CUSINS. My dear Lady Brit: there are things in the family prayer book that I couldnt bear to hear you say.

LADY BRITOMART. What things, pray?

CUSINS. Well, you would have to say before all the servants that we have done things we ought not to have done, and left undone things we ought to have done, and that there is no health in us. I cannot bear to hear you doing yourself such an injustice, and Barbara such an injustice. As for myself, I flatly deny it: I have done my best. I shouldnt dare to marry Barbara—I couldnt look you in the face—if it were true. So I must go to the drawing-room.

LADY BRITOMART. [Offended.] Well, go. [He starts for the door.] And remember this, Adolphus. [He turns to listen.] I have a very strong suspicion that you went to the Salvation Army to worship Barbara and nothing else. And I quite appreciate the very clever way in which you systematically humbug me. I have found you out. Take care Barbara doesnt. That's all.

CUSINS. [*With unruffled sweetness.*] Dont tell on me.   [*He steals out.*

LADY BRITOMART. Sarah: if you want to go, go. Anything's better than to sit there as if you wished you were a thousand miles away.

SARAH. [*Languidly.*] Very well, mamma.   [*She goes.*

    Lady Britomart, with a sudden flounce, gives way to a little gust of tears.

STEPHEN. [*Going to her.*] Mother: what's the matter?

LADY BRITOMART. [*Swishing away her tears with her handkerchief.*] Nothing. Foolishness. You can go with him, too, if you like, and leave me with the servants.

STEPHEN. Oh, you mustnt think that, mother. I—I dont like him.

LADY BRITOMART. The others do. That is the injustice of a woman's lot. A woman has to bring up her children; and that means to restrain them, to deny them things they want, to set them tasks, to punish them when they do wrong, to do all the unpleasant things. And the the father, who has nothing to do but pet them and spoil them, comes in when all her work is done and steals their affection from her.

STEPHEN. He has not stolen our affection from you. It is only curiosity.

LADY BRITOMART. [*Violently.*] I wont be consoled, Stephen. There is nothing the matter with me.

                    [*She rises and goes towards the door.*

STEPHEN. Where are you going, mother?

LADY BRITOMART. To the drawing-room, of course. [*She goes out.* 'Onward, Christian Soldiers', on the concertina, with tambourine accompaniment, is heard when the door opens.*] Are you coming, Stephen?

STEPHEN. No. Certainly not.

    [*She goes. He sits down on the settee, with compressed lips and an expression of strong dislike.*

*The yard of the West Ham shelter of the Salvation Army is a cold place
on a January morning. The building itself, an old warehouse, is newly
whitewashed. Its gabled end projects into the yard in the middle, with a
door on the ground floor, and another in the loft above it without any
balcony or ladder, but with a pulley rigged over it for hoisting sacks.
Those who come from this central gable end into the yard have the gateway
leading to the street on their left, with a stone horse-trough just beyond it,
and, on the right, a penthouse shielding a table from the weather. There
are forms at the table; and on them are seated a man and a woman, both
much down on their luck, finishing a meal of bread (one thick slice each,
with margarine and golden syrup) and diluted milk.*

*The man, a workman out of employment, is young, agile, a talker, a poser,
sharp enough to be capable of anything in reason except honesty or
altruistic considerations of any kind. The woman is a commonplace old
bundle of poverty and hard-worn humanity. She looks sixty and probably
is forty-five. If they were rich people, gloved and muffed and well wrapped
up in furs and overcoats, they would be numbed and miserable; for it is a
grindingly cold raw January day; and a glance at the background of grimy
warehouses and leaden sky visible over the whitewashed walls of the yard
would drive any idle rich person straight to the Mediterranean. But these
two, being no more troubled with visions of the Mediterranean than of the
moon, and being compelled to keep more of their clothes in the pawnshop,
and less on their persons, in winter than in summer, are not depressed by
the cold: rather are they stung into vivacity, to which their meal has just
now given an almost jolly turn. The man takes a pull at his mug, and
then gets up and moves about the yard with his hands deep in his pockets,
occasionally breaking into a stepdance.*

THE WOMAN. Feel better arter your meal, sir?

THE MAN. No. Call that a meal! Good enough for you, praps; but
wot is it to me, an intelligent workin man?

THE WOMAN. Workin man! Wot are you?

THE MAN. Painter.

THE WOMAN. [*Sceptically.*] Yus, I dessay.

THE MAN. Yus, you dessay! I know. Every loafer that cant do
nothink calls issself a painter. Well, I'm a real painter: grainer,
finisher, thirty-eight bob a week when I can get it.

THE WOMAN. Then why dont you go and get it?

THE MAN. I'll tell you why. Fust: I'm intelligent—fffff! it's rotten

83

cold here. [*He dances a step or two.*] Yes: intelligent beyond the station o life into which it has pleased the capitalists to call me; and they dont like a man that sees through em. Second, an intelligent bein needs a doo share of appiness; so I drink something cruel when I get the chawnce. Third, I stand by my class and do as little as I can so's to leave arf the job for me fellow workers. Fourth, I'm fly enough to know wots inside the law and wots outside it; and inside it I do as the capitalists do: pinch wot I can lay me ands on. In a proper state of society I am sober, industrious and honest: in Rome, so to speak, I do as the Romans do. Wots the consequence? When trade is bad—and it's rotten bad just now—and the employers az to sack arf their men, they generally start on me.

THE WOMAN. Whats your name?

THE MAN. Price. Bronterre O'Brien Price. Usually called Snobby Price, for short.

THE WOMAN. Snobby's a carpenter, aint it? You said you was a painter.

PRICE. Not that kind of snob, but the genteel sort. I'm too uppish, owing to my intelligence, and my father being a Chartist and a reading, thinking man: a stationer, too. I'm none of your common hewers of wood and drawers of water; and dont you forget it. [*He returns to his seat at the table, and takes up his mug.*] Wots your name?

THE WOMAN. Rummy Mitchens, sir.

PRICE. [*Quaffing the remains of his milk to her.*] Your elth, Miss Mitchens.

RUMMY. [*Correcting him.*] Missis Mitchens.

PRICE. Wot! Oh Rummy, Rummy. Respectable married woman, Rummy, gittin rescued by the Salvation Army by pretendin to be a bad un. Same old game!

RUMMY. What am I to do? I cant starve. Them Salvation lasses is dear good girls; but the better you are, the worse they likes to think you were before they rescued you. Why shouldnt they av a bit o credit, poor loves? Theyre worn to rags by their work. And where would they get the money to rescue us if we was to let on we're no worse than other people? You know what ladies and gentlemen are.

PRICE. Thievin swine! Wish I ad their job, Rummy, all the same. Wot does Rummy stand for? Pet name praps?

RUMMY. Short for Romola.

PRICE. For wot?

RUMMY. Romola. It was out of a new book. Somebody me mother wanted me to grow up like.

PRICE. We're companions in misfortune, Rummy. Both on us got names that nobody cawnt pronounce. Consequently I'm Snobby and youre Rummy because Bill and Sally wasnt good enough for our parents. Such is life!

RUMMY. Who saved you, Mr Price? Was it Major Barbara?

PRICE. No: I come here on my own. I'm going to be Bronterre O'Brien Price, the converted painter. I know wot they like. I'll tell em how I blasphemed and gambled and wopped my poor old mother—

RUMMY. [*Shocked.*] Used you to beat your mother?

PRICE. Not likely. She used to beat me. No matter: you come and listen to the converted painter, and youll hear how she was a pious woman that taught me me prayers at er knee, an how I used to come home drunk and drag her out o bed be er snow white airs, an lam into er with the poker.

RUMMY. Thats whats so unfair to us women. Your confessions is just as big lies as ours: you dont tell what you really done no more than us; but you men can tell your lies right out at the meetins and be made much of for it; while the sort o confessions we az to make to be wispered to one lady at a time. It aint right, spite of all their piety.

PRICE. Right! Do you spose the Army'd be allowed if it went and did right? Not much. It combs our air and makes us good little blokes to be robbed and put upon. But I'll play the game as good as any of em. I'll see somebody struck by lightnin, or hear a voice sayin 'Snobby Price: where will you spend eternity?' I'll av a time of it, I tell you.

RUMMY. You wont be let drink, though.

PRICE. I'll take it out in gorspellin, then. I dont want to drink if I can get fun enough any other way.

Jenny Hill, a pale, overwrought, pretty Salvation lass of eighteen, comes in through the yard gate, leading Peter Shirley, a half hardened, half worn-out elderly man, weak with hunger.

JENNY. [*Supporting him.*] Come! Pluck up. I'll get you something to eat. Youll be all right then.

PRICE. [*Rising and hurrying officiously to take the old man off Jenny's hands.*] Poor old man! Cheer up, brother: youll find rest and peace and appiness ere. Hurry up with the food, miss: e's fair done. [*Jenny hurries into the shelter.*] Ere, buck up, daddy! She's fetchin y'a thick slice o breadn treacle, an a mug o skyblue.
    [*He seats him at the corner of the table.*

RUMMY. [*Gaily.*] Keep up your old art! Never say die!

SHIRLEY. I'm not an old man. I'm only forty-six. I'm as good as ever I was. The grey patch come in my hair before I was thirty. All it wants is three pennorth o hair dye: am I to be turned on the streets to starve for it? Holy God! Ive worked ten to twelve

hours a day since I was thirteen, and paid my way all through;
and now am I to be thrown into the gutter and my job given to
a young man that can do it no better than me because Ive black
hair that goes white at the first change?

PRICE. [*Cheerfully.*] No good jawrin about it. Youre only a jumped-
up, jerked-off, orspittle-turned-out incurable of an ole workin
man: who cares about you? Eh? Make the thievin swine give you
a meal: theyve stole many a one from you. Get a bit o your own
back. [*Jenny returns with the usual meal.*] There you are, brother.
Awsk a blessin an tuck that into you.

SHIRLEY. [*Looking at it ravenously but not touching it, and crying like a
child.*] I never took anything before.

JENNY. [*Petting him.*] Come, come! The Lord sends it to you: he
wasnt above taking bread from his friends; and why should you
be? Besides, when we find you a job you can pay us for it if
you like.

SHIRLEY. [*Eagerly.*] Yes, yes: that's true. I can pay you back: it's
only a loan. [*Shivering.*] Oh Lord! Oh Lord!
            [*He turns to the table and attacks the meal ravenously.*]

JENNY. Well, Rummy, are you more comfortable now?

RUMMY. God bless you, lovey! Youve fed my body and saved my
soul havent you? [*Jenny, touched, kisses her.*] Sit down and rest a
bit: you must be ready to drop.

JENNY. Ive been going hard since morning. But theres more work
than we can do. I mustnt stop.

RUMMY. Try a prayer for just two minutes. Youll work all the
better after.

JENNY. [*Her eyes lighting up.*] Oh, isnt it wonderful how a few
minutes prayer revives you! I was quite lightheaded at twelve
o'clock, I was so tired; but Major Barbara just sent me to pray
for five minutes; and I was able to go on as if I had only just
begun. [*To Price.*] Did you have a piece of bread?

PRICE. [*With unction.*] Yes, miss; but Ive got the piece that I value
more; and thats the peace that passeth hall hannerstennin.

RUMMY. [*Fervently.*] Glory, Hallelujah!

*Bill Walker, a rough customer of about twenty-five, appears at the
    yard gate and looks malevolently at Jenny.*

JENNY. That makes me so happy. When you say that, I feel wicked
for loitering here. I must get to work again.

[*She is hurrying to the shelter, when the newcomer moves quickly up
to the door and intercepts her. His manner is so threatening that she
retreats as he comes at her truculently, driving her down the yard.*

BILL. Aw knaow you. Youre the one that took awy maw girl.
Youre the one that set er agen me. Well, I'm gowing to ev er
aht. Not that Aw care a carse for er or you: see? Bat Aw'll let

er knaow; and Aw'll let you knaow. Aw'm gowing to give her
a doin thatll teach er to cat awy from me. Nah in wiv you and
tell er to cam aht afore Aw cam in and kick er aht. Tell her Bill
Walker wants her. She'll knaow wot thet means; and if she
keeps me witin itll be worse. You stop to jawr beck at me; and
Aw'll stawt on you: d'ye eah? Theres your wy. In you gow.

> [*He takes her by the arm and slings her towards the door of the shelter.
> She falls on her hand and knee. Rummy helps her up again.*

PRICE. [*Rising, and venturing irresolutely towards Bill.*] Easy there,
mate. She aint doin you no arm.

BILL. Oo are you calling mite? [*Standing over him threateningly.*]
Youre gowin to stend ap for er, aw yer? Put ap your ends.

RUMMY. [*Running indignantly to him to scold him.*] Oh, you great
brute——

> [*He instantly swings his left hand back against her face. She screams
> and reels back to the trough, where she sits down, covering her
> bruised face with her hands and rocking herself and moaning with
> pain.*

JENNY. [*Going to her.*] Oh, God forgive you! How could you strike
an old woman like that?

BILL. [*Seizing her by the hair so violently that she also screams, and
tearing her away from the old woman.*] You Gawd forgimme again
an Aw'll Gawd forgive you one on the jawr thetll stop you
pryin for a week. [*Holding her and turning fiercely on Price.*] Ev you
ennything to sy agen it?

PRICE. [*Intimidated.*] No, matey: she aint anything to do with me.

BILL. Good job for you! Aw'd pat two meals into you and fawt
you with one finger arter, you stawved cur. [*To Jenny.*] Nah are
you gowin to fetch aht Mog Ebbijem; or em Aw to knock your
fice off you and fetch her meself?

JENNY. [*Writhing in his grasp.*] Oh, please someone go in and tell
Major Barbara——

> [*She screams again as he wrenches her head down; and Price and
> Rummy flee into the shelter.*

BILL. You want to gow in and tell your Mijor of me, do you?

JENNY. Oh, please dont drag my hair. Let me go.

BILL. Do you or downt you? [*She stifles a scream.*] Yus or nao?

JENNY. God give me strength——

BILL. [*Striking her with his fist in the face.*] Gow an shaow her thet,
and tell her if she wants one lawk it to cam and interfere with me.
[*Jenny, crying with pain, goes into the shed. He goes to the form and
addresses the old man.*] Eah: finish your mess; an git aht o maw wy.

SHIRLEY. [*Springing up and facing him fiercely, with the mug in his hand.*]
You take a liberty with me, and I'll smash you over the face with
the mug and cut your eye out. Aint you satisfied—young whelps

like you—with taking the bread out o the mouths of your elders
that have brought you up and slaved for you, but you must come
shovin and cheekin and bullyin in here, where the bread o
charity is sickenin in our stummicks?

BILL. [*Contemptuously, but backing a little.*] Wot good are you, you
aold palsy mag? Wot good are you?

SHIRLEY. As good as you and better. I'll do a day's work agen you
or any fat young soaker of your age. Go and take my job at
Horrockses, where I worked for ten year. They want young
men there: they cant afford to keep men over forty-five. Theyre
very sorry—give you a character and happy to help you to get
anything suited to your years—sure a steady man wont be long
out of a job. Well, let em try you. Theyll find the differ. What do
you know? Not as much as how to beeyave yourself—layin your
dirty fist across the mouth of a respectable woman!

BILL. Downt provowk me to ly it acrost yours: d' ye eah?

SHIRLEY. [*With blighting contempt.*] Yes: you like an old man to
hit, dont you, when youve finished with the women. I aint seen
you hit a young one yet.

BILL. [*Stung.*] You loy, you aold soupkitchener, you. There was
a yang menn eah. Did Aw offer to itt him or did Aw not?

SHIRLEY. Was he starvin or was he not? Was he a man or only a cross-
eyed thief an a loafer? Would you hit my son-in-law's brother?

BILL. Oo's ee?

SHIRLEY. Todger Fairmile o Balls Pond. Him that won £20 off the
Japanese wrastler at the music hall by standin out 17 minutes
4 seconds agen him.

BILL. [*Sullenly.*] Aw'm nao music awl wrastler. Ken he box?

SHIRLEY. Yes: an you cant.

BILL. Wot! Aw cawnt, cawnt Aw? Wots thet you sy?

[*Threatening him.*

SHIRLEY. [*Not budging an inch.*] Will you box Todger Fairmile if I
put him on to you? Say the word.

BILL. [*Subsiding with a slouch.*] Aw'll stend ap to enny menn alawv,
if he was ten Todger Fairmawls. But Aw dont set ap to be a
perfeshnal.

SHIRLEY. [*Looking down on him with unfathomable disdain.*] You box!
Slap an old woman with the back o your hand! You hadnt even
the sense to hit her where a magistrate couldnt see the mark of it,
you silly young lump of conceit and ignorance. Hit a girl in the
jaw and ony make her cry! If Todger Fairmile'd done it, she
wouldnt a got up inside o ten minutes, no more than you would if
he got on to you. Yah! I'd set about you myself if I had a week's
feedin in me instead o two months' starvation.

[*He turns his back on him and sits down moodily at the table.*

BILL. [*Following him and stooping over him to drive the taunt in.*] You loy! Youve the bread and treacle in you that you cam eah to beg.

SHIRLEY. [*Bursting into tears.*] Oh God! It's true: I'm only an old pauper on the scrap heap. [*Furiously.*] But youll come to it yourself; and then youll know. Youll come to it sooner than a teetotaller like me, fillin yourself with gin at this hour o the mornin!

BILL. Aw'm nao gin drinker, you oald lawr; bat wen Aw want to give my girl a bloomin good awdin Aw lawk to ev a bit o devil in me: see? An eah Aw emm, talkin to a rotten aold blawter like you sted o giving her wot for. [*Working himself into a rage.*] Aw'm gowin in there to fetch her aht.

> [*He makes vengefully for the shelter door.*

SHIRLEY. Youre going to the station on a stretcher, more likely; and theyll take the gin and the devil out of you there when they get you inside. You mind what youre about: the major here is the Earl o Stevenage's grand-daughter.

BILL. [*Checked.*] Garn!

SHIRLEY. Youll see.

BILL. [*His resolution oozing.*] Well, Aw aint dan nathin to er.

SHIRLEY. Spose she said you did! Who'd believe you?

BILL. [*Very uneasy, skulking back to the corner of the penthouse.*] Gawd! Theres no jastice in this cantry. To think wot them people can do! Aw'm as good as er.

SHIRLEY. Tell her so. It's just what a fool like you would do.

Barbara, brisk and businesslike, comes from the shelter with a note-book, and addresses herself to Shirley. Bill, cowed, sits down in the corner on a form, and turns his back on them.

BARBARA. Good morning.

SHIRLEY. [*Standing up and taking off his hat.*] Good morning, miss.

BARBARA. Sit down: make yourself at home. [*He hesitates; but she puts a friendly hand on his shoulder and makes him obey.*] Now then, since youve made friends with us, we want to know all about you. Names and addresses and trades.

SHIRLEY. Peter Shirley. Fitter. Chucked out two months ago because I was too old.

BARBARA. [*Not at all surprised.*] Youd pass still. Why didnt you dye your hair?

SHIRLEY. I did. Me age come out at a coroner's inquest on me daughter.

BARBARA. Steady?

SHIRLEY. Teetotaller. Never out of a job before. Good worker. And sent to the knackers like an old horse!

BARBARA. No matter: if you did your part God will do his.

SHIRLEY. [*Suddenly stubborn.*] My religion's no concern of anybody but myself.

BARBARA. [*Guessing.*] I know. Secularist?

SHIRLEY. [*Hotly.*] Did I offer to deny it?

BARBARA. Why should you? My own father's a Secularist, I think. Our Father—yours and mine—fulfils himself in many ways; and I dare say he knew what he was about when he made a Secularist of you. So buck up, Peter! We can always find a job for a steady man like you. [*Shirley, disarmed and a little bewildered, touches his hat. She turns from him to Bill.*] What's your name?

BILL. [*Insolently.*] Wot's thet to you?

BARBARA. [*Calmly making a note.*] Afraid to give his name. Any trade?

BILL. Oo's afride to give his nime? [*Doggedly, with a sense of heroically defying the House of Lords in the person of Lord Stevenage.*] If you want to bring a chawge agen me, bring it. [*She waits, unruffled.*] Moy nime's Bill Walker.

BARBARA. [*As if the name were familiar; trying to remember how.*] Bill Walker? [*Recollecting.*] Oh, I know: youre the man that Jenny Hill was praying for inside just now.

[*She enters his name in her notebook.*

BILL. Oo's Jenny Ill? And wot call as she to pry for me?

BARBARA. I dont know. Perhaps it was you that cut her lip.

BILL. [*Defiantly.*] Yus, it was me that cat her lip. Aw aint afride o you.

BARBARA. How could you be, since youre not afraid of God? Youre a brave man, Mr Walker. It takes some pluck to do our work here; but none of us dare lift our hand against a girl like that, for fear of her father in heaven.

BILL. [*Sullenly.*] I want nan o your kentin jawr. I spowse you think Aw cam eah to beg from you, like this demmiged lot eah. Not me. Aw downt want your bread and scripe and ketlep. Aw dont blieve in your Gawd, no more than you do yourself.

BARBARA. [*Sunnily apologetic and ladylike, as on a new footing with him.*] Oh, I beg your pardon for putting your name down, Mr Walker. I didn't understand. I'll strike it out.

BILL. [*Taking this as a slight, and deeply wounded by it.*] Eah! You let maw nime alown. Aint it good enaff to be in your book?

BARBARA. [*Considering.*] Well, you see, there's no use putting down your name unless I can do something for you, is there? Whats your trade?

BILL. [*Still smarting.*] Thets nao concern o yours.

BARBARA. Just so. [*Very businesslike.*] I'll put you down as [*writing*] the man who—struck—poor little Jenny Hill—in the mouth.

BILL. [*Rising threateningly.*] See eah. Awve ed enaff o this.

BARBARA. [*Quite sunny and fearless.*] What did you come to us for?

BILL. Aw cam for maw gel, see? Aw cam to tike her aht o this and to brike er jawr for er.

BARBARA. [*Complacently.*] You see I was right about your trade. [*Bill, on the point of retorting furiously, finds himself, to his great shame and terror, in danger of crying instead. He sits down again suddenly.*] What's her name?

BILL. [*Dogged.*] Er nime's Mog Ebbijem: thets wot her nime is.

BARBARA. Mog Habbijam! Oh, she's gone to Canning Town, to our barracks there.

BILL. [*Fortified by his resentment of Mog's perfidy.*] Is she? [*Vindictively.*] Then Aw'm gowin to Kennintahn arter her. [*He crosses to the gate; hesitates; finally comes back at Barbara.*] Are you loyin to me to git shat o me?

BARBARA. I dont want to get shut of you. I want to keep you here and save your soul. Youd better stay: youre going to have a bad time today, Bill.

BILL. Oo's gowin to give it to me? You, preps?

BARBARA. Someone you dont believe in. But youll be glad afterwards.

BILL. [*Slinking off.*] Aw'll gow to Kennintahn to be aht o reach o your tangue. [*Suddenly turning on her with intense malice.*] And if Aw downt fawnd Mog there, Aw'll cam beck and do two years for you, selp me Gawd if Aw downt!

BARBARA. [*A shade kindlier, if possible.*] It's no use, Bill. She's got another bloke.

BILL. Wot!

BARBARA. One of her own converts. He fell in love with her when he saw her with her soul saved, and her face clean and her hair washed.

BILL. [*Surprised.*] Wottud she wash it for, the carroty slat? It's red.

BARBARA. It's quite lovely now, because she wears a new look in her eyes with it. It's a pity youre too late. The new bloke has put your nose out of joint, Bill.

BILL. Aw'll put his nowse aht o joint for him. Not that Aw care a carse for er, mawnd thet. But Aw'll teach her to drop me as if Aw was dirt. And Aw'll teach him to meddle with maw judy. Wots iz bleedin nime?

BARBARA. Sergeant Todger Fairmile.

SHIRLEY. [*Rising with grim joy.*] I'll go with him, miss. I want to see them two meet. I'll take him to the infirmary when it's over.

BILL. [*To Shirley, with undissembled misgiving.*] Is thet im you was speakin on?

SHIRLEY. Thats him.

BILL. Im that wrastled in the music awl?

SHIRLEY. The competitions at the National Sportin Club was worth nigh a hundred a year to him. He's gev em up now for religion; so he's a bit fresh for want of the exercise he was accustomed to. He'll be glad to see you. Come along.

BILL. Wot's is wight?

SHIRLEY. Thirteen four.   [*Bill's last hope expires.*

BARBARA. Go and talk to him, Bill. He'll convert you.

SHIRLEY. He'll convert your head into a mashed potato.

BILL. [*Sullenly.*] Aw aint afride of im. Aw aint afride of ennybody. Bat e can lick me. She's dan me.

[*He sits down moodily on the edge of the horse trough.*

SHIRLEY. You aint going. I thought not.   [*He resumes his seat.*

BARBARA. [*Calling.*] Jenny!

JENNY. [*Appearing at the shelter door with a plaster on the corner of her mouth.*] Yes, Major.

BARBARA. Send Rummy Mitchens out to clear away here.

JENNY. I think she's afraid.

BARBARA. [*Her resemblance to her mother flashing out for a moment.*] Nonsense! She must do as she's told.

JENNY. [*Calling into the shelter.*] Rummy: the Major says you must come.

[*Jenny comes to Barbara, purposely keeping on the side next Bill, lest he suppose that she shrank from him or bore malice.*

BARBARA. Poor little Jenny! Are you tired? [*Looking at the wounded cheek.*] Does it hurt?

JENNY. No: it's all right now. It was nothing.

BARBARA. [*Critically.*] It was as hard as he could hit, I expect. Poor Bill! You dont feel angry with him, do you?

JENNY. Oh no, no, no: indeed I dont, Major, bless his poor heart!

[*Barbara kisses her; and she runs away merrily into the shelter. Bill writhes with an agonizing return of his new and alarming symptoms, but says nothing. Rummy Mitchens comes from the shelter.*

BARBARA. [*Going to meet Rummy.*] Now Rummy, bustle. Take in those mugs and plates to be washed; and throw the crumbs about for the birds.

[*Rummy takes the three plates and mugs; but Shirley takes back his mug from her, as there is still some milk left in it.*

RUMMY. There aint any crumbs. This aint a time to waste good bread on birds.

PRICE. [*Appearing at the shelter door.*] Gentleman come to see the shelter, Major. Says he's your father.

BARBARA. All right. Coming.

[*Snobby goes back into the shelter, followed by Barbara.*

RUMMY. [*Stealing across to Bill and addressing him in a subdued voice, but with intense conviction.*] I'd av the lor of you, you flat-eared pignosed potwalloper, if she'd let me. Youre no gentleman, to hit a lady in the face.

[*Bill, with greater things moving in him, takes no notice.*

SHIRLEY. [*Following her.*] Here! In with you and dont get yourself into more trouble by talking.

RUMMY. [*With hauteur.*] I aint ad the pleasure o being hintroduced to you, as I can remember.

[*She goes into the shelter with the plates.*

SHIRLEY. That's the——

BILL. [*Savagely.*] Downt you talk to me, d'ye eah? You lea me alown, or Aw'll do you a mischief. Aw'm not dirt under your feet, ennywy.

SHIRLEY. [*Calmly.*] Dont you be afeerd. You aint such prime company that you need expect to be sought after.

[*He is about to go into the shelter when Barbara comes out, with Undershaft on her right.*

BARBARA. Oh, there you are, Mr Shirley! [*Between them.*] This is my father: I told you he was a Secularist, didnt I? Perhaps youll be able to comfort one another.

UNDERSHAFT. [*Startled.*] A Secularist! Not the least in the world: on the contrary, a confirmed mystic.

BARBARA. Sorry, I'm sure. By the way, papa, what is your religion —in case I have to introduce you again?

UNDERSHAFT. My religion? Well, my dear, I am a Millionaire. That is my religion.

BARBARA. Then I'm afraid you and Mr Shirley wont be able to comfort one another after all. Youre not a Millionaire, are you, Peter?

SHIRLEY. No; and proud of it.

UNDERSHAFT. [*Gravely.*] Poverty, my friend, is not a thing to be proud of.

SHIRLEY. [*Angrily.*] Who made your millions for you? Me and my like. What's kep us poor? Keepin you rich. I wouldnt have your conscience, not for all your income.

UNDERSHAFT. I wouldnt have your income, not for all your conscience, Mr Shirley.

[*He goes to the penthouse and sits down on a form.*

BARBARA. [*Stopping Shirley adroitly as he is about to retort.*] You wouldnt think he was my father, would you, Peter? Will you go into the shelter and lend the lasses a hand for a while: we're worked off our feet.

SHIRLEY. [*Bitterly.*] Yes: I'm in their debt for a meal, aint I?

BARBARA. Oh, not because youre in their debt, but for love of them, Peter, for love of them. [*He cannot understand, and is rather scandalized.*] There! Dont stare at me. In with you; and give that conscience of yours a holiday.

[*Bustling him into the shelter.*

SHIRLEY. [*As he goes in.*] Ah! it's a pity you never was trained to use your reason, miss. Youd have been a very taking lecturer on Secularism.

[*Barbara turns to her father.*

UNDERSHAFT. Never mind me, my dear. Go about your work; and let me watch it for a while.

BARBARA. All right.

UNDERSHAFT. For instance, whats the matter with that out-patient over there?

BARBARA. [*Looking at Bill, whose attitude has never changed, and whose expression of brooding wrath has deepened.*] Oh, we shall cure him in no time. Just watch. [*She goes over to Bill and waits. He glances up at her and casts his eyes down again, uneasy, but grimmer than ever.*] It would be nice to just stamp on Mog Habbigam's face, wouldnt it, Bill?

BILL. [*Starting up from the trough in consternation.*] It's a loy: Aw never said so. [*She shakes her head.*] Oo taold you wot was in moy mawnd?

BARBARA. Only your new friend.

BILL. Wot new friend?

BARBARA. The devil, Bill. When he gets round people they get miserable, just like you.

BILL. [*With a heartbreaking attempt at devil-may-care cheerfulness.*] Aw aint miserable.

[*He sits down again, and stretches his legs in an attempt to seem indifferent.*

BARBARA. Well, if youre happy, why dont you look happy, as we do?

BILL. [*His legs curling back in spite of him.*] Aw'm eppy enaff, Aw tell you. Woy cawnt you lea me alown? Wot ev I dan to you? Aw aint smashed your fice, ev Aw?

BARBARA. [*Softly; wooing his soul.*] It's not me that's getting at you, Bill.

BILL. Oo else is it?

BARBARA. Somebody that doesnt intend you to smash women's faces, I suppose. Somebody or something that wants to make a man of you.

BILL. [*Blustering.*] Mike a menn o me! Aint Aw a menn? eh? Oo sez Aw'm not a menn?

BARBARA. Theres a man in you somewhere, I suppose. But why did he let you hit poor little Jenny Hill? That wasnt very manly of him, was it?

BILL. [*Tormented.*] Ev dan wiv it, Aw tell you. Chack it. Aw'm
sick o your Jenny Ill and er silly little fice.

BARBARA. Then why do you keep thinking about it? Why does it
keep coming up against you in your mind? Youre not getting
converted, are you?

BILL. [*With conviction.*] Not ME. Not lawkly.

BARBARA. Thats right, Bill. Hold out against it. Put out your
strength. Dont lets get you cheap. Todger Fairmile said he
wrestled for three nights against his salvation harder than he ever
wrestled with the Jap at the music hall. He gave in to the Jap
when his arm was going to break. But he didnt give in to his
salvation until his heart was going to break. Perhaps youll
escape that. You havnt any heart, have you?

BILL. Wot d' ye mean? Woy aint Aw got a awt the sime as ennybody else?

BARBARA. A man with a heart wouldnt have bashed poor little
Jenny's face, would he?

BILL. [*Almost crying.*] Ow, will you lea me alown? Ev Aw ever
offered to meddle with you, that you cam neggin and pro-
vowking me lawk this?

> [*He writhes convulsively from his eyes to his toes.*

BARBARA. [*With a steady soothing hand on his arm and a gentle voice
that never lets him go.*] It's your soul thats hurting you, Bill, and
not me. Weve been through it all ourselves. Come with us, Bill.
[*He looks wildly round.*] To brave manhood on earth and eternal
glory in heaven. [*He is on the point of breaking down.*] Come. [*A
drum is heard in the shelter; and Bill, with a gasp, escapes from the spell
as Barbara turns quickly. Adolphus enters from the shelter with a big
drum.*] Oh! There you are, Dolly. Let me introduce a new friend
of mine, Mr Bill Walker. This is my bloke, Bill: Mr Cusins.

> [*Cusins salutes with his drumstick.*

BILL. Gowin to merry im?

BARBARA. Yes.

BILL. [*Fervently.*] Gawd elp im! Gaw-aw-aw-awd elp im!

BARBARA. Why? Do you think he wont be happy with me?

BILL. Awve aony ed to stend it for a mawnin: e'll ev to stend it for
a lawftawm.

CUSINS. That is a frightful reflection, Mr Walker. But I cant tear
myself away from her.

BILL. Well, Aw ken. [*To Barbara.*] Eah! Do you knaow where
Aw'm gowin to, and wot Aw'm gowin to do?

BARBARA. Yes: youre going to heaven; and youre coming back
here before the week's out to tell me so.

BILL. You loy. Aw'm gowin to Kenningtahn, to spit in Todger
Fairmawl's eye. Aw beshed Jenny Ill's fice; an nar Aw'll git

me aown fice beshed and cam beck and shaow it to er. Ee'll itt me ardern Aw itt her. Thatll mike us square. [*To Adolphus.*] Is thet fair or is it not? Youre a genlmn: you oughter knaow.

BARBARA. Two black eyes wont make one white one, Bill.

BILL. Aw didnt awst you. Cawnt you never keep your mahth shat? Oy awst the genlmn.

CUSINS. [*Reflectively.*] Yes: I think youre right, Mr Walker. Yes: I should do it. It's curious: it's exactly what an ancient Greek would have done.

BARBARA. But what good will it do?

CUSINS. Well, it will give Mr Fairmile some exercise; and it will satisfy Mr Walker's soul.

BILL. Rot! There aint nao sach a thing as a saoul. Ah kin you tell wevver Awve a saoul or not? You never seen it.

BARBARA. Ive seen it hurting you when you went against it.

BILL. [*With compressed aggravation.*] If you was maw gel and took the word aht o me mahth lawk thet, Aw'd give you sathink youd feel urtin, Aw would. [*To Adolphus.*] You tike maw tip, mite. Stop er jawr; or youll doy afoah your tawm. [*With intense expression.*] Wore aht: thets wot youll be: wore aht.

[*He goes away through the gate.*

CUSINS. [*Looking after him.*] I wonder!

BARBARA. Dolly!   [*Indignant, in her mother's manner.*

CUSINS. Yes, my dear, it's very wearing to be in love with you. If it lasts, I quite think I shall die young.

BARBARA. Should you mind?

CUSINS. Not at all.

[*He is suddenly softened, and kisses her over the drum, evidently not for the first time, as people cannot kiss over a big drum without practice. Undershaft coughs.*

BARBARA. It's all right, papa, weve not forgotten you. Dolly: explain the place to papa: I havnt time.

[*She goes busily into the shelter.*

[*Undershaft and Adolphus now have the yard to themselves. Undershaft, seated on a form, and still keenly attentive, looks hard at Adolphus. Adolphus looks hard at him.*

UNDERSHAFT. I fancy you guess something of what is in my mind, Mr Cusins. [*Cusins flourishes his drumsticks as if in the act of beating a lively rataplan, but makes no sound.*] Exactly so. But suppose Barbara finds you out!

CUSINS. You know, I do not admit that I am imposing on Barbara. I am quite genuinely interested in the views of the Salvation Army. The fact is, I am a sort of collector of religions; and the curious thing is that I find I can believe them all. By the way, have you any religion?

UNDERSHAFT. Yes.

CUSINS. Anything out of the common?

UNDERSHAFT. Only that there are two things necessary to Salvation.

CUSINS. [*Disappointed, but polite.*] Ah, the Church Catechism. Charles Lomax also belongs to the Established Church.

UNDERSHAFT. The two things are——

CUSINS. Baptism and——

UNDERSHAFT. No. Money and gunpowder.

CUSINS. [*Surprised, but interested.*] That is the general opinion of our governing classes. The novelty is in hearing any man confess it.

UNDERSHAFT. Just so.

CUSINS. Excuse me: is there any place in your religion for honor, justice, truth, love, mercy and so forth?

UNDERSHAFT. Yes: they are the graces and luxuries of a rich, strong and safe life.

CUSINS. Suppose one is forced to choose between them and money or gunpowder?

UNDERSHAFT. Choose money and gunpowder; for without enough of both you cannot afford the others.

CUSINS. That is your religion?

UNDERSHAFT. Yes.

> [*The cadence of this reply makes a full close in the conversation, Cusins twists his face dubiously and contemplates Undershaft. Undershaft contemplates him.*

CUSINS. Barbara wont stand that. You will have to choose between your religion and Barbara.

UNDERSHAFT. So will you, my friend. She will find out that that drum of yours is hollow.

CUSINS. Father Undershaft: you are mistaken: I am a sincere Salvationist. You do not understand the Salvation Army. It is the army of joy, of love, of courage: it has banished the fear and remorse and despair of the old hell-ridden evangelical sects: it marches to fight the devil with trumpet and drum, with music and dancing, with banner and palm, as becomes a sally from heaven by its happy garrison. It picks the waster out of the public house and makes a man of him: it finds a worm wriggling in a back kitchen, and lo! a woman! Men and women of rank too, sons and daughters of the Highest. It takes the poor professor of Greek, the most artificial and self-suppressed of human creatures, from his meal of roots, and lets loose the rhapsodist in him; reveals the true worship of Dionysos to him; sends him down the public street drumming dithyrambs.

> [*He plays a thundering flourish on the drum.*

UNDERSHAFT. You will alarm the shelter.

CUSINS. Oh, they are accustomed to these sudden ecstasies. How-
ever, if the drum worries you——
   [*He pockets the drumsticks, unhooks the drum, and stands it on the
   ground opposite the gateway.*
UNDERSHAFT. Thank you.
CUSINS. You remember what Euripides says about your money
and gunpowder?
CUSINS. [*Declaiming.*]

                    One and another
   In money and guns may outpass his brother;
   And men in their millions float and flow
   And seethe with a million hopes as leaven;
   And they win their will; or they miss their will;
   And their hopes are dead or are pined for still;
             But whoe'er can know
             As the long days go
   That to live is happy, has found his heaven.

My translation: what do you think of it?
UNDERSHAFT. I think, my friend, that if you wish to know, as the
long days go, that to live is happy, you must first acquire
money enough for a decent life, and power enough to be your
own master.
CUSINS. You are damnably discouraging.
                              [*He resumes his declamation.*
             Is it so hard a thing to see
             That the spirit of God—whate'er it be—
   The law that abides and changes not, ages long,
   The Eternal and Nature-born: these things be strong?
   What else is Wisdom? What of Man's endeavor,
   Or God's high grace so lovely and so great?
   To stand from fear set free? To breathe and wait?
   To hold a hand uplifted over Fate?
   And shall not Barbara be loved for ever?

UNDERSHAFT. Euripides mentions Barbara, does he?
CUSINS. It is a fair translation. The word means Loveliness.
UNDERSHAFT. May I ask—as Barbara's father—how much a year
she is to be loved for ever on?
CUSINS. As for Barbara's father, that is more your affair than mine.
I can feed her by teaching Greek: that is about all.
UNDERSHAFT. Do you consider it a good match for her?
CUSINS. [*With polite obstinacy.*] Mr Undershaft: I am in many ways
a weak, timid, ineffectual person; and my health is far from
satisfactory. But whenever I feel that I must have anything, I
get it, sooner or later. I feel that way about Barbara. I dont like

marriage: I feel intensely afraid of it; and I dont know what I shall do with Barbara or what she will do with me. But I feel that I and nobody else must marry her. Please regard that as settled—not that I wish to be arbitrary; but why should I waste your time in discussing what is inevitable?

UNDERSHAFT. You mean that you will stick at nothing: not even the conversion of the Salvation Army to the worship of Dionysos.

CUSINS. The business of the Salvation Army is to save, not to wrangle about the name of the pathfinder. Dionysos or another: what does it matter?

UNDERSHAFT. [*Rising and approaching him.*] Professor Cusins: you are a young man after my own heart.

CUSINS. Mr Undershaft: you are, as far as I am able to gather, a most infernal old rascal: but you appeal very strongly to my sense of ironic humor.

> [*Undershaft mutely offers his hand. They shake.*

UNDERSHAFT. [*Suddenly concentrating himself.*] And now to business.

CUSINS. Pardon me. We are discussing religion. Why go back to such an uninteresting and unimportant subject as business?

UNDERSHAFT. Religion is our business at present, because it is through religion alone that we can win Barbara.

CUSINS. Have you, too, fallen in love with Barbara?

UNDERSHAFT. Yes, with a father's love.

CUSINS. A father's love for a grown-up daughter is the most dangerous of all infatuations. I apologize for mentioning my own pale, coy, mistrustful fancy in the same breath with it.

UNDERSHAFT. Keep to the point. We have to win her; and we are neither of us Methodists.

CUSINS. That doesnt matter. The power Barbara wields here—the power that wields Barbara herself—is not Calvinism, not Presbyterianism, not Methodism——

UNDERSHAFT. Not Greek Paganism either, eh?

CUSINS. I admit that. Barbara is quite original in her religion.

UNDERSHAFT. [*Triumphantly.*] Aha! Barbara Undershaft would be. Her inspiration comes from within herself.

CUSINS. How do you suppose it got there?

UNDERSHAFT. [*In towering excitement.*] It is the Undershaft inheritance. I shall hand on my torch to my daughter. She shall make my converts and preach my gospel——

CUSINS. What! Money and gunpowder!

UNDERSHAFT. Yes, money and gunpowder. Freedom and power. Command of life and command of death.

CUSINS. [*Urbanely; trying to bring him down to earth.*] This is extremely interesting, Mr Undershaft. Of course you know that you are mad.

UNDERSHAFT. [*With redoubled force.*] And you?

CUSINS. Oh, mad as a hatter. You are welcome to my secret since I have discovered yours. But I am astonished. Can a madman make cannons?

UNDERSHAFT. Would anyone else than a madman make them? And now [*with surging energy*] question for question. Can a sane man translate Euripides?

CUSINS. No.

UNDERSHAFT. [*Seizing him by the shoulder.*] Can a sane woman make a man of a waster or a woman of a worm?

CUSINS. [*Reeling before the storm.*] Father Colossus—Mammoth Millionaire——

UNDERSHAFT. [*Pressing him.*] Are there two mad people or three in this Salvation shelter today?

CUSINS. You mean Barbara is as mad as we are?

UNDERSHAFT. [*Pushing him lightly off and resuming his equanimity suddenly and completely.*] Pooh, Professor! let us call things by their proper names. I am a millionaire; you are a poet; Barbara is a savior of souls. What have we three to do with the common mob of slaves and idolators?

[*He sits down again with a shrug of contempt for the mob.*

CUSINS. Take care! Barbara is in love with the common people. So am I. Have you never felt the romance of that love?

UNDERSHAFT. [*Cold and sardonic.*] Have you ever been in love with Poverty, like St Francis? Have you ever been in love with Dirt, like St Simeon? Have you ever been in love with disease and suffering, like our nurses and philanthropists? Such passions are not virtues, but the most unnatural of all the vices. This love of the common people may please an earl's grand-daughter and a university professor; but I have been a common man and a poor man; and it has no romance for me. Leave it to the poor to pretend that poverty is a blessing: leave it to the coward to make a religion of his cowardice by preaching humility: we know better than that. We three must stand together above the common people: how else can we help their children to climb up beside us? Barbara must belong to us, not to the Salvation Army.

CUSINS. Well, I can only say that if you think you will get her away from the Salvation Army by talking to her as you have been talking to me, you dont know Barbara.

UNDERSHAFT. My friend: I never ask for what I can buy.

CUSINS. [*In a white fury.*] Do I understand you to imply that you can buy Barbara?

UNDERSHAFT. No; but I can buy the Salvation Army.

CUSINS. Quite impossible.

UNDERSHAFT. You shall see. All religious organizations exist by selling themselves to the rich.

CUSINS. Not the Army. That is the Church of the poor.

UNDERSHAFT. All the more reason for buying it.

CUSINS. I dont think you quite know what the Army does for the poor.

UNDERSHAFT. Oh yes, I do. It draws their teeth: that is enough for me as a man of business.

CUSINS. Nonsense! It makes them sober——

UNDERSHAFT. I prefer sober workmen. The profits are larger.

CUSINS. —honest——

UNDERSHAFT. Honest workmen are the most economical.

CUSINS. —attached to their homes——

UNDERSHAFT. So much the better: they will put up with anything sooner than change their shop.

CUSINS. —happy——

UNDERSHAFT. An invaluable safeguard against revolution.

CUSINS. —unselfish——

UNDERSHAFT. Indifferent to their own interests, which suits me exactly.

CUSINS. —with their thoughts on heavenly things——

UNDERSHAFT. [*Rising.*] And not on Trade Unionism nor Socialism. Excellent.

CUSINS. [*Revolted.*] You really are an infernal old rascal.

UNDERSHAFT. [*Indicating Peter Shirley, who has just come from the shelter and strolled dejectedly down the yard between them.*] And this is an honest man!

SHIRLEY. Yes; and what av I got by it?

[*He passes on bitterly and sits on the form, in the corner of the penthouse.*

[*Snobby Price, beaming sanctimoniously, and Jenny Hill, with a tambourine full of coppers, come from the shelter and go to the drum, on which Jenny begins to count the money.*

UNDERSHAFT. [*Replying to Shirley.*] Oh, your employers must have got a good deal by it from first to last.

[*He sits on the table, with one foot on the side form. Cusins, overwhelmed, sits down on the same form nearer the shelter. Barbara comes from the shelter to the middle of the yard. She is excited and a little overwrought.*

BARBARA. Weve just had a splendid experience meeting at the other gate in Cripps's Lane. Ive hardly ever seen them so much moved as they were by your confession, Mr Price.

PRICE. I could almost be glad of my past wickedness if I could believe that it would elp to keep hathers stright.

BARBARA. So it will, Snobby. How much, Jenny?

JENNY. Four and tenpence, Major.

BARBARA. Oh, Snobby, if you had given your poor mother

just one more kick, we should have got the whole five shillings!

PRICE. If she heard you say that, miss, she'd be sorry I didnt. But I'm glad. Oh, what a joy it will be to her when she hears I'm saved!

UNDERSHAFT. Shall I contribute the odd twopence, Barbara? The millionaire's mite, eh?

> [He takes a couple of pennies from his pocket.

BARBARA. How did you make that twopence?

UNDERSHAFT. As usual. By selling cannons, torpedoes, submarines and my new patent Grand Duke hand grenade.

BARBARA. Put it back in your pocket. You cant buy your salvation here for twopence: you must work it out.

UNDERSHAFT. Is twopence not enough? I can afford a little more, if you press me.

BARBARA. Two million millions would not be enough. There is bad blood on your hands; and nothing but good blood can cleanse them. Money is no use. Take it away. [She turns to Cusins.] Dolly: you must write another letter for me to the papers. [He makes a wry face.] Yes: I know you dont like it; but it must be done. The starvation this winter is beating us: everybody is unemployed. The General says we must close this shelter if we cant get more money. I force the collections at the meetings until I am ashamed: dont I, Snobby?

PRICE. It's a fair treat to see you work it, miss. The way you got them up from three-and-six to four-and-ten with that hymn, penny by penny and verse by verse, was a caution. Not a Cheap Jack on Mile End Waste could touch you at it.

BARBARA. Yes; but I wish we could do without it. I am getting at last to think more of the collection than of the people's souls. And what are those hatfuls of pence and halfpence? We want thousands! tens of thousands! hundreds of thousands! I want to convert people, not to be always begging for the Army in a way I'd die sooner than beg for myself.

UNDERSHAFT. [In profound irony.] Genuine unselfishness is capable of anything, my dear.

BARBARA. [Unsuspectingly, as she turns away to take the money from the drum and put it in a cash bag she carries.] Yes, isn't it?

> [Undershaft looks sardonically at Cusins.

CUSINS. [Aside to Undershaft.] Mephistopheles! Machiavelli!

BARBARA. [Tears coming into her eyes as she ties the bag and pockets it.] How are we to feed them? I cant talk religion to a man with bodily hunger in his eyes. [Almost breaking down.] It's frightful.

JENNY. [Running to her.] Major, dear——

BARBARA. [*Rebounding.*] No: dont comfort me. It will be all right. We shall get the money.

UNDERSHAFT. How?

JENNY. By praying for it, of course. Mrs Baines says she prayed for it last night; and she has never prayed for it in vain: never once.   [*She goes to the gate and looks out into the street.*

BARBARA. [*Who has dried her eyes and regained her composure.*] By the way, dad, Mrs Baines has come to march with us to our big meeting this afternoon; and she is very anxious to meet you, for some reason or other. Perhaps she'll convert you.

UNDERSHAFT. I shall be delighted, my dear.

JENNY. [*At the gate: excitedly.*] Major! Major! heres that man back again.

BARBARA. What man?

JENNY. The man that hit me. Oh, I hope he's coming back to join us.

[*Bill Walker, with frost on his jacket, comes through the gate, his hands deep in his pockets and his chin sunk between his shoulders, like a cleaned-out gambler. He halts between Barbara and the drum.*

BARBARA. Hallo, Bill! Back already!

BILL. [*Nagging at her.*] Bin talkin ever sence, ev you?

BARBARA. Pretty nearly. Well, has Todger paid you out for poor Jenny's jaw?

BILL. Nao e aint.

BARBARA. I thought your jacket looked a bit snowy.

BILL. Sao it is snaowy. You want to knaow where the snaow cam from, downt you?

BARBARA. Yes.

BILL. Well, it cam from orf the grahnd in Pawkinses Corner in Kennintahn. It got rabbed orf be maw shaoulders: see?

BARBARA. Pity you didnt rub some off with your knees, Bill! That would have done you a lot of good.

BILL. [*With sour mirthless humor.*] Aw was sivin anather menn's knees at the tawm. E was kneelin on moy ed, e was.

JENNY. Who was kneeling on your head?

BILL. Todger was. E was pryin for me: pryin camfortable wiv me as a cawpet. Sow was Mog. Sao was the aol bloomin meetin. Mog she sez, 'Ow Lawd, brike is stabborn sperrit; bat downt urt is dear art.' Thet was wot she said. 'Downt urt is dear art'! An er blowk—thirteen stun four!—kneelin wiv all is wight on me. Fanny, aint it?

JENNY. Oh no. We're so sorry, Mr Walker.

BARBARA. [*Enjoying it frankly.*] Nonsense! Of course it's funny. Served you right, Bill! You must have done something to him first.

BILL. [*Doggedly.*] Aw did wot Aw said Aw'd do. Aw spit in is eye.
E looks ap at the skoy and sez, 'Ow that Aw should be fahnd
worthy to be spit upon for the gospel's sike!' e sez; an Mog
sez, 'Glaory, Allelloolier!'; an then e called me Braddher, an
dahned me as if Aw was a kid and e was me mather worshin me
a Setterda nawt. Aw ednt jast nao shaow wiv im at all. Arf the
street pryed; an the tather arf larfed fit to split theirselves. [*To
Barbara.*] There! Are you settisfawd nah?

BARBARA. [*Her eyes dancing.*] Wish I'd been there, Bill.

BILL. Yus: youd a got in a hextra bit o talk on me, wouldnt
you?

JENNY. I'm so sorry, Mr Walker.

BILL. [*Fiercely.*] Downt you gow being sorry for me: youve no call.
Listen eah. Aw browk your jawr.

JENNY. No, it didnt hurt me: indeed it didnt, except for a moment.
It was only that I was frightened.

BILL. Aw downt want to be forgive be you, or be ennybody. Wot
Aw did Aw'll py for. Aw trawd to gat me aown jawr browk to
settisfaw you——

JENNY. [*Distressed.*] Oh no——

BILL. [*Impatiently.*] Tell y' Aw did: cawnt you listen to wots
bein taold you? All Aw got be it was being mide a sawt of in
the pablic street for me pines. Well, if Aw cawnt settisfaw you
one wy, Aw ken anather. Listen eah! Aw ed two quid sived agen
the frost; an Awve a pahnd of it left. A mite o mawn last week
ed words with the judy e's gowing to merry. E give er wot-for;
an e's bin fawnd fifteen bob. E ed a rawt to itt er cause they was
gowin to be merrid; but Aw ednt nao rawt to itt you; sao put
anather fawv bob on an call it a pahnd's worth. [*He produces a
sovereign.*] Eahs the manney. Tike it; and lets ev no more o your
forgivin an prying and your Mijor jawrin me. Let wot Aw dan
be dan an pide for; and let there be a end of it.

JENNY. Oh, I couldnt take it, Mr Walker. But if you would give a
shilling or two to poor Rummy Mitchens! You really did hurt
her; and she's old.

BILL. [*Contemptuously.*] Not lawkly. Aw'd give her anather as soon
as look at er. Let her ev the lawr o me as she threatened! S h e
aint forgiven me: not mach. Wot Aw dan to er is not on me
mawnd—wot she [*indicating Barbara*] mawt call on me conscience
—no more than stickin a pig. It's this Christian gime o yours
that Aw wownt ev plyed agen me: this bloomin forgivin an
neggin an jawrin that mikes a menn thet sore that iz lawf's a
burdn to im. Aw wownt ev it, Aw tell you; sao tike your manney
and stop thraowing your silly beshed fice hap agen me.

JENNY. Major: may I take a little of it for the Army?

BARBARA. No: the Army is not to be bought. We want your soul, Bill; and we'll take nothing less.

BILL. [*Bitterly.*] Aw knaow. Me an maw few shillins is not good enaff for you. Youre a earl's grendorter, you are. Nathink less than a andered pahnd for you.

UNDERSHAFT. Come, Barbara! You could do a great deal of good with a hundred pounds. If you will set this gentleman's mind at ease by taking his pound, I will give the other ninety-nine.

[*Bill, dazed by such opulence, instinctively touches his cap.*]

BARBARA. Oh, youre too extravagant, papa. Bill offers twenty pieces of silver. All you need offer is the other ten. That will make the standard price to buy anybody who's for sale. I'm not; and the Army's not. [*To Bill.*] Youll never have another quiet moment, Bill, until you come round to us. You cant stand out against your salvation.

BILL. [*Sullenly.*] Aw cawnt stend aht agen music awl wrastlers and awful tangued women. Awve offered to py. Aw can do no more. Tike it or leave it. There it is.

[*He throws the sovereign on the drum, and sits down on the horse-trough. The coin fascinates Snobby Price, who takes an early opportunity of dropping his cap on it.*
Mrs Baines comes from the shelter. She is dressed as a Salvation Army Commissioner. She is an earnest looking woman of about forty, with a caressing, urgent voice, and an appealing manner.]

BARBARA. This is my father, Mrs Baines. [*Undershaft comes from the table, taking his hat off with marked civility.*] Try what you can do with him. He wont listen to me, because he remembers what a fool I was when I was a baby.

[*She leaves them together and chats with Jenny.*]

MRS BAINES. Have you been shewn over the shelter, Mr Undershaft? You know the work we're doing, of course.

UNDERSHAFT. [*Very civilly.*] The whole nation knows it, Mrs Baines.

MRS BAINES. No, sir: the whole nation does not know it, or we should not be crippled as we are for want of money to carry our work through the length and breadth of the land. Let me tell you that there would have been rioting this winter in London but for us.

UNDERSHAFT. You really think so?

MRS BAINES. I know it. I remember 1886, when you rich gentlemen hardened your hearts against the cry of the poor. They broke the windows of your clubs in Pall Mall.

UNDERSHAFT. [*Gleaming with approval of their method.*] And the Mansion House Fund went up next day from thirty thousand pounds to seventy-nine thousand! I remember quite well.

MRS BAINES. Well, wont you help me to get at the people? They wont break windows then. Come here, Price. Let me shew you to this gentleman. [*Price comes to be inspected.*] Do you remember the window breaking?

PRICE. My ole father thought it was the revolution, maam.

MRS BAINES. Would you break windows now?

PRICE. Oh no, maam. The windows of eaven av bin opened to me. I know now that the rich man is a sinner like myself.

RUMMY. [*Appearing above the loft door.*] Snobby Price!

SNOBBY. Wot is it?

RUMMY. Your mother's askin for you at the other gate in Cripps's Lane. She's heard about your confession.   [*Price turns pale.*

MRS BAINES. Go, Mr Price; and pray with her.

JENNY. You can go through the shelter, Snobby.

PRICE. [*To Mrs Baines.*] I couldnt face her now, maam, with all the weight of my sins fresh on me. Tell her she'll find her son at ome, waitin for her in prayer.

[*He skulks off through the gate, incidentally stealing the sovereign on his way out by picking up his cap from the drum.*

MRS BAINES. [*With swimming eyes.*] You see how we take the anger and the bitterness against you out of their hearts, Mr Undershaft.

UNDERSHAFT. It is certainly most convenient and gratifying to all large employers of labor, Mrs Baines.

MRS BAINES. Barbara: Jenny: I have good news: most wonderful news. [*Jenny runs to her.*] My prayers have been answered. I told you they would, Jenny, didnt I?

JENNY. Yes, yes.

BARBARA. [*Moving nearer to the drum.*] Have we got money enough to keep the shelter open?

MRS BAINES. I hope we shall have enough to keep all the shelters open. Lord Saxmundham has promised us five thousand pounds——

BARBARA. Hooray!

JENNY. Glory!

MRS BAINES. —if——

BARBARA. 'If!' If what?

MRS BAINES. —if five other gentlemen will give a thousand each to make it up to ten thousand.

BARBARA. Who is Lord Saxmundham? I never heard of him.

UNDERSHAFT. [*Who has pricked up his ears at the peer's name, and is now watching Barbara curiously.*] A new creation, my dear. You have heard of Sir Horace Bodger?

BARBARA. Bodger! Do you mean the distiller? Bodger's whisky!

UNDERSHAFT. That is the man. He is one of the greatest of our public benefactors. He restored the cathedral at Hakington.

They made him a baronet for that. He gave half a million to the funds of his party: they made him a baron for that.

SHIRLEY. What will they give him for the five thousand?

UNDERSHAFT. There is nothing left to give him. So the five thousand, I should think, is to save his soul.

MRS BAINES. Heaven grant it may! Oh Mr Undershaft, you have some very rich friends. Cant you help us towards the other five thousand? We are going to hold a great meeting this afternoon at the Assembly Hall in the Mile End Road. If I could only announce that one gentleman had come forward to support Lord Saxmundham, others would follow. Dont you know somebody? Couldnt you? Wouldnt you? [*Her eyes fill with tears.*] Oh, think of those poor people, Mr Undershaft: think of how much it means to them, and how little to a great man like you.

UNDERSHAFT. [*Sardonically gallant.*] Mrs Baines: you are irresistible. I cant disappoint you; and I cant deny myself the satisfaction of making Bodger pay up. You shall have your five thousand pounds.

MRS BAINES. Thank God!

UNDERSHAFT. You dont thank me?

MRS BAINES. Oh sir, dont try to be cynical: dont be ashamed of being a good man. The Lord will bless you abundantly; and our prayers will be like a strong fortification round you all the days of your life. [*With a touch of caution.*] You will let me have the cheque to shew at the meeting, wont you? Jenny: go in and fetch a pen and ink.   [*Jenny runs to the shelter door.*]

UNDERSHAFT. Do not disturb Miss Hill: I have a fountain pen. [*Jenny halts. He sits at the table and writes the cheque. Cusins rises to make room for him. They all watch him silently.*]

BILL. [*Cynically, aside to Barbara, his voice and accent horribly debased.*] Wot prawce selvytion nah?

BARBARA. Stop. [*Undershaft stops writing; they all turn to her in surprise.*] Mrs Baines: are you really going to take this money?

MRS BAINES. [*Astonished.*] Why not, dear?

BARBARA. Why not! Do you know what my father is? Have you forgotten that Lord Saxmundham is Bodger the whisky man? Do you remember how we implored the County Council to stop him from writing Bodger's Whisky in letters of fire against the sky; so that the poor drink-ruined creatures on the Embankment could not wake up from their snatches of sleep without being reminded of their deadly thirst by that wicked sky sign? Do you know that the worst thing I have had to fight here is not the devil, but Bodger, Bodger, Bodger, with his whisky, his distilleries, and his tied houses? Are you going to make our shelter another tied house for him, and ask me to keep it?

BILL. Rotten dranken whisky it is too.

MRS BAINES. Dear Barbara: Lord Saxmundham has a soul to be saved like any of us. If heaven has found the way to make a good use of his money, are we to set ourselves up against the answer to our prayers?

BARBARA. I know he has a soul to be saved. Let him come down here; and I'll do my best to help him to his salvation. But he wants to send his cheque down to buy us, and go on being as wicked as ever.

UNDERSHAFT. [*With a reasonableness which Cusins alone perceives to be ironical.*] My dear Barbara: alcohol is a very necessary article. It heals the sick——

BARBARA. It does nothing of the sort.

UNDERSHAFT. Well, it assists the doctor: that is perhaps a less questionable way of putting it. It makes life bearable to millions of people who could not endure their existence if they were quite sober. It enables Parliament to do things at eleven at night that no sane person would do at eleven in the morning. Is it Bodger's fault that this inestimable gift is deplorably abused by less than one per cent of the poor?

[*He turns again to the table; signs the cheque; and crosses it.*

MRS BAINES. Barbara: will there be less drinking or more if all those poor souls we are saving come tomorrow and find the doors of our shelters shut in their faces? Lord Saxmundham gives us the money to stop drinking—to take his own business from him.

CUSINS. [*Impishly.*] Pure self-sacrifice on Bodger's part, clearly! Bless dear Bodger!

[*Barbara almost breaks down as Adolphus, too, fails her.*

UNDERSHAFT. [*Tearing out the cheque and pocketing the book as he rises and goes past Cusins to Mrs Baines.*] I also, Mrs Baines, may claim a little disinterestedness. Think of my business! think of the widows and orphans! The men and lads torn to pieces with shrapnel and poisoned with lyddite! [*Mrs Baines shrinks; but he goes on remorselessly.*] The oceans of blood, not one drop of which is shed in a really just cause! The ravaged crops! The peaceful peasants forced, women and men, to till their fields under the fire of opposing armies on pain of starvation! The bad blood of the fierce little cowards at home who egg on others to fight for the gratification of their national vanity! All this makes money for me: I am never richer, never busier than when the papers are full of it. Well, it is your work to preach peace on earth and good will to men. [*Mrs Baines's face lights up again.*] Every convert you make is a vote against war. [*Her lips move in prayer.*] Yet I give you this money to help you to hasten my own commercial ruin.

[*He gives her the cheque.*

CUSINS. [*Mounting the form in an ecstasy of mischief.*] The millenium will be inaugurated by the unselfishness of Undershaft and Bodger. Oh, be joyful!

[*He takes the drumsticks from his pocket and flourishes them.*

MRS BAINES. [*Taking the cheque.*] The longer I live the more proof I see that there is an Infinite Goodness that turns everything to the work of salvation sooner or later. Who would have thought that any good could have come out of war and drink? And yet their profits are brought today to the feet of salvation to do its blessed work.   [*She is affected to tears.*

JENNY. [*Running to Mrs Baines and throwing her arms round her.*] Oh dear! How blessed, how glorious it all is!

CUSINS. [*In a convulsion of irony.*] Let us seize this unspeakable moment. Let us march to the great meeting at once. Excuse me just an instant.

[*He rushes into the shelter. Jenny takes her tambourine from the drum head.*

MRS BAINES. Mr Undershaft: have you ever seen a thousand people fall on their knees with one impulse and pray? Come with us to the meeting. Barbara shall tell them thàt the Army is saved, and saved through you.

CUSINS. [*Returning impetuously from the shelter with a flag and a trombone, and coming between Mrs Baines and Undershaft.*] You shall carry the flag down the first street, Mrs Baines. [*He gives her the flag.*] Mr Undershaft is a gifted trombonist: he shall intone an Olympian diapason to the West Ham Salvation March. [*Aside to Undershaft, as he forces the trombone on him.*] Blow, Machiavelli, blow.

UNDERSHAFT. [*Aside to him, as he takes the trombone.*] The trumpet in Zion! [*Cusins rushes to the drum, which he takes up and puts on. Undershaft continues, aloud.*] I will do my best. I could vamp a bass if I knew the tune.

CUSINS. It is a wedding chorus from one of Donizetti's operas; but we have converted it. We convert everything to good here, including Bodger. You remember the chorus. 'For thee immense rejoicing—immenso giubilo—immenso giubilo.' [*With drum obbligato.*] Rum tum ti tum tum, tum tum ti ta——

BARBARA. Dolly: you are breaking my heart.

CUSINS. What is a broken heart more or less here? Dionysos Undershaft has descended. I am possessed.

MRS BAINES. Come, Barbara: I must have my dear Major to carry the flag with me.

JENNY. Yes, yes, Major darling.

[*Cusins snatches the tambourine out of Jenny's hand and mutely offers it to Barbara.*

BARBARA. [*Coming forward a little as she puts the offer behind her with*

*a shudder, whilst Cusins recklessly tosses the tambourine back to Jenny
and goes to the gate.*] I cant come.

JENNY. Not come!

MRS BAINES. [*With tears in her eyes.*] Barbara: do you think I am
wrong to take the money?

BARBARA. [*Impulsively going to her and kissing her.*] No, no: God help
you, dear, you must: you are saving the Army. Go; and may you
have a great meeting!

JENNY. But arnt you coming?

BARBARA. No.

[*She begins taking off the silver S brooch from her collar.*

MRS BAINES. Barbara: what are you doing?

JENNY. Why are you taking your badge off? You cant be going to
leave us, Major.

BARBARA. [*Quietly.*] Father: come here.

UNDERSHAFT. [*Coming to her.*] My dear!

[*Seeing that she is going to pin the badge on his collar, he retreats to the
penthouse in some alarm.*

BARBARA. [*Following him.*] Dont be frightened. [*She pins the badge on
and steps back towards the table, shewing him to the others.*] There!
It's not much for £5000, is it?

MRS BAINES. Barbara: if you wont come and pray with us, promise me you will pray for us.

BARBARA. I cant pray now. Perhaps I shall never pray again.

MRS BAINES. Barbara!

JENNY. Major!

BARBARA. [*Almost delirious.*] I cant bear any more. Quick march!

CUSINS. [*Calling to the procession in the street outside.*] Off we go. Play
up, there! Immenso giubilo.

[*He gives the time with his drum; and the band strikes up the march,
which rapidly becomes more distant as the procession moves briskly
away.*

MRS BAINES. I must go, dear. Youre overworked: you will be all
right tomorrow. We'll never lose you. Now Jenny: step out with
the old flag. Blood and Fire!

[*She marches out through the gate with her flag.*

JENNY. Glory Hallelujah!

[*Flourishing her tambourine and marching.*

UNDERSHAFT. [*To Cusins, as he marches out past him easing the slide of
his trombone.*] 'My ducats and my daughter'!

CUSINS. [*Following him out.*] Money and gunpowder!

BARBARA. Drunkenness and Murder! My God: why hast thou
forsaken me?

[*She sinks on the form with her face buried in her hands. The march
passes away into silence. Bill Walker steals across to her.*

BILL. [*Taunting.*] Wot prawce selvytion nah?

SHIRLEY. Dont you hit her when she's down.

BILL. She itt me wen aw wiz dahn. Waw shouldnt Aw git a bit o me aown beck?

BARBARA. [*Raising her head.*] I didnt take your money, Bill.

> [*She crosses the yard to the gate and turns her back on the two men to hide her face from them.*

BILL. [*Sneering after her.*] Naow, it warnt enaff for you. [*Turning to the drum, he misses the money.*] Ellow! If you aint took it sammun else ez. Weres it gorn? Bly me if Jenny Ill didnt tike it arter all!

RUMMY. [*Screaming at him from the loft.*] You lie, you dirty black-guard! Snobby Price pinched it off the drum when he took up his cap. I was up here all the time an see im do it.

BILL. Wot! Stowl maw manney! Waw didnt you call thief on him, you silly aold macker you?

RUMMY. To serve you aht for ittin me acrost the fice. It's cost y' pahnd, that az. [*Raising a paean of squalid triumph.*] I done you. I'm even with you. Uve ad it aht o y——

> [*Bill snatches up Shirley's mug and hurls it at her. She slams the loft door and vanishes. The mug smashes against the door and falls in fragments.*

BILL. [*Beginning to chuckle.*] Tell us, aol menn, wot o'clock this mawnin was it wen im as they call Snobby Prawce was sived?

BARBARA. [*Turning to him more composedly, and with unspoiled sweetness.*] About half past twelve, Bill. And he pinched your pound at a quarter to two. *I* know. Well, you cant afford to lose it. I'll send it to you.

BILL. [*His voice and accent suddenly approving.*] Not if Aw wiz to stawve for it. Aw aint to be bought.

SHIRLEY. Aint you? Youd sell yourself to the devil for a pint o beer; only there aint no devil to make the offer.

BILL. [*Unashamed.*] Sao Aw would, mite, and often ev, cheerful. But she cawnt baw me. [*Approaching Barbara.*] You wanted maw saoul, did you? Well, you aint got it.

BARBARA. I nearly got it, Bill. But weve sold it back to you for ten thousand pounds.

SHIRLEY. And dear at the money!

BARBARA. No, Peter: it was worth more than money.

BILL. [*Salvationproof.*] It's nao good: you cawnt get rahnd me nah. Aw downt blieve in it; and Awve seen tody that Aw was rawt. [*Going.*] Sao long, aol soup-kitchener! Ta, ta, Mijor Earl's Grendorter! [*Turning at the gate.*] Wot prawce selvytion nah? Snobby Prawce! Ha! ha!

BARBARA. [*Offering her hand.*] Goodbye, Bill.

BILL. [*Taken aback, half plucks his cap off; then shoves it on again defiantly.*] Git aht. [*Barbara drops her hand, discouraged. He has a twinge of remorse.*] But thets aw rawt, you knaow. Nathink pasnl. Naow mellice. Sao long, Judy.   [*He goes.*

BARBARA. No malice. So long, Bill.

SHIRLEY. [*Shaking his head.*] You make too much of him, miss, in your innocence.

BARBARA. [*Going to him.*] Peter: I'm like you now. Cleaned out, and lost my job.

SHIRLEY. Youve youth an hope. Thats two better than me.

BARBARA. I'll get you a job, Peter. Thats hope for you: the youth will have to be enough for me. [*She counts her money.*] I have just enough left for two teas at Lockharts, a Rowton doss for you, and my tram and bus home. [*He frowns and rises with offended pride. She takes his arm.*] Dont be proud, Peter: it's sharing between friends. And promise me youll talk to me and not let me cry.
                    [*She draws him towards the gate.*

SHIRLEY. Well I'm not accustomed to talk to the like of you——

BARBARA. [*Urgent.*] Yes, yes: you must talk to me. Tell me about Tom Paine's books and Bradlaugh's lectures. Come along.

SHIRLEY. Ah, if you would only read Tom Paine in the proper spirit, miss!   [*They go out through the gate together.*

Next day after lunch Lady Britomart is writing in the library in Wilton Crescent. Sarah is reading in the armchair near the window. Barbara, in ordinary fashionable dress, pale and brooding, is on the settee. Charles Lomax enters. He starts on seeing Barbara fashionably attired and in low spirits.

LOMAX. Youve left off your uniform!

[*Barbara says nothing; but an expression of pain passes over her face.*

LADY BRITOMART. [*Warning him in low tones to be careful.*] Charles!

LOMAX. [*Much concerned, coming behind the settee and bending sympathetically over Barbara.*] I'm awfully sorry, Barbara. You know I helped you all I could with the concertina and so forth. [*Momentously.*] Still, I have never shut my eyes to the fact that there is a certain amount of tosh about the Salvation Army. Now the claims of the Church of England——

LADY BRITOMART. That's enough, Charles. Speak of something suited to your mental capacity.

LOMAX. But surely the Church of England is suited to all our capacities.

BARBARA. [*Pressing his hand.*] Thank you for your sympathy, Cholly. Now go and spoon with Sarah.

LOMAX. [*Dragging a chair from the writing table and seating himself affectionately by Sarah's side.*] How is my ownest today?

SARAH. I wish you wouldnt tell Cholly to do things, Barbara. He always comes straight and does them. Cholly: we're going to the works this afternoon.

LOMAX. What works?

SARAH. The cannon works.

LOMAX. What? Your governor's shop!

SARAH. Yes.

LOMAX. Oh I say!

[*Cusins enters in poor condition. He also starts visibly when he sees Barbara without her uniform.*

BARBARA. I expected you this morning. Dolly. Didn't you guess that?

CUSINS. [*Sitting down beside her.*] I'm sorry. I have only just breakfasted.

SARAH. But weve just finished lunch.

BARBARA. Have you had one of your bad nights?

CUSINS. No: I had rather a good night: in fact, one of the most remarkable nights I have ever passed.

BARBARA. The meeting?

CUSINS. No: after the meeting.

LADY BRITOMART. You should have gone to bed after the meeting. What were you doing?

CUSINS. Drinking.

LADY BRITOMART.	Adolphus!
SARAH.	Dolly!
BARBARA.	Dolly!
LOMAX.	Oh I say!

LADY BRITOMART. What were you drinking, may I ask?

CUSINS. A most devilish kind of Spanish burgundy, warranted free from added alcohol: a Temperance burgundy in fact. Its richness in natural alcohol made any addition superfluous.

BARBARA. Are you joking, Dolly?

CUSINS. [*Patiently.*] No. I have been making a night of it with the nominal head of this household: that is all.

LADY BRITOMART. Andrew made you drunk!

CUSINS. No: he only provided the wine. I think it was Dionysos who made me drunk. [*To Barbara.*] I told you I was possessed.

LADY BRITOMART. Youre not sober yet. Go home to bed at once.

CUSINS. I have never before ventured to reproach you, Lady Brit; but how could you marry the Prince of Darkness?

LADY BRITOMART. It was much more excusable to marry him than to get drunk with him. That is a new accomplishment of Andrew's, by the way. He usent to drink.

CUSINS. He doesnt now. He only sat there and completed the wreck of my moral basis, the rout of my convictions, the purchase of my soul. He cares for you, Barbara. That is what makes him so dangerous to me.

BARBARA. That has nothing to do with it, Dolly. There are larger loves and diviner dreams than the fireside ones. You know that, dont you?

CUSINS. Yes: that is our understanding. I know it. I hold to it. Unless he can win me on that holier ground he may amuse me for a while; but he can get no deeper hold, strong as he is.

BARBARA. Keep to that; and the end will be right. Now tell me what happened at the meeting?

CUSINS. It was an amazing meeting. Mrs Baines almost died of emotion. Jenny Hill simply gibbered with hysteria. The Prince of Darkness played his trombone like a madman: its brazen roarings were like the laughter of the damned. 117 conversions took place then and there. They prayed with the most touching sincerity and gratitude for Bodger, and for the anonymous donor of the £5000. Your father would not let his name be given.

LOMAX. That was rather fine of the old man, you know. Most chaps would have wanted the advertisement.

CUSINS. He said all the charitable institutions would be down on him like kites on a battlefield if he gave his name.

LADY BRITOMART. Thats Andrew all over. He never does a proper thing without giving an improper reason for it.

CUSINS. He convinced me that I have all my life been doing improper things for proper reasons.

LADY BRITOMART. Adolphus: now that Barbara has left the Salvation Army, you had better leave it too. I will not have you playing that drum in the streets.

CUSINS. Your orders are already obeyed, Lady Brit.

BARBARA. Dolly: were you ever really in earnest about it? Would you have joined if you had never seen me?

CUSINS. [Disingenuously.] Well—er—well, possibly, as a collector of religions——

LOMAX. [Cunningly.] Not as a drummer, though, you know. You are a very clearheaded brainy chap, Dolly; and it must have been apparent to you that there is a certain amount of tosh about——

LADY BRITOMART. Charles: if you must drivel, drivel like a grown-up man and not like a schoolboy.

LOMAX. [Out of countenance.] Well, drivel is drivel, dont you know, whatever a man's age.

LADY BRITOMART. In good society in England, Charles, men drivel at all ages by repeating silly formulas with an air of wisdom. Schoolboys make their own formulas out of slang, like you. When they reach your age, and get political private secretary-ships and things of that sort, they drop slang and get their formulas out of the *Spectator* or *The Times*. You had better confine yourself to *The Times*. You will find that there is a certain amount of tosh about *The Times*; but at least its language is reputable.

LOMAX. [Overwhelmed.] You are so awfully strong-minded, Lady Brit——

LADY BRITOMART. Rubbish! [Morrison comes in.] What is it?

MORRISON. If you please, my lady, Mr Undershaft has just drove up to the door.

LADY BRITOMART. Well, let him in. [Morrison hesitates.] Whats the matter with you?

MORRISON. Shall I announce him, my lady; or is he at home here, so to speak, my lady?

LADY BRITOMART. Announce him.

MORRISON. Thank you, my lady. You wont mind my asking, I hope. The occasion is in a manner of speaking new to me.

LADY BRITOMART. Quite right. Go and let him in.

MORRISON. Thank you, my lady.   [*He withdraws.*

LADY BRITOMART. Children: go and get ready. [*Sarah and Barbara go upstairs for their out-of-door wraps.*] Charles: go and tell Stephen to come down here in five minutes: you will find him in the drawing-room. [*Charles goes.*] Adolphus: tell them to send round the carriage in about fifteen minutes.   [*Adolphus goes.*

MORRISON. [*At the door.*] Mr Undershaft.

        [*Undershaft comes in. Morrison goes out.*

UNDERSHAFT. Alone! How fortunate!

LADY BRITOMART. [*Rising.*] Dont be sentimental, Andrew. Sit down. [*She sits on the settee; he sits beside her, on her left. She comes to the point before he has time to breathe.*] Sarah must have £800 a year until Charles Lomax comes into his property. Barbara will need more, and need it permanently, because Adolphus hasnt any property.

UNDERSHAFT. [*Resignedly.*] Yes, my dear: I will see to it. Anything else—for yourself, for instance?

LADY BRITOMART. I want to talk to you about Stephen.

UNDERSHAFT. [*Rather wearily.*] Dont, my dear. Stephen doesnt interest me.

LADY BRITOMART. He does interest me. He is our son.

UNDERSHAFT. Do you really think so? He has induced us to bring him into the world; but he chose his parents very incongruously, I think. I see nothing of myself in him, and less of you.

LADY BRITOMART. Andrew: Stephen is an excellent son, and a most steady, capable, highminded young man. You are simply trying to find an excuse for disinheriting him.

UNDERSHAFT. My dear Biddy: the Undershaft tradition disinherits him. It would be dishonest of me to leave the cannon foundry to my son.

LADY BRITOMART. It would be most unnatural and improper of you to leave it to anyone else, Andrew. Do you suppose this wicked and immoral tradition can be kept up for ever? Do you pretend that Stephen could not carry on the foundry just as well as all the other sons of the big business houses?

UNDERSHAFT. Yes: he could learn the office routine without understanding the business, like all the other sons; and the firm would go on by its own momentum until the real Undershaft— probably an Italian or a German—would invent a new method and cut him out.

LADY BRITOMART. There is nothing that any Italian or German could do that Stephen could not do. And Stephen at least has breeding.

UNDERSHAFT. The son of a foundling! Nonsense!

LADY BRITOMART. My son, Andrew! And even you may have good blood in your veins for all you know.

UNDERSHAFT. True. Probably I have. That is another argument in favour of a foundling.

LADY BRITOMART. Andrew: dont be aggravating. And dont be wicked. At present you are both.

UNDERSHAFT. This conversation is part of the Undershaft tradition, Biddy. Every Undershaft's wife has treated him to it ever since the house was founded. It is mere waste of breath. If the tradition be ever broken it will be for an abler man than Stephen.

LADY BRITOMART. [*Pouting.*] Then go away.

UNDERSHAFT. [*Deprecatory.*] Go away!

LADY BRITOMART. Yes: go away. If you will do nothing for Stephen, you are not wanted here. Go to your foundling, whoever he is; and look after him.

UNDERSHAFT. The fact is, Biddy——

LADY BRITOMART. Dont call me Biddy. I dont call you Andy.

UNDERSHAFT. I will not call my wife Britomart: it is not good sense. Seriously, my love, the Undershaft tradition has landed me in a difficulty. I am getting on in years; and my partner Lazarus has at last made a stand and insisted that the succession must be sttled one way or the other; and of course he is quite right. You see, I havent found a fit successor yet.

LADY BRITOMART. [*Obstinately.*] There is Stephen.

UNDERSHAFT. Thats just it: all the foundlings I can find are exactly like Stephen.

LADY BRITOMART. Andrew!!

UNDERSHAFT. I want a man with no relations and no schooling: that is, a man who would be out of the running altogether if he were not a strong man. And I cant find him. Every blessed foundling nowadays is snapped up in his infancy by Barnardo homes, or School Board officers, or Boards of Guardians; and if he shews the least ability he is fastened on by schoolmasters; trained to win scholarships like a racehorse; crammed with secondhand ideas; drilled and disciplined in docility and what they call good taste; and lamed for life so that he is fit for nothing but teaching. If you want to keep the foundry in the family, you had better find an eligible foundling and marry him to Barbara.

LADY BRITOMART. Ah! Barbara! Your pet! You would sacrifice Stephen to Barbara.

UNDERSHAFT. Cheerfully. And you, my dear, would boil Barbara to make soup for Stephen.

LADY BRITOMART. Andrew: this is not a question of our likings and dislikings: it is a question of duty. It is your duty to make Stephen your successor.

UNDERSHAFT. Just as much as it is your duty to submit to your husband. Come, Biddy! These tricks of the governing class are of no use with me. I am one of the governing class myself; and it is waste of time giving tracts to a missionary. I have the power in this matter; and I am not to be humbugged into using it for your purposes.

LADY BRITOMART. Andrew: you can talk my head off; but you cant change wrong into right. And your tie is all on one side. Put it straight.

UNDERSHAFT. [*Disconcerted.*] It wont stay unless it's pinned——
　　　　　　　　　　　　　　[*He fumbles at it with childish grimaces.*
　　　　　　　　　　　　　　[*Stephen comes in.*

STEPHEN. [*At the door.*] I beg your pardon.　　[*About to retire.*

LADY BRITOMART. No: come in, Stephen.
　　　　　　　[*Stephen comes forward to his mother's writing table.*

UNDERSHAFT. [*Not very cordially.*] Good afternoon.

STEPHEN. [*Coldly.*] Good afternoon.

UNDERSHAFT. [*To Lady Britomart.*] He knows all about the tradition, I suppose?

LADY BRITOMART. Yes. [*To Stephen.*] It is what I told you last night, Stephen.

UNDERSHAFT. [*Sulkily.*] I understand you want to come into the cannon business.

STEPHEN. *I* go into trade! Certainly not.

UNDERSHAFT. [*Opening his eyes, greatly eased in mind and manner.*] Oh! In that case——

LADY BRITOMART. Cannons are not trade, Stephen. They are enterprise.

STEPHEN. I have no intention of becoming a man of business in any sense. I have no capacity for business and no taste for it. I intend to devote myself to politics.

UNDERSHAFT. [*Rising.*] My dear boy: this is an immense relief to me. And I trust it may prove an equally good thing for the country. I was afraid you would consider yourself disparaged and slighted.
　　　　　　[*He moves towards Stephen as if to shake hands with him.*

LADY BRITOMART. [*Rising and interposing.*] Stephen: I cannot allow you to throw away an enormous property like this.

STEPHEN. [*Stiffly.*] Mother: there must be an end of treating me as a child, if you please. [*Lady Britomart recoils, deeply wounded by his tone.*] Until last night I did not take your attitude seriously, because I did not think you meant it seriously. But I find now that you left me in the dark as to matters which you should have explained to me years ago. I am extremely hurt and offended.

Any further discussion of my intentions had better take place with my father, as between one man and another.

LADY BRITOMART. Stephen!

[*She sits down again, her eyes filling with tears.*

UNDERSHAFT. [*With grave compassion.*] You see, my dear, it is only the big men who can be treated as children.

STEPHEN. I am sorry, mother, that you have forced me——

UNDERSHAFT. [*Stopping him.*] Yes, yes, yes, yes: thats all right, Stephen. She wont interfere with you any more: your independence is achieved: you have won your latchkey. Dont rub it in; and above all, dont apologize. [*He resumes his seat.*] Now what about your future, as between one man and another—I beg your pardon, Biddy: as between two men and a woman.

LADY BRITOMART. [*Who has pulled herself together strongly.*] I quite understand, Stephen. By all means go your own way if you feel strong enough.

[*Stephen sits down magisterially in the chair at the writing table with an air of affirming his majority.*

UNDERSHAFT. It is settled that you do not ask for the succession to the cannon business.

STEPHEN. I hope it is settled that I repudiate the cannon business.

UNDERSHAFT. Come, come! Dont be so devilishly sulky: it's boyish. Freedom should be generous. Besides, I owe you a fair start in life in exchange for disinheriting you. You cant become prime minister all at once. Havnt you a turn for something? What about literature, art, and so forth?

STEPHEN. I have nothing of the artist about me, either in faculty or character, thank Heaven!

UNDERSHAFT. A philosopher, perhaps? Eh?

STEPHEN. I make no such ridiculous pretension.

UNDERSHAFT. Just so. Well, there is the army, the navy, the Church, the Bar. The Bar requires some ability. What about the Bar?

STEPHEN. I have not studied law. And I am afraid I have not the necessary push—I believe that is the name barristers give to their vulgarity—for success in pleading.

UNDERSHAFT. Rather a difficult case, Stephen. Hardly anything left but the stage, is there? [*Stephen makes an impatient movement.*] Well, come! Is there anything you know or care for?

STEPHEN. [*Rising and looking at him steadily.*] I know the difference between right and wrong.

UNDERSHAFT. [*Hugely tickled.*] You dont say so! What! No capacity for business, no knowledge of law, no sympathy with art, no pretension to philosophy; only a simple knowledge of the secret that has puzzled all the philosophers, baffled all the lawyers, muddled all the men of business, and ruined most of the artists:

the secret of right and wrong. Why, man, youre a genius, a master of masters, a god! At twenty-four, too!

STEPHEN. [*Keeping his temper with difficulty.*] You are pleased to be facetious. I pretend to nothing more than any honourable English gentleman claims as his birthright.

[*He sits down angrily.*

UNDERSHAFT. Oh, thats everybody's birthright. Look at poor little Jenny Hill, the Salvation lassie! She would think you were laughing at her if you asked her to stand up in the street and teach grammar or geography or mathematics or even drawing-room dancing; but it never occurs to her to doubt that she can teach morals and religion. You are all alike, you respectable people. You cant tell me the bursting strain of a ten-inch gun, which is a very simple matter; but you all think you can tell me the bursting strain of a man under temptation. You darent handle high explosives; but youre all ready to handle honesty and truth and justice and the whole duty of man, and kill one another at that game. What a country! What a world!

LADY BRITOMART. [*Uneasily.*] What do you think he had better do, Andrew?

UNDERSHAFT. Oh, just what he wants to do. He knows nothing and he thinks he knows everything. That points clearly to a political career. Get him a private secretaryship to someone who can get him an Under Secretaryship; and then leave him alone. He will find his natural and proper place in the end on the Treasury Bench.

STEPHEN. [*Springing up again.*] I am sorry, sir, that you force me to forget the respect due to you as my father. I am an Englishman and I will not hear the Government of my country insulted.

[*He thrusts his hands in his pockets, and walks angrily across to the window.*

UNDERSHAFT. [*With a touch of brutality.*] The government of your country! *I* am the government of your country: I, and Lazarus. Do you suppose that you and half a dozen amateurs like you, sitting in a row in that foolish gabble shop, can govern Undershaft and Lazarus? No, my friend: you will do what pays us. You will make war when it suits us, and keep peace when it doesnt. You will find out that trade requires certain measures when we have decided on those measures. When I want anything to keep my dividends up, you will discover that my want is a national need. When other people want something to keep my dividends down, you will call out the police and military. And in return you shall have the support and applause of my newspapers, and the delight of imagining that you are a great statesman. Government of your country! Be off with you, my boy, and play with your caucuses and leading articles and historic parties and great leaders and burning questions and the rest of your toys. *I* am going back to my counting-house to pay the piper and call the tune.

STEPHEN. [*Actually smiling, and putting his hand on his father's shoulder with indulgent patronage.*] Really, my dear father, it is impossible to be angry with you. You dont know how absurd all this sounds to me. You are very properly proud of having been industrious enough to make money; and it is greatly to your credit that you have made so much of it. But it has kept you in circles where you are valued for your money and deferred to for it, instead of in the doubtless very old-fashioned and behind-the-times public school and university where I formed my habits of mind. It is natural for you to think that money governs England; but you must allow me to think I know better.

UNDERSHAFT. And what does govern England, pray?

STEPHEN. Character, father, character.

UNDERSHAFT. Whose character? Yours or mine?

STEPHEN. Neither yours nor mine, father, but the best elements in the English national character.

UNDERSHAFT. Stephen: Ive found your profession for you. Youre a born jounalist. I'll start you with a high-toned weekly review. There!

[*Before Stephen can reply Sarah, Barbara, Lomax and Cusins come in ready for walking. Barbara crosses the room to the window and looks out. Cusins drifts amiably to the armchair. Lomax remains near the door, whilst Sarah comes to her mother.*

[*Stephen goes to the smaller writing table and busies himself with his letters.*

SARAH. Go and get ready, mamma: the carriage is waiting.

[*Lady Britomart leaves the room.*

UNDERSHAFT. [*To Sarah.*] Good day, my dear. Good afternoon, Mr Lomax.

LOMAX. [*Vaguely.*] Ahdedoo.

UNDERSHAFT. [*To Cusins.*] Quite well after last night, Euripides, eh?

CUSINS. As well as can be expected.

UNDERSHAFT. Thats right. [*To Barbara.*] So you are coming to see my death and devastation factory, Barbara?

BARBARA. [*At the window.*] You came yesterday to see my salvation factory. I promised you a return visit.

LOMAX. [*Coming forward between Sarah and Undershaft.*] Youll find it awfully interesting. Ive been through the Woolwich Arsenal; and it gives you a ripping feeling of security, you know, to think of the lot of beggars we could kill if it came to fighting. [*To Undershaft, with sudden solemnity.*] Still, it must be rather an awful reflection for you, from the religious point of view as it were. Youre getting on, you know, and all that.

SARAH. You dont mind Cholly's imbecility, papa, do you?

LOMAX. [*Much taken aback.*] Oh, I say!

UNDERSHAFT. Mr Lomax looks at the matter in a very proper spirit, my dear.

LOMAX. Just so. Thats all I meant, I assure you.

SARAH. Are you coming, Stephen?

STEPHEN. Well, I am rather busy—er— [*Magnanimously.*] Oh well, yes: I'll come. That is, if there is room for me.

UNDERSHAFT. I can take two with me in a little motor I am experimenting with for field use. You wont mind its being rather unfashionable. It's not painted yet; but it's bullet proof.

LOMAX. [*Appalled at the prospect of confronting Wilton Crescent in an unpainted motor.*] Oh, I say!

SARAH. The carriage for me, thank you. Barbara doesnt mind what she's seen in.

LOMAX. I say, Dolly, old chap: do you really mind the car being a guy? Because of course if you do I'll go in it. Still——

CUSINS. I prefer it.

LOMAX. Thanks awfully, old man, Come, my ownest.

[*He hurries out to secure his seat in the carriage. Sarah follows him.*

CUSINS. [*Moodily walking across to Lady Britomart's writing table.*] Why are we two coming to this Works Department of Hell? That is what I ask myself.

BARBARA. I have always thought of it as a sort of pit where lost creatures with blackened faces stirred up smoky fires and were driven and tormented by my father. Is it like that, dad?

UNDERSHAFT. [*Scandalized.*] My dear! It is a spotlessly clean and beautiful hillside town.

CUSINS. With a Methodist chapel? Oh do say theres a Methodist chapel.

UNDERSHAFT. There are two: a Primitive one and a sophisticated one. There is even an Ethical Society; but it is not much patronized, as my men are all strongly religious. In the High Explosives Sheds they object to the presence of Agnostics as unsafe.

CUSINS. And yet they dont object to you!

BARBARA. Do they obey all your orders?

UNDERSHAFT. I never give them any orders. When I speak to one of them it is 'Well, Jones, is the baby doing well? and has Mrs Jones made a good recovery?' 'Nicely, thank you, sir.' And that's all.

CUSINS. But Jones has to be kept in order. How do you maintain discipline among your men?

UNDERSHAFT. I dont. They do. You see, the one thing Jones

wont stand is any rebellion from the man under him, or any assertion of social equality between the wife of the man with four shillings a week less than himself, and Mrs Jones! Of course they all rebel against me, theoretically. Practically, every man of them keeps the man just below him in his place. I never meddle with them. I never bully them. I dont even bully Lazarus. I say that certain things are to be done; but I dont order anybody to do them. I dont say, mind you, that there is no ordering about and snubbing and even bullying. The men snub the boys and order them about; the carmen snub the sweepers; the artisans snub the unskilled laborers; the foremen drive and bully both the laborers and artisans; the assistant engineers find fault with the foremen; the chief engineers drop on the assistants; the departmental managers worry the chiefs; and the clerks have tall hats and hymn-books and keep up the social tone by refusing to associate on equal terms with anybody. The result is a colossal profit, which comes to me.

CUSINS. [Revolted.] You really are a—well, what I was saying yesterday.

BARBARA. What was he saying yesterday?

UNDERSHAFT. Never mind, my dear. He thinks I have made you unhappy. Have I?

BARBARA. Do you think I can be happy in this vulgar silly dress? I, who have worn the uniform! Do you understand what you have done to me? Yesterday I had a man's soul in my hand. I set him in the way of life with his face to salvation. But when we took your money he turned back to drunkenness and derision. [With intense conviction.] I will never forgive you that. If I had a child, and you destroyed its body with your explosives—if you murdered Dolly with your horrible guns—I could forgive you if my forgiveness would open the gates of heaven to you. But to take a human soul from me, and turn it into the soul of a wolf! That is worse than any murder.

UNDERSHAFT. Does my daughter despair so easily? Can you strike a man to the heart and leave no mark on him?

BARBARA. [Her face lighting up.] Oh, you are right: he can never be lost now: where was my faith?

CUSINS. Oh, clever, clever devil!

BARBARA. You may be a devil; but God speaks through you sometimes. [She takes her father's hands and kisses them.] You have given me back my happiness: I feel it deep down now, though my spirit is troubled.

UNDERSHAFT. You have learnt something. That always feels at first as if you had lost something.

BARBARA. Well, take me to the factory of death; and let me learn

something more. There must be some truth or other behind all
this frightful irony. Come, Dolly.   [*She goes out.*

CUSINS. My guardian angel! [*To Undershaft.*] Avaunt!

[*He follows Barbara.*

STEPHEN. [*Quietly, at the writing table.*] You must not mind Cusins,
father. He is a very amiable good fellow; but he is a Greek
scholar and naturally a little eccentric.

UNDERSHAFT. Ah, quite so. Thank you, Stephen. Thank you.

[*He goes out.*

[*Stephen smiles patronizingly; buttons his coat responsibly; and
crosses the room to the door. Lady Britomart, dressed for out-of-
doors, opens it before he reaches it. She looks round for others; looks
at Stephen; and turns to go without a word.*

STEPHEN. [*Embarrassed.*] Mother——

LADY BRITOMART. Dont be apologetic, Stephen. And dont forget
that you have outgrown your mother.   [*She goes out.*

[*Perivale St Andrews lies between two Middlesex hills, half climbing
the northern one. It is an almost smokeless town of white walls,
roofs of narrow green slates or red tiles, tall trees, domes, campaniles
and slender chimney shafts, beautifully situated and beautiful in
itself. The best view of it is obtained from the crest of a slope about
half a mile to the east, where the high explosives are dealt with.
The foundry lies hidden in the depths between, the tops of its
chimneys sprouting like huge skittles into the middle distance.
Across the crest runs an emplacement of concrete, with a firestep,
and a parapet which suggests a fortification, because there is a huge
cannon of the obsolete Woolwich Infant pattern peering across it at
the town. The cannon is mounted on an experimental gun-carriage:
possibly the original model of the Undershaft disappearing rampart
gun alluded to by Stephen. The firestep, being a convenient place to
sit, is furnished here and there with straw disk cushions; and at one
place there is the additional luxury of a fur rug.*

*Barbara is standing on the firestep, looking over the parapet towards
the town. On her right is the cannon; on her left the end of a shed
raised on piles, with a ladder of three or four steps up to the door,
which opens outwards and has a little wooden landing at the threshold,
with a fire bucket in the corner of the landing. Several dummy
soldiers more or less mutilated, with straw protruding from their
gashes, have been shoved out of the way under the landing. A few
others are nearly upright against the shed; and one has fallen
forward and lies, like a grotesque corpse, on the emplacement. The
parapet stops short of the shed, leaving a gap which is the beginning
of the path down the hill through the foundry to the town. The rug
is on the firestep near this gap. Down on the emplacement behind the
cannon is a trolley carrying a huge conical bombshell with a red band*

painted on it. Farther to the right is the door of an office, which, like the sheds, is of the lightest possible construction.

Cusins arrives by the path from the town.

BARBARA. Well?

CUSINS. Not a ray of hope. Everything perfect! Wonderful! Real! It only needs a cathedral to be a heavenly city instead of a hellish one.

BARBARA. Have you found out whether they have done anything for old Peter Shirley?

CUSINS. They have found him a job as gatekeeper and time-keeper. He's frightfully miserable. He calls the time-keeping brainwork, and says he isnt used to it; and his gate lodge is so splendid that he's ashamed to use the rooms, and skulks in the scullery.

BARBARA. Poor Peter!

[Stephen arrives from the town. He carries a field-glass.

STEPHEN. [*Enthusiastically.*] Have you two seen the place? Why did you leave us?

CUSINS. I wanted to see everything I was not intended to see; and Barbara wanted to make the men talk.

STEPHEN. Have you found anything discreditable?

CUSINS. No. They call him Dandy Andy and are proud of his being a cunning old rascal; but it's all horribly, frightfully, immorally, unanswerably perfect.

[Sarah arrives.

SARAH. Heavens! What a place! [*She crosses to the trolley.*] Did you see the nursing home!?   [*She sits down on the shell.*

STEPHEN. Did you see the libraries and schools?

SARAH. Did you see the ballroom and the banqueting chamber in the Town Hall?

STEPHEN. Have you gone into the insurance fund, the pension fund, the building society, the various applications of co-operation?

[Undershaft comes from the office, with a sheaf of telegrams in his hand.

UNDERSHAFT. Well, have you seen everything? I'm sorry I was called away. [*Indicating the telegrams.*] Good news from Manchuria.

STEPHEN. Another Japanese victory?

UNDERSHAFT. Oh, I dont know. Which side wins does not concern us here. No: the good news is that the aerial battleship is a tremendous success. At the first trial it has wiped out a fort with three hundred soldiers in it.

CUSINS. [*From the platform.*] Dummy soldiers?

UNDERSHAFT. [*Striding across to Stephen and kicking the prostrate dummy brutally out of his way.*] No: the real thing.

[Cusins and Barbara exchange glances. Then Cusins sits on the step

*and buries his face in his hands. Barbara gravely lays her hand on
his shoulder. He looks up at her in whimsical desperation.*

UNDERSHAFT. Well, Stephen, what do you think of the place?

STEPHEN. Oh, magnificent. A perfect triumph of modern industry.
Frankly, my dear father, I have been a fool: I had no idea of
what it all meant: of the wonderful forethought, the power of
organization, the administrative capacity, the financial genius,
the colossal capital it represents. I have been repeating to myself
as I came through your streets 'Peace hath her victories no less
renowned than War.' I have only one misgiving about it all.

UNDERSHAFT. Out with it.

STEPHEN. Well, I cannot help thinking that all this provision for
every want of your workmen may sap their independence and
weaken their sense of responsibility. And greatly as we enjoyed
our tea at that splendid restaurant—how they gave us all that
luxury and cake and jam and cream for threepence I really cannot
imagine!—still you must remember that restaurants break up
home life. Look at the Continent, for instance! Are you sure so
much pampering is really good for the men's characters?

UNDERSHAFT. Well you see, my dear boy, when you are organizing
civilization you have to make up your mind whether trouble and
anxiety are good things or not. If you decide that they are, then,
I take it, you simply dont organize civilization; and there you are,
with trouble and anxiety enough to make us all angels! But if
you decide the other way, you may as well go through with it.
However, Stephen, our characters are safe here. A sufficient dose
of anxiety is always provided by the fact that we may be blown
to smithereens at any moment.

SARAH. By the way, papa, where do you make the explosives?

UNDERSHAFT. In separate little sheds, like that one. When one of
them blows up, it costs very little; and only the people quite
close to it are killed.

[*Stephen, who is quite close to it, looks at it rather scaredly, and
moves away quickly to the cannon. At the same moment the door of
the shed is thrown abruptly open; and a foreman in overalls and list
slippers comes out on the little landing and holds the door for Lomax,
who appears in the doorway.*

LOMAX. [*With studied coolness.*] My good fellow: you neednt get
into a state of nerves. Nothing's going to happen to you; and I
suppose it wouldnt be the end of the world if anything did. A
little bit of British pluck is what you want, old chap.

[*He descends and strolls across to Sarah.*

UNDERSHAFT. [*To the foreman.*] Anything wrong, Bilton?

BILTON. [*With ironic calm.*] Gentleman walked into the high
explosives shed and lit a cigaret, sir: that's all.

UNDERSHAFT. Ah, quite so. [*Going over to Lomax.*] Do you happen to remember what you did with the match?

LOMAX. Oh come! I'm not a fool. I took jolly good care to blow it out before I chucked it away.

BILTON. The top of it was red hot inside, sir.

LOMAX. Well, suppose it was! I didnt chuck it into any of your messes.

UNDERSHAFT. Think no more of it, Mr Lomax. By the way, would you mind lending me your matches?

LOMAX. [*Offering his box.*] Certainly.

UNDERSHAFT. Thanks.   [*He pockets the matches.*

LOMAX. [*Lecturing to the company generally.*] You know, these high explosives dont go off like gunpowder, except when theyre in a gun. When theyre spread loose, you can put a match to them without the least risk: they just burn quietly like a bit of paper. [*Warming to the scientific interest of the subject.*] Did you know that, Undershaft? Have you ever tried?

UNDERSHAFT. Not on a large scale, Mr Lomax. Bilton will give you a sample of gun-cotton when you are leaving if you ask him. You can experiment with it at home.   [*Bilton looks puzzled.*

SARAH. Bilton will do nothing of the sort, papa. I suppose it's your business to blow up the Russians and Japs; but you might really stop short of blowing up poor Cholly.

[*Bilton gives it up and retires into the shed.*

LOMAX. My ownest, there is no danger.

[*He sits beside her on the shell.*
[*Lady Britomart arrives from the town with a bouquet.*

LADY BRITOMART. [*Impetuously.*] Andrew: you shouldnt have let me see this place.

UNDERSHAFT. Why, my dear?

LADY BRITOMART. Never mind why: you shouldnt have: thats all. To think of all that [*indicating the town*] being yours! And that you have kept it to yourself all these years!

UNDERSHAFT. It does not belong to me. I belong to it. It is the Undershaft inheritance.

LADY BRITOMART. It is not. Your ridiculous cannons and that noisy banging foundry may be the Undershaft inheritance; but all that plate and linen, all that furniture and those houses and orchards and gardens belong to us. They belong to me: they are not a man's business. I wont give them up. You must be out of your senses to throw them all away; and if you persist in such folly I will call in a doctor .

UNDERSHAFT. [*Stooping to smell the bouquet.*] Where did you get the flowers, my dear?

LADY BRITOMART. Your men presented them to me in your William Morris Labor Church.

CUSINS. Oh! It needed only that. A Labor Church.

　　[*He mounts the firestep distractedly, and leans with his elbows on the parapet, turning his back to them.*

LADY BRITOMART. Yes, with Morris's words in mosaic letters ten feet high round the dome. NO MAN IS GOOD ENOUGH TO BE ANOTHER MAN'S MASTER. The cynicism of it!

UNDERSHAFT. It shocked the men at first, I am afraid. But now they take no more notice of it than of the ten commandments in church.

LADY BRITOMART. Andrew: you are trying to put me off the subject of the inheritance by profane jokes. Well, you shant. I dont ask it any longer, for Stephen: he has inherited far too much of your perversity to be fit for it. But Barbara has rights as well as Stephen. Why should not Adolphus succeed to the inheritance? I could manage the town for him; and he can look after the cannons, if they are really necessary.

UNDERSHAFT. I should ask nothing better if Adolphus were a foundling. He is exactly the sort of new blood that is wanted in English business. But he's not a foundling; and theres an end of it.　　　　　　　　　　　　　　[*He makes for the office door.*

CUSINS. [*Turning to them.*] Not quite. [*They all turn and stare at him.*] I think—Mind! I am not committing myself in any way as to my future course—but I think the foundling difficulty can be got over.　　　　　　　　　　　　　[*He jumps down to the emplacement.*

UNDERSHAFT. [*Coming back to him.*] What do you mean?

CUSINS. Well, I have something to say which is in the nature of a confession.

SARAH.
LADY BRITOMART.　⎬　Confession!
BARBARA.
STEPHEN.

LOMAX. Oh, I say!

CUSINS. Yes, a confession. Listen, all. Until I met Barbara I thought myself in the main an honorable, truthful man, because I wanted the approval of my conscience more than I wanted anything else. But the moment I saw Barbara, I wanted her far more than the approval of my conscience.

LADY BRITOMART. Adolphus!

CUSINS. It is true. You accused me yourself, Lady Brit, of joining the Army to worship Barbara; and so I did. She bought my soul like a flower at a street corner; but she bought it for herself.

UNDERSHAFT. What! Not for Dionysos or another?

CUSINS. Dionysos and all the others are in herself. I adored what was divine in her, and was therefore a true worshipper. But I was romantic about her too. I thought she was a woman of the people, and that a marriage with a professor of Greek would be far beyond the wildest social ambitions of her rank.

LADY BRITOMART. Adolphus!!

LOMAX. Oh, I say!!!

CUSINS. When I learnt the horrible truth——

LADY BRITOMART. What do you mean by the horrible truth, pray?

CUSINS. That she was enormously rich; that her grandfather was an earl; that her father was the Prince of Darkness——

UNDERSHAFT. Chut!

CUSINS. —and that I was only an adventurer trying to catch a rich wife, then I stooped to deceive her about my birth.

BARBARA. [*Rising.*] Dolly!

LADY BRITOMART. Your birth! Now Adolphus, dont dare to make up a wicked story for the sake of these wretched cannons. Remember: I have seen photographs of your parents; and the Agent General for South Western Australia knows them personally and has assured me that they are most respectable married people.

CUSINS. So they are in Australia; but here they are outcasts. Their marriage is legal in Australia, but not in England. My mother is my father's deceased wife's sister; and in this island I am consequently a foundling. [*Sensation.*

BARBARA. Silly!

 [*She climbs to the cannon, and leans, listening, in the angle it makes with the parapet.*

CUSINS. Is the subterfuge good enough, Machiavelli?

UNDERSHAFT. [*Thoughtfully.*] Biddy: this may be a way out of the difficulty.

LADY BRITOMART. Stuff! A man cant make cannons any the better for being his own cousin instead of his proper self.

 [*She sits down on the rug with a bounce that expresses her downright contempt for their casuistry.*

UNDERSHAFT. [*To Cusins.*] You are an educated man. That is against the tradition.

CUSINS. Once in ten thousand times it happens that the schoolboy is a born master of what they try to teach him. Greek has not destroyed my mind: it has nourished it. Besides, I did not learn it at an English public school.

UNDERSHAFT. Hm! Well, I cannot afford to be too particular: you have cornered the foundling market. Let it pass. You are eligible, Euripides: you are eligible.

BARBARA. Dolly: yesterday morning, when Stephen told us all about the tradition, you became very silent; and you have been

strange and excited ever since. Were you thinking of your birth
then?

CUSINS. When the finger of Destiny suddenly points at a man in
the middle of his breakfast, it makes him thoughtful.

UNDERSHAFT. Aha! You have had your eye on the business, my
young friend, have you?

CUSINS. Take care! There is an abyss of moral horror between me
and your accursed aerial battleships.

UNDERSHAFT. Never mind the abyss for the present. Let us settle
the practical details and leave your final decision open. You
know that you will have to change your name. Do you object
to that?

CUSINS. Would any man named Adolphus—any man called Dolly!
—object to be called something else?

UNDERSHAFT. Good. Now, as to money! I propose to treat you
handsomely from the beginning. You shall start at a thousand a
year.

CUSINS. [*With sudden heat, his spectacles twinkling with mischief.*] A
thousand! You dare offer a miserable thousand to the son-in-
law of a millionaire! No, by Heavens, Machiavelli, you shall not
cheat me! You cannot do without me; and I can do without you.
I must have two thousand five hundred a year for two years.
At the end of that time, if I am a failure, I go. But if I am a success,
and stay on, you must give me the other five thousand.

UNDERSHAFT. What other five thousand?

CUSINS. To make the two years up to five thousand a year. The
two thousand five hundred is only half pay in case I should turn
out a failure. The third year I must have ten per cent on the
profits.

UNDERSHAFT. [*Taken aback.*] Ten per cent! Why, man, do you
know what my profits are?

CUSINS. Enormous, I hope: otherwise I shall require twenty-five
per cent.

UNDERSHAFT. But, Mr Cusins, this is a serious matter of business.
You are not bringing any capital into the concern.

CUSINS. What! No capital! Is my mastery of Greek no capital? Is
my access to the subtlest thought, the loftiest poetry yet attained
by humanity, no capital? My character! my intellect! my life!
my career! what Barbara calls my soul!—are these no capital?
Say another word: and I double my salary.

UNDERSHAFT. Be reasonable——

CUSINS. [*Peremptorily.*] Mr Undershaft: you have my terms. Take
them or leave them.

UNDERSHAFT. [*Recovering himself.*] Very well. I note your terms;
and I offer you half.

CUSINS. [*Disgusted.*] Half!

UNDERSHAFT. [*Firmly.*] Half.

CUSINS. You call yourself a gentleman; and you offer me half!!

UNDERSHAFT. I do not call myself a gentleman; but I offer you half.

CUSINS. This to your future partner! your successor! your son-in-law!

BARBARA. You are selling your own soul, Dolly, not mine. Leave me out of the bargain, please.

UNDERSHAFT. Come! I will go a step further for Barbara's sake. I will give you three fifths; but that is my last word.

CUSINS. Done!

LOMAX. Done in the eye! Why, *I* get only eight hundred, you know.

CUSINS. By the way, Mac, I am a classical scholar, not an arithmetical one. Is three fifths more than half or less?

UNDERSHAFT. More, of course.

CUSINS. I would have taken two hundred and fifty. How you can succeed in business when you are willing to pay all that money to a University don who is obviously not worth a junior clerk's wages! Well! What will Lazarus say?

UNDERSHAFT. Lazarus is a gentle romantic Jew who cares for nothing but string quartets and stalls at fashionable theatres. He will be blamed for your rapacity in money matters, poor fellow, as he has hitherto been blamed for mine. You are a shark of the first order, Euripides. So much the better for the firm!

BARBARA. Is the bargain closed, Dolly! Does your soul belong to him now?

CUSINS. No: the price is settled: that is all. The real tug of war is still to come. What about the moral question?

LADY BRITOMART. There is no moral question in the matter at all, Adolphus. You must simply sell cannons and weapons to people whose cause is right and just, and refuse them to foreigners and criminals.

UNDERSHAFT. [*Determinedly.*] No: none of that. You must keep the true faith of an Armorer, or you dont come in here.

CUSINS. What on earth is the true faith of an Armorer?

UNDERSHAFT. To give arms to all men who offer an honest price for them, without respect of persons or principles: to aristocrat and republican, to Nihilist and Tsar, to Capitalist and Socialist, to Protestant and Catholic, to burglar and policeman, to black man, white man and yellow man, to all sorts and conditions, all nationalities, all faiths, all follies, all causes and all crimes. The first Undershaft wrote up in his shop IF GOD GAVE THE HAND, LET NOT MAN WITHHOLD THE SWORD. The second wrote up ALL HAVE THE RIGHT TO FIGHT: NONE HAVE THE RIGHT TO JUDGE. The third wrote up TO MAN THE WEAPON: TO HEAVEN THE

VICTORY. The forth had no literary turn; so he did not write up anything; but he sold cannons to Napoleon under the nose of George the Third. The fifth wrote up PEACE SHALL NOT PREVAIL SAVE WITH A SWORD IN HER HAND. The sixth, my master, was the best of all. He wrote up NOTHING IS EVER DONE IN THIS WORLD UNTIL MEN ARE PREPARED TO KILL ONE ANOTHER IF IT IS NOT DONE. After that, there was nothing left for the seventh to say. So he wrote up, simply, UNASHAMED.

CUSINS. My good Machiavelli, I shall certainly write something up on the wall; only, as I shall write it in Greek, you wont be able to read it. But as to your Armorer's faith, if I take my neck out of the noose of my own morality I am not going to put it into the noose of yours. I shall sell cannons to whom I please and refuse them to whom I please. So there!

UNDERSHAFT. From the moment when you become Andrew Undershaft, you will never do as you please again. Dont come here lusting for power, young man.

CUSINS. If power were my aim I should not come here for it. You have no power.

UNDERSHAFT. None of my own, certainly.

CUSINS. I have more power than you, more will. You do not drive this place: it drives you. And what drives the place?

UNDERSHAFT. [*Enigmatically.*] A will of which I am a part.

BARBARA. [*Startled.*] Father! Do you know what you are saying; or are you laying a snare for my soul?

CUSINS. Dont listen to his metaphysics, Barbara. The place is driven by the most rascally part of society, the money hunters, the pleasure hunters, the military promotion hunters; and he is their slave.

UNDERSHAFT. Not necessarily. Remember the Armorer's faith. I will take an order from a good man as cheerfully as from a bad one. If you good people prefer preaching and shirking to buying my weapons and fighting the rascals, dont blame me. I can make cannons: I cannot make courage and conviction. Bah! You tire me, Euripides, with your morality mongering. Ask Barbara: she understands. [*He suddenly reaches up and takes Barbara's hands, looking powerfully into her eyes.*] Tell him, my love, what power really means.

BARBARA. [*Hypnotized.*] Before I joined the Salvation Army, I was in my own power; and the consequence was that I never knew what to do with myself. When I joined it, I had not time enough for all the things I had to do.

UNDERSHAFT. [*Approvingly.*] Just so. And why was that, do you suppose?

BARBARA. Yesterday I should have said, because I was in the power of God. [*She resumes her self-possession, withdrawing her hands from his with a power equal to his own.*] But you came and shewed me that I was in the power of Bodger and Undershaft. Today I feel —oh! how can I put it into words? Sarah: do you remember the earthquake at Cannes, when we were little children?—How little the surprise of the first shock mattered compared to the dread and horror of waiting for the second? That is how I feel in this place today. I stood on the rock I thought eternal; and without a word of warning it reeled and crumbled under me. I was safe with an infinite wisdom watching me, an army marching to Salvation with me; and in a moment, at a stroke of your pen in a cheque book, I stood alone; and the heavens were empty. That was the first shock of the earthquake: I am waiting for the second.

UNDERSHAFT. Come, come, my daughter! Dont make too much of your little tinpot tragedy. What do we do here when we spend years of work and thought and thousands of pounds of solid cash on a new gun or an aerial battleship that turns out just a hairsbreadth wrong after all? Scrap it. Scrap it without wasting another hour or another pound on it. Well, you have made for yourself something that you call a morality or a religion or what not. It doesnt fit the facts. Well, scrap it. Scrap it and get one that does fit. That is what is wrong with the world at present. It scraps its obsolete steam engines and dynamos; but it wont scrap its old prejudices and its old moralities and its old religions and its old political constitutions. Whats the result? In machinery it does very well; but in morals and religion and politics it is working at a loss that brings it nearer bankruptcy every year. Dont persist in that folly. If your old religion broke down yesterday, get a newer and a better one for tomorrow.

BARBARA. Oh, how gladly I would take a better one to my soul! But you offer me a worse one. [*Turning on him with sudden vehemence.*] Justify yourself: shew me some light through the darkness of this dreadful place, with its beautifully clean workshops, and respectable workmen and model homes.

UNDERSHAFT. Cleanliness and respectability do not need justification, Barbara: they justify themselves. I see no darkness here, no dreadfulness. In your Salvation shelter I saw poverty, misery, cold and hunger. You gave them bread and treacle and dreams of heaven. I give from thirty shillings a week to twelve thousand a year. They find their own dreams; but I look after the drainage.

BARBARA. And their souls?

UNDERSHAFT. I save their souls just as I saved yours.

BARBARA. [*Revolted.*] You saved my soul! What do you mean?

UNDERSHAFT. I fed you and clothed you and housed you. I took care that you should have money enough to live handsomely—

more than enough; so that you could be wasteful, careless, generous. That saved your soul from the seven deadly sins.

BARBARA. [*Bewildered.*] The seven deadly sins!

UNDERSHAFT. Yes, the deadly seven. [*Counting on his fingers.*] Food, clothing, firing, rent, taxes, respectability and children. Nothing can lift those seven millstones from Man's neck but money; and the spirit cannot soar until the millstones are lifted. I lifted them from your spirit. I enabled Barbara to become Major Barbara; and I saved her from the crime of poverty.

CUSINS. Do you call poverty a crime?

UNDERSHAFT. The worst of crimes. All the other crimes are virtues beside it: all the other dishonors are chivalry itself by comparison. Poverty blights whole cities; spreads horrible pestilences; strikes dead the very souls of all who come within sight, sound or smell of it. What you call crime is nothing: a murder here and a theft there, a blow now and a curse then: what do they matter? They are only the accidents and illnesses of life: there are not fifty genuine professional criminals in London. But there are millions of poor people, abject people, dirty people, ill fed, ill clothed people. They poison us morally and physically: they kill the happiness of society: they force us to do away with our own liberties and to organize unnatural cruelties for fear they should rise against us and drag us down into their abyss. Only fools fear crime: we all fear poverty. Pah! [*Turning on Barbara.*] You talk of your half-saved ruffian in West Ham: you accuse me of dragging his soul back to perdition. Well, bring him to me here; and I will drag his soul back again to salvation for you. Not by words and dreams; but by thirty-eight shillings a week, a sound house in a handsome street, and a permanent job. In three weeks he will have a fancy waistcoat; in three months a tall hat and a chapel sitting; before the end of the year he will shake hands with a duchess at a Primrose League meeting, and join the Conservative Party.

BARBARA. And will he be the better for that?

UNDERSHAFT. You know he will. Dont be a hypocrite, Barbara. He will be better fed, better housed, better clothed, better behaved; and his children will be pounds heavier and bigger. That will be better than an American cloth mattress in a shelter, chopping firewood, eating bread and treacle, and being forced to kneel down from time to time to thank heaven for it: knee drill, I think you call it. It is cheap work converting starving men with a Bible in one hand and a slice of bread in the other. I will undertake to convert West Ham to Mahometanism on the same terms. Try your hand on my men: their souls are hungry because their bodies are full.

BARBARA. And leave the East End to starve?

UNDERSHAFT. [*His energetic tone dropping into one of bitter and brooding remembrance.*] I was an East Ender. I moralized and starved until one day I swore that I would be a full-fed free man at all costs; that nothing should stop me except a bullet, neither reason nor morals nor the lives of other men. I said, 'Thou shalt starve ere I starve'; and with that word I became free and great. I was a dangerous man until I had my will: now I am a useful, beneficent, kindly person. That is the history of most self-made millionaires, I fancy. When it is the history of every Englishman we shall have an England worth living in.

LADY BRITOMART. Stop making speeches, Andrew. This is not the place for them.

UNDERSHAFT. [*Punctured.*] My dear: I have no other means of conveying my ideas.

LADY BRITOMART. Your ideas are nonsense. You got on because you were selfish and unscrupulous.

UNDERSHAFT. Not at all. I had the strongest scruples about poverty and starvation. Your moralists are quite unscrupulous about both: they make virtues of them. I had rather be a thief than a pauper. I had rather be a murderer than a slave. I dont want to be either; but if you force the alternative on me, then, by Heaven, I'll choose the braver and more moral one. I hate poverty and slavery worse than any other crimes whatsoever. And let me tell you this. Poverty and slavery have stood up for centuries to your sermons and leading articles: they will not stand up to my machine-guns. Dont preach at them: dont reason with them. Kill them.

BARBARA. Killing. Is that your remedy for everything?

UNDERSHAFT. It is the final test of conviction, the only lever strong enough to overturn a social system, the only way of saying Must. Let six hundred and seventy fools loose in the streets; and three policemen can scatter them. But huddle them together in a certain house in Westminster; and let them go through certain ceremonies and call themselves certain names until at last they get the courage to kill; and your six hundred and seventy fools become a government. Your pious mob fills up ballot papers and imagines it is governing its masters; but the ballot paper that really governs is the paper that has a bullet wrapped up in it.

CUSINS. That is perhaps why, like most intelligent people, I never vote.

UNDERSHAFT. Vote! Bah! When you vote, you only change the names of the Cabinet. When you shoot, you pull down governments, inaugurate new epochs, abolish old orders and set up new. Is that historically true, Mr Learned Man, or is it not?

CUSINS. It is historically true. I loathe having to admit it. I repudiate your sentiments. I abhor your nature. I defy you in every possible way. Still, it is true. But it ought not to be true.

UNDERSHAFT. Ought! ought! ought! ought! ought! Are you going to spend your life saying ought, like the rest of our moralists? Turn your oughts into shalls, man. Come and make explosives with me. Whatever can blow men up can blow society up. The history of the world is the history of those who had courage enough to embrace this truth. Have you the courage to embrace it, Barbara?

LADY BRITOMART. Barbara: I positively forbid you to listen to your father's abominable wickedness. And you, Adolphus, ought to know better than to go about saying that wrong things are true. What does it matter whether they are true if they are wrong?

UNDERSHAFT. What does it matter whether they are wrong if they are true?

LADY BRITOMART. [Rising.] Children: come home instantly. Andrew: I am exceedingly sorry I allowed you to call on us. You are wickeder than ever. Come at once.

BARBARA. [Shaking her head.] It's no use running away from wicked people, mamma.

LADY BRITOMART. It is every use. It shews your disapprobation of them.

BARBARA. It does not save them.

LADY BRITOMART. I can see that you are going to disobey me. Sarah: are you coming home or are you not?

SARAH. I daresay it's very wicked of papa to make cannons; but I dont think I shall cut him on that account.

LOMAX. [Pouring oil on the troubled waters.] The fact is, you know, there is a certain amount of tosh about this notion of wickedness. It doesnt work. You must look at facts. Not that I would say a word in favor of anything wrong; but then, you see, all sorts of chaps are always doing all sorts of things; and we have to fit them in somehow, dont you know. What I mean is that you cant go cutting everybody; and thats about what it comes to. [Their rapt attention to his eloquence makes him nervous.] Perhaps I dont make myself clear.

LADY BRITOMART. You are lucidity itself, Charles. Because Andrew is successful and has plenty of money to give to Sarah, you will flatter him and encourage him in his wickedness.

LOMAX. [Unruffled.] Well, where the carcase is, there will the eagles be gathered, dont you know. [To Undershaft.] Eh? What?

UNDERSHAFT. Precisely. By the way, may I call you Charles?

LOMAX. Delighted. Cholly is the usual ticket.

UNDERSHAFT. [To Lady Britomart.] Biddy——

LADY BRITOMART. [*Violently.*] Dont dare call me Biddy. Charles Lomax: you are a fool. Adolphus Cusins: you are a Jesuit. Stephen: you are a prig. Barbara: you are a lunatic. Andrew: you are a vulgar tradesman. Now you all know my opinion; and my conscience is clear, at all events.

[*She sits down with a vehemence that the rug fortunately softens.*

UNDERSHAFT. My dear: you are the incarnation of morality. [*She snorts.*] Your conscience is clear and your duty done when you have called everybody names. Come, Euripides! It is getting late; and we all want to go home. Make up your mind.

CUSINS. Understand this, you old demon——

LADY BRITOMART. Adolphus!

UNDERSHAFT. Let him alone, Biddy. Proceed, Euripides.

CUSINS. You have me in a horrible dilemma. I want Barbara.

UNDERSHAFT. Like all young men, you greatly exaggerate the difference between one young woman and another.

BARBARA. Quite true, Dolly.

CUSINS. I also want to avoid being a rascal.

UNDERSHAFT. [*With biting contempt.*] You lust for personal righteousness, for self-approval, for what you call a good conscience, for what Barbara calls salvation, for what I call patronizing people who are not so lucky as yourself.

CUSINS. I do not: all the poet in me recoils from being a good man. But there are things in me that I must reckon with. Pity——

UNDERSHAFT. Pity! The scavenger of misery.

CUSINS. Well, love.

UNDERSHAFT. I know. You love the needy and the outcast: you love the oppressed races, the negro, the Indian ryot, the underdog everywhere. Do you love the Japanese? Do you love the French? Do you love the English?

CUSINS. No. Every true Englishman detests the English. We are the wickedest nation on earth; and our success is a moral horror.

UNDERSHAFT. That is what comes of your gospel of love, is it?

CUSINS. May I not love even my father-in-law?

UNDERSHAFT. Who wants your love, man? By what right do you take the liberty of offering it to me? I will have your due heed and respect, or I will kill you. But your love! Damn your impertinence!

CUSINS. [*Grinning.*] I may not be able to control my affections, Mac.

UNDERSHAFT. You are fencing, Euripides. You are weakening: your grip is slipping. Come! Try your last weapon. Pity and love have broken in your hand: forgiveness is still left.

CUSINS. No: forgiveness is a beggar's refuge. I am with you there: we must pay our debts.

UNDERSHAFT. Well said. Come! You will suit me. Remember the words of Plato.

CUSINS. [*Starting.*] You dare quote Plato to me!

UNDERSHAFT. Plato says, my friend, that society cannot be saved until either the professors of Greek take to making gunpowder or else the makers of gunpowder become professors of Greek.

CUSINS. Oh, tempter, cunning tempter!

UNDERSHAFT. Come! Choose, man, choose.

CUSINS. But perhaps Barbara will not marry me if I make the wrong choice.

BARBARA. Perhaps not.

CUSINS. [*Desperately perplexed.*] You hear!

BARBARA. Father: do you love nobody?

UNDERSHAFT. I love my best friend.

LADY BRITOMART. And who is that, pray?

UNDERSHAFT. My bravest enemy. That is the man who keeps me up to the mark.

CUSINS. You know, the creature is really a sort of poet in his way. Suppose he is a great man, after all!

UNDERSHAFT. Suppose you stop talking and make up your mind, my young friend.

CUSINS. But you are driving me against my nature. I hate war.

UNDERSHAFT. Hatred is the coward's revenge for being intimidated. Dare you make war on war? Here are the means: my friend Mr Lomax is sitting on them.

LOMAX. [*Springing up.*] Oh, I say! You dont mean that this thing is loaded, do you? My ownest: come off it.

SARAH. [*Sitting placidly on the shell.*] If I am to be blown up, the more thoroughly it is done the better. Dont fuss, Cholly.

LOMAX. [*To Undershaft, strongly remonstrant.*] Your own daughter, you know!

UNDERSHAFT. So I see. [*To Cusins.*] Well, my friend, may we expect you here at six tomorrow morning?

CUSINS. [*Firmly.*] Not on any account. I will see the whole establishment blown up with its own dynamite before I will get up at five. My hours are healthy, rational hours: eleven to five.

UNDERSHAFT. Come when you please: before a week you will come at six and stay until I turn you out for the sake of your health. [*Calling.*] Bilton! [*He turns to Lady Britomart, who rises.*] My dear: let us leave these two young people to themselves for a moment. [*Bilton comes from the shed.*] I am going to take you through the gun-cotton shed.

BILTON. [*Barring the way.*] You cant take anything explosive in here, sir.

LADY BRITOMART. What do you mean? Are you alluding to me?

BILTON. [*Unmoved.*] No, maam. Mr Undershaft has the other gentleman's matches in his pocket.

LADY BRITOMART. [*Abruptly.*] Oh! I beg your pardon.

[*She goes into the shed.*

UNDERSHAFT. Quite right, Bilton, quite right: here you are. [*He gives Bilton the box of matches.*] Come, Stephen. Come, Charles. Bring Sarah.   [*He passes into the shed.*

[*Bilton opens the box and deliberately drops the matches into the fire-bucket.*

LOMAX. Oh! I say. [*Bilton stolidly hands him the empty box.*] Infernal nonsense! Pure scientific ignorance!   [*He goes in.*

SARAH. Am I all right, Bilton?

BILTON. Youll have to put on list slippers, miss: thats all. Weve got em inside.   [*She goes in.*]

STEPHEN. [*Very seriously to Cusins.*] Dolly, old fellow, think. Think before you decide. Do you feel that you are a sufficiently practical man? It is a huge undertaking, an enormous responsibility. All this mass of business will be Greek to you.

CUSINS. Oh, I think it will be much less difficult than Greek.

STEPHEN. Well, I just want to say this before I leave you to yourselves. Dont let anything I have said about right and wrong prejudice you against this great chance in life. I have satisfied myself that the business is one of the highest character and a credit to our country. [*Emotionally.*] I am very proud of my father. I——

[*Unable to proceed, he presses Cusins' hand and goes hastily into the shed, followed by Bilton.*

[*Barbara and Cusins, left alone together, look at one another silently.*

CUSINS. Barbara: I am going to accept this offer.

BARBARA. I thought you would.

CUSINS. You understand, dont you, that I had to decide without consulting you. If I had thrown the burden of the choice on you, you would sooner or later have despised me for it.

BARBARA. Yes: I did not want you to sell your soul for me any more than for this inheritance.

CUSINS. It is not the sale of my soul that troubles me: I have sold it too often to care about that. I have sold it for a professorship. I have sold it for an income. I have sold it to escape being imprisoned for refusing to pay taxes for hangmen's ropes and unjust wars and things that I abhor. What is all human conduct but the daily and hourly sale of our souls for trifles? What I am now selling it for is neither money nor position nor comfort, but for reality and for power.

BARBARA. You know that you will have no power, and that he has none.

CUSINS. I know. It is not for myself alone. I want to make power for the world.

BARBARA. I want to make power for the world too; but it must be spiritual power.

CUSINS. I think all power is spiritual: these cannons will not go off by themselves. I have tried to make spiritual power by teaching Greek. But the world can never be really touched by a dead language and a dead civilization. The people must have power; and the people cannot have Greek. Now the power that is made here can be wielded by all men.

BARBARA. Power to burn women's houses down and kill their sons and tear their husbands to pieces.

CUSINS. You cannot have power for good without having power for evil too. Even mother's milk nourishes murderers as well as heroes. This power which only tears men's bodies to pieces has never been so horribly abused as the intellectual power, the imaginative power, the poetic, religious power that can enslave men's souls. As a teacher of Greek I gave the intellectual man weapons against the common man. I now want to give the common man weapons against the intellectual man. I love the common people. I want to arm them against the lawyers, the doctors, the priests, the literary men, the professors, the artists and the politicians, who, once in authority, are more disastrous and tyrannical than all the fools, rascals and impostors. I want a power simple enough for common men to use, yet strong enough to force the intellectual oligarchy to use its genius for the general good.

BARBARA. Is there no higher power than that [*pointing to the shell*]?

CUSINS. Yes; but that power can destroy the higher powers just as a tiger can destroy a man: therefore Man must master that power first. I admitted this when the Turks and Greeks were last at war. My best pupil went out to fight for Hellas. My parting gift to him was not a copy of Plato's Republic, but a revolver and a hundred Undershaft cartridges. The blood of every Turk he shot—if he shot any—is on my head as well as on Undershaft's. That act committed me to this place for ever. Your father's challenge has beaten me. Dare I make war on war? I must. I will. And now, is it all over between us?

BARBARA. [*Touched by his evident dread of her answer.*] Silly baby Dolly! How could it be!

CUSINS. [*Overjoyed.*] Then you—you—you—Oh for my drum!
                    [*He flourishes imaginary drumsticks.*

BARBARA. [*Angered by his levity.*] Take care, Dolly, take care. Oh, if only I could get away from you and from father and from it all! If I could have the wings of a dove and fly away to heaven!

CUSINS. And leave m e !

BARBARA. Yes, you, and all the other naughty mischievous children of men. But I cant. I was happy in the Salvation Army for a moment. I escaped from the world into a paradise of enthusiasm and prayer and soul saving; but the moment our money ran short, it all came back to Bodger: it was he who saved our people: he, and the Prince of Darkness, my papa. Undershaft and Bodger: their hands stretch everywhere: when we feed a starving fellow creature, it is with their bread, because there is no other bread; when we tend the sick, it is in the hospitals they endow; if we turn from the churches they build, we must kneel on the stones of the streets they pave. As long as that lasts, there is no getting away from them. Turning our backs on Bodger and Undershaft is turning our backs on life.

CUSINS. I thought you were determined to turn your back on the wicked side of life.

BARBARA. There is no wicked side: life is all one. And I never wanted to shirk my share in whatever evil must be endured, whether it be sin or suffering. I wish I could cure you of middle-class ideas, Dolly.

CUSINS. [Gasping.] Middle cl—! A snub! A social snub to me! From the daughter of a foundling!

BARBARA. That is why I have no class. Dolly: I come straight out of the heart of the whole people. If I were middle-class I should turn my back on my father's business; and we should both live in an artistic drawing-room, with you reading the reviews in one corner, and I in the other at the piano, playing Schumann: both very superior persons, and neither of us a bit of use. Sooner than that, I would sweep out the gun-cotton shed, or be one of Bodger's barmaids. Do you know what would have happened if you had refused papa's offer?

CUSINS. I wonder!

BARBARA. I should have given you up and married the man who accepted it. After all, my dear old mother has more sense than any of you. I felt like her when I saw this place—felt that I must have it—that never, never, never could I let it go; only she thought it was the houses and the kitchen ranges and the linen and china, when it was really all the human souls to be saved: not weak souls in starved bodies, sobbing with gratitude for a scrap of bread and treacle, but fullfed, quarrelsome, snobbish, uppish creatures, all standing on their little rights and dignities, and thinking that my father ought to be greatly obliged to them for making so much money for him—and so he ought. That is where salvation is really wanted. My father shall never throw it in my teeth again that my converts were bribed with bread. [She *is transfigured.*] I have got rid of the bribe of bread. I have got rid of the bribe of heaven. Let God's work be done for its own sake: the work he had to create us to do because it cannot be done except by living men and women. When I die, let him be in my debt, not I in his; and let me forgive him as becomes a woman of my rank.

CUSINS. Then the way of life lies through the factory of death?

BARBARA. Yes, through the raising of hell to heaven and of man to God, through the unveiling of an eternal light in the Valley of The Shadow. [*Seizing him with both hands.*] Oh, did you think my courage would never come back? Did you believe that I was a deserter? That I, who have stood in the streets, and taken my people to my heart, and talked of the holiest and greatest things with them, could ever turn back and chatter foolishly to fashionable people about nothing in a drawing-room? Never, never, never, never: Major Barbara will die with the colors. Oh! and I have my dear little Dolly boy still; and he has found me my place and my work. Glory, Hallelujah!   [*She kisses him.*

CUSINS. My dearest: consider my delicate health. I cannot stand as much happiness as you can.

BARBARA. Yes: it is not easy work being in love with me, is it? But it's good for you. [*She runs to the shed, and calls, childlike.*] Mamma! Mamma! [*Bilton comes out of the shed, followed by Undershaft.*] I want Mamma.

UNDERSHAFT. She is taking off her list slippers, dear. [*He passes on to Cusins.*] Well? What does she say?

CUSINS. She has gone right up into the skies.

LADY BRITOMART. [*Coming from the shed and stopping on the steps, obstructing Sarah, who follows with Lomax. Barbara clutches like a baby at her mother's skirt.*] Barbara: when will you learn to be independent and to act and think for yourself? I know as well as possible what that cry of 'Mamma, Mamma,' means. Always running to me!

SARAH. [*Touching Lady Britomart's ribs with her finger-tips and imitating a bicycle horn.*] Pip! pip!

LADY BRITOMART. [*Highly indignant.*] How dare you say Pip! pip! to me, Sarah? You are both very naughty children. What do you want, Barbara?

BARBARA. I want a house in the village to live in with Dolly. [*Dragging at the skirt.*] Come and tell me which one to take.

UNDERSHAFT. [*To Cusins.*] Six o'clock tomorrow morning, Euripides.

SAINT JOAN

A CHRONICLE PLAY IN SIX SCENES
AND AN EPILOGUE

NOTE

If Joan had been malicious, selfish, cowardly or stupid, she would have been one of the most odious persons known to history instead of one of the most attractive. If she had been old enough to know the effect she was producing on the men whom she humiliated by being right when they were wrong, and had learned to flatter and manage them, she might have lived as long as Queen Elizabeth.

Joan got a fairer trial from the Church and the Inquisition than any prisoner of her type and in her situation gets nowadays in any official secular court; and the decision was strictly according to law. And she was not a melodramatic heroine: that is, a physically beautiful lovelorn parasite on an equally beautiful hero, but a genius and a saint.

To understand Joan's history it is not enough to understand her character: you must understand her environment as well. . . . To see her in her proper perspective you must understand Christendom and the Catholic Church, the Holy Roman Empire and the Feudal System. . . . If you confuse the Middle Ages with the Dark Ages, and are in the habit of ridiculing your aunt for wearing 'medieval clothes' . . . and are quite convinced that the world has progressed enormously, both morally and mechanically, since Joan's time, then you will never understand why Joan was burnt, much less feel that you might have voted for burning her yourself . . . and until you feel that you know nothing essential about her.

Still, there was a great wrong done to Joan and to the conscience of the world by her burning. *Tout comprendre, c'est tout pardonner*, which is the Devil's sentimentality, cannot excuse it. When we have admitted that the tribunal was not only honest and legal, but exceptionally merciful in respect of sparing Joan the torture which was customary when she was obdurate as to taking the oath . . . the human fact remains that the burning of Joan of Arc was a horror, and that a historian who would defend it would defend anything.

G. B. S.

SAINT JOAN

A fine spring morning on the River Meuse, between Lorraine and Cham-
pagne, in the year A.D. 1429, in the castle of Vaucouleurs.
Captain Robert de Baudricourt, a military squire, handsome and physically
energetic, but with no will of his own, is disguising that defect in his usual
fashion by storming terribly at his steward, a trodden worm, scanty of
flesh, scanty of hair, who might be any age from eighteen to fifty-five, being
the sort of man whom age cannot wither because he has never bloomed.
The two are in a sunny stone chamber on the first floor of the castle. At a
plain strong oak table, seated in chair to match, the captain presents his
left profile. The steward stands facing him at the other side of the table,
if so deprecatory a stance as his can be called standing. The mullioned
thirteenth-century window is open behind him. Near it in the corner is a
turret with a narrow arched doorway leading to a winding stair which
descends to the courtyard. There is a stout four-legged stool under the
table, and a wooden chest under the window.

ROBERT. No eggs! No eggs!! Thousand thunders, man, what do
you mean by no eggs?

STEWARD. Sir: it is not my fault. It is the act of God.

ROBERT. Blasphemy. You tell me there are no eggs; and you blame
your Maker for it.

STEWARD. Sir: what can I do? I cannot lay eggs.

ROBERT. [*Sarcastic.*] Ha! You jest about it.

STEWARD. No, sir, God knows. We all have to go without eggs
just as you have, sir. The hens will not lay.

ROBERT. Indeed! [*Rising.*] Now listen to me, you.

STEWARD. [*Humbly.*] Yes, sir.

ROBERT. What am I?

STEWARD. What are you, sir?

ROBERT. [*Coming at him.*] Yes: what am I? Am I Robert, squire of
Baudricourt and captain of this castle of Vaucouleurs; or am I
a cowboy?

STEWARD. Oh, sir, you know you are a greater man here than the
king himself.

ROBERT. Precisely. And now, do you know what you are?

145

STEWARD. I am nobody, sir, except that I have the honour to be your steward.

ROBERT. [*Driving him to the wall, adjective by adjective.*] You have not only the honor of being my steward, but the privilege of being the worst, most incompetent, drivelling snivelling jibbering jabbering idiot of a steward in France.

[*He strides back to the table.*

STEWARD. [*Cowering on the chest.*] Yes, sir: to a great man like you I must seem like that.

ROBERT. [*Turning.*] My fault, I suppose. Eh?

STEWARD. [*Coming to him deprecatingly.*] Oh, sir: you always give my most innocent words such a turn!

ROBERT. I will give your neck a turn if you dare tell me, when I ask you how many eggs there are, that you cannot lay any.

STEWARD. [*Protesting.*] Oh sir, oh sir——

ROBERT. No: not oh sir, oh sir, but no sir, no sir. My three Barbary hens and the black are the best layers in Champagne. And you come and tell me that there are no eggs! Who stole them? Tell me that, before I kick you out through the castle gate for a liar and a seller of my goods to thieves. The milk was short yesterday, too: do not forget that.

STEWARD. [*Desperate*]. I know, sir. I know only too well. There is no milk: there are no eggs: tomorrow there will be nothing.

ROBERT. Nothing! You will steal the lot: eh?

STEWARD. No, sir: nobody will steal anything. But there is a spell on us: we are bewitched.

ROBERT. That story is not good enough for me. Robert de Baudricourt burns witches and hangs thieves. Go. Bring me four dozen eggs and two gallons of milk here in this room before noon, or Heaven have mercy on your bones! I will teach you to make a fool of me.   [*He resumes his seat with an air of finality.*

STEWARD. Sir: I tell you there are no eggs. There will be none—not if you were to kill me for it—as long as The Maid is at the door.

ROBERT. The Maid! What maid? What are you talking about?

STEWARD. The girl from Lorraine, sir. From Domrémy.

ROBERT. [*Rising in fearful wrath.*] Thirty thousand thunders! Fifty thousand devils! Do you mean to say that that girl, who had the impudence to ask to see me two days ago, and whom I told you to send back to her father with my orders that he was to give her a good hiding, is here still?

STEWARD. I have told her to go, sir. She wont.

ROBERT. I did not tell you to tell her to go: I told you to throw her out. You have fifty men-at-arms and a dozen lumps of able-bodied servants to carry out my orders. Are they afraid of her?

STEWARD. She is so positive, sir.

ROBERT. [*Seizing him by the scruff of the neck.*] Positive! Now see here. I am going to throw you downstairs.

STEWARD. No, sir. Please.

ROBERT. Well, stop me by being positive. It's quite easy: any slut of a girl can do it.

STEWARD. [*Hanging limp in his hands.*] Sir, sir: you cannot get rid of her by throwing me out. [*Robert has to let him drop. He squats on his knees on the floor, contemplating his master resignedly.*] You see, sir, you are much more positive than I am. But so is she.

ROBERT. I am stronger than you are, you fool.

STEWARD. No, sir: it isnt that: it's your strong character, sir. She is weaker than we are: she is only a slip of a girl; but we cannot make her go.

ROBERT. You parcel of curs: you are afraid of her.

STEWARD. [*Rising cautiously.*] No, sir: we are afraid of you; but she puts courage into us. She really doesnt seem to be afraid of anything. Perhaps you could frighten her, sir.

ROBERT. [*Grimly.*] Perhaps. Where is she now?

STEWARD. Down in the courtyard, sir, talking to the soldiers as usual. She is always talking to the soldiers except when she is praying.

ROBERT. Praying! Ha! You believe she prays, you idiot. I know the sort of girl that is always talking to soldiers. She shall talk to me a bit. [*He goes to the window and shouts fiercely through it.*] Hallo, you there!

A GIRL'S VOICE. [*Bright, strong and rough.*] Is it me, sir?

ROBERT. Yes, you.

THE VOICE. Be you captain?

ROBERT. Yes, damn your impudence, I be captain. Come up here. [*To the soldiers in the yard.*] Shew her the way, you. And shove her along quick.

[*He leaves the window, and returns to his place at the table, where he sits magisterially.*

STEWARD. [*Whispering.*] She wants to go and be a soldier herself. She wants you to give her soldier's clothes. Armor, sir! And a sword! Actually!   [*He steals behind Robert.*

[*Joan appears in the turret doorway. She is an able-bodied country girl of seventeen or eighteen, respectably dressed in red, with an uncommon face; eyes very wide apart and bulging as they often do in very imaginative people, a long, well-shaped nose with wide nostrils, a short upper lip, resolute but full-lipped mouth, and handsome fighting chin. She comes eagerly to the table, delighted at having penetrated to Baudricourt's presence at last, and full of hope as to the result. His scowl does not check or frighten her in the least.*

Her voice is normally a hearty coaxing voice, very confident, very appealing, very hard to resist.

JOAN. [*Bobbing a curtsey.*] Good morning, captain squire. Captain: you are to give me a horse and armor and some soldiers, and send me to the Dauphin. Those are your orders from my Lord.

ROBERT. [*Outraged.*] Orders from your lord! And who the devil may your lord be? Go back to him, and tell him that I am neither duke nor peer at his orders: I am squire of Baudricourt; and I take no orders except from the king.

JOAN. [*Reassuringly.*] Yes, squire: that is all right. My Lord is the King of Heaven.

ROBERT. Why, the girl's mad. [*To the steward.*] Why didnt you tell me so, you blockhead?

STEWARD. Sir: do not anger her: give her what she wants.

JOAN. [*Impatient, but friendly.*] They all say I am mad until I talk to them, squire. But you see that it is the will of God that you are to do what He has put into my mind.

ROBERT. It is the will of God that I shall send you back to your father with orders to put you under lock and key and thrash the madness out of you. What have you to say to that?

JOAN. You think you will, squire; but you will find it all coming quite different. You said you would not see me; but here I am.

STEWARD. [*Appealingly.*] Yes, sir. You see, sir.

ROBERT. Hold your tongue, you.

STEWARD. [*Abjectly.*] Yes, sir.

ROBERT. [*To Joan, with a sour loss of confidence.*] So you are presuming on my seeing you, are you?

JOAN. [*Sweetly.*] Yes, squire.

ROBERT. [*Feeling that he has lost ground, brings down his two fists squarely on the table, and inflates his chest imposingly to cure the unwelcome and only too familiar sensation.*] Now listen to me. I am going to assert myself.

JOAN. [*Busily.*] Please do, squire. The horse will cost sixteen francs. It is a good deal of money; but I can save it on the armor. I can find a soldier's armor that will fit me well enough: I am very hardy; and I do no need beautiful armor made to my measure like you wear. I shall not want many soldiers: the Dauphin will give me all I need to raise the siege of Orleans.

ROBERT. [*Flabbergasted.*] To raise the siege of Orleans!

JOAN. [*Simply.*] Yes, squire: that is what God is sending me to do. Three men will be enough for you to send with me if they are good men and gentle to me. They have promised to come with me. Polly and Jack and——

ROBERT. Polly!! You impudent baggage, do you dare call squire Bertrand de Poulengey Polly to my face?

JOAN. His friends call him so, squire: I did not know he had any other name. Jack——

ROBERT. That is Monsieur John of Metz, I suppose?

JOAN. Yes, squire. Jack will come willingly: he is a very kind gentleman, and gives me money to give to the poor. I think John Godsave will come, and Dick the Archer, and their servants John of Honecourt and Julian. There will be no trouble for you, squire: I have arranged it all: you have only to give the order.

ROBERT. [*Contemplating her in a stupor of amazement.*] Well, I am damned!

JOAN. [*With unruffled sweetness.*] No, squire: God is very merciful; and the blessed saints Catherine and Margaret, who speak to me every day [*he gapes*], will intercede for you. You will go to paradise; and your name will be remembered for ever as my first helper.

ROBERT. [*To the steward, still much bothered, but changing his tone as he pursues a new clue.*] Is this true about Monsieur de Poulengey?

STEWARD. [*Eagerly.*] Yes, sir, and about Monsieur de Metz too. They both want to go with her.

ROBERT. [*Thoughtfully.*] Mf! [*He goes to the window, and shouts into the courtyard.*] Hallo! You there: send Monsieur de Poulengey to me, will you? [*He turns to Joan.*] Get out; and wait in the yard.

JOAN. [*Smiling brightly at him.*] Right, squire.   [*She goes out.*

ROBERT. [*To the steward.*] Go with her, you dithering imbecile. Stay within call; and keep your eye on her. I shall have her up here again.

STEWARD. Do so in God's name, sir. Think of those hens, the best layers in Champagne; and——

ROBERT. Think of my boot; and take your backside out of reach of it.

[*The steward retreats hastily and finds himself confronted in the doorway by Bertrand de Poulengey, a lymphatic French gentleman-at-arms, aged thirty-six or thereabouts, employed in the department of the provost-marshal, dreamily absent-minded, seldom speaking unless spoken to, and then slow and obstinate in reply: altogether in contrast to the self-assertive, loud-mouthed, superficially energetic, fundamentally will-less Robert. The steward makes way for him, and vanishes.*

Poulengey salutes, and stands awaiting orders.

ROBERT. [*Genially.*] It isnt service, Polly. A friendly talk. Sit down.
          [*He hooks the stool from under the table with his instep.*
[*Poulengey, relaxing, comes into the room; places the stool between the table and the window; and sits down ruminatively. Robert, half sitting on the end of the table, begins the friendly talk.*

ROBERT. Now listen to me, Polly. I must talk to you like a father.
          [*Poulengey looks up at him gravely for a moment, but says nothing.*

ROBERT. It's about this girl you are interested in. Now, I have seen
her. I have talked to her. First, she's mad. That doesnt matter.
Second, she's not a farm wench. She's a bourgeoise. That matters
a good deal. I know her class exactly. Her father came here last
year to represent his village in a lawsuit: he is one of their
notables. A farmer. Not a gentleman farmer: he makes money by
it, and lives by it. Still, not a laborer. Not a mechanic. He might
have a cousin a lawyer, or in the Church. People of this sort may
be of no account socially; but they can give a lot of bother to
the authorities. That is to say, to me. Now, no doubt it seems
to you a very simple thing to take this girl away, humbugging
her into the belief that you are taking her to the Dauphin. But
if you get her into trouble, you may get me into no end of a
mess, as I am her father's lord, and responsible for her protection.
So friends or no friends, Polly, hands off her.

POULENGEY. [*With deliberate impressiveness.*] I should as soon think
of the Blessed Virgin herself in that way, as of this girl.

ROBERT. [*Coming off the table.*] But she says you and Jack and Dick
have offered to go with her. What for? You are not going to tell
me that you take her crazy notion of going to the Dauphin
seriously, are you?

POULENGEY. [*Slowly.*] There is something about her. They are
pretty foul-mouthed and foul-minded down there in the guard-
room, some of them. But there hasnt been a word that has anything to do with her being a woman. They have stopped swearing
before her. There is something. Something. It may be worth
trying.

ROBERT. Oh, come, Polly! Pull yourself together. Common sense
was never your strong point; but this is a little too much.
                                        [*He retreats disgustedly.*

POULENGEY. [*Unmoved.*] What is the good of common sense? If
we had any common sense we should join the Duke of Burgundy
and the English king. They hold half the country, right down to
the Loire. They have Paris. They have this castle: you know very
well that we had to surrender it to the Duke of Bedford, and that
you are holding it on parole. The Dauphin is in Chinon, like
a rat in a corner, except that he wont fight. We dont even know
that he is the Dauphin: his mother says he isnt; and she ought
to know. Think of that! The queen denying the legitimacy of
her own son!

ROBERT. Well, she married her daughter to the English king. Can
you blame the woman?

POULENGEY. I blame nobody. But thanks to her, the Dauphin is
down and out; and we may as well face it. The English will take
Orleans: the Bastard will not be able to stop them.

ROBERT. He beat the English the year before last at Montargis. I was with him.

POULENGEY. No matter: his men are cowed now; and he cant work miracles. And I tell you that nothing can save our side now but a miracle.

ROBERT. Miracles are all right, Polly. The only difficulty about them is that they dont happen nowadays.

POULENGEY. I used to think so. I am not so sure now. [*Rising, and moving ruminatively towards the window.*] At all events this is not a time to leave any stone unturned. There is something about the girl.

ROBERT. Oh! You think the girl can work miracles, do you?

POULENGEY. I think the girl herself is a bit of a miracle. Anyhow, she is the last card left in our hand. Better play her than throw up the game.   [*He wanders to the turret.*

ROBERT. [*Wavering.*] You really think that?

POULENGEY. [*Turning.*] Is there anything else left for us to think?

ROBERT. [*Going to him.*] Look here, Polly. If you were in my place would you let a girl like that do you out of sixteen francs for a horse?

POULENGEY. I will pay for the horse.

ROBERT. You will!

POULENGEY. Yes: I will back my opinion.

ROBERT. You will really gamble on a forlorn hope to the tune of sixteen francs?

POULENGEY. It is not a gamble.

ROBERT. What else is it?

POULENGEY. It is a certainty. Her words and her ardent faith in God have put fire into me.

ROBERT. [*Giving him up.*] Whew! You are as mad as she is.

POULENGEY. [*Obstinately.*] We want a few mad people now. See where the sane ones have landed us!

ROBERT. [*His irresoluteness now openly swamping his affected decisiveness.*] I shall feel like a precious fool. Still, if you feel sure——?

POULENGEY. I feel sure enough to take her to Chinon—unless you stop me.

ROBERT. This is not fair. You are putting the responsibility on me.

POULENGEY. It is on you whichever way you decide.

ROBERT. Yes: thats just it. Which way am I to decide? You dont see how awkward this is for me. [*Snatching at a dilatory step with an unconscious hope that Joan will make up his mind for him.*] Do you think I ought to have another talk to her?

POULGENEY. [*Rising.*] Yes. [*He goes to the window and calls.*] Joan!

JOAN'S VOICE. Will he let us go, Polly?

POULENGEY. Come up. Come in. [*Turning to Robert.*] Shall I leave you with her?

ROBERT. No: stay here; and back me up.

[*Poulengey sits down on the chest. Robert goes back to his magisterial chair, but remains standing to inflate himself more imposingly. Joan comes in, full of good news.*]

JOAN. Jack will go halves for the horse.

ROBERT. Well!!   [*He sits, deflated.*]

POULENGEY. [*Gravely.*] Sit down, Joan.

JOAN. [*Checked a little, and looking to Robert.*] May I?

ROBERT. Do what you are told.

[*Joan curtsies and sits down on the stool between them. Robert outfaces his perplexity with his most peremptory air.*]

ROBERT. What is your name?

JOAN. [*Chattily.*] They always call me Jenny in Lorraine. Here in France I am Joan. The soldiers call me The Maid.

ROBERT. What is your surname?

JOAN. Surname? What is that? My father sometimes calls himself d'Arc; but I know nothing about it. You met my father. He——

ROBERT. Yes, yes: I remember. You come from Domrémy in Lorraine, I think.

JOAN. Yes; but what does it matter? We all speak French.

ROBERT. Dont ask questions: answer them. How old are you?

JOAN. Seventeen: so they tell me. It might be nineteen. I dont remember.

ROBERT. What did you mean when you said that St Catherine and St Margaret talked to you every day?

JOAN. They do.

ROBERT. What are they like?

JOAN. [*Suddenly obstinate.*] I will tell you nothing about that: they have not given me leave.

ROBERT. But you actually see them; and they talk to you just as I am talking to you?

JOAN. No: it is quite different. I cannot tell you: you must not talk to me about my voices.

ROBERT. How do you mean—voices?

JOAN. I hear voices telling me what to do. They come from God.

ROBERT. They come from your imagination.

JOAN. Of course. That is how the messages of God come to us.

POULENGEY. Checkmate.

ROBERT. No fear! [*To Joan.*] So God says you are to raise the siege of Orleans?

JOAN. And to crown the Dauphin in Rheims Cathedral.

ROBERT. [*Gasping.*] Crown the D——! Gosh!

JOAN. And to make the English leave France.

ROBERT. [*Sarcastic.*] Anything else?

JOAN. [*Charming.*] Not just at present, thank you, squire.

ROBERT. I suppose you think raising a siege is as easy as chasing a cow out of a meadow. You think soldiering is anybody's job?

JOAN. I do not think it can be very difficult if God is on your side, and you are willing to put your life in His hand. But many soldiers are very simple.

ROBERT. [*Grimly.*] Simple! Did you ever see English soldiers fighting?

JOAN. They are only men. God made them just like us; but He gave them their own country and their own language; and it is not His will that they should come into our country and try to speak our language.

ROBERT. Who has been putting such nonsense into your head? Dont you know that soldiers are subject to their feudal lord, and that it is nothing to them or to you whether he is the duke of Burgundy or the king of England or the king of France? What has their language to do with it?

JOAN. I do not understand that a bit. We are all subject to the King of Heaven; and He gave us our countries and our languages, and meant us to keep to them. If it were not so it would be murder to kill an Englishman in battle; and you, squire, would be in great danger of hell fire. You must not think about your duty to your feudal lord, but about your duty to God.

POULENGEY. It's no use, Robert: she can choke you like that every time.

ROBERT. Can she, by Saint Dennis! We shall see. [*To Joan.*] We are not talking about God: we are talking about practical affairs. I ask you again, girl, have you ever seen English soldiers fighting? Have you ever seen them plundering, burning, turning the countryside into a desert? Have you heard no tales of their Black Prince who was blacker than the devil himself, or of the English king's father?

JOAN. You must not be afraid, Robert——

ROBERT. Damn you, I am not afraid. And who gave you leave to call me Robert?

JOAN. You were called so in church in the name of our Lord. All the other names are your father's or your brother's or anybody's.

ROBERT. Tcha!

JOAN. Listen to me, squire. At Domrémy we had to fly to the next village to escape from the English soldiers. Three of them were left behind, wounded. I came to know these three poor goddams quite well. They had not half my strength.

ROBERT. Do you know why they are called goddams?

JOAN. No. Everyone calls them goddams.

ROBERT. It is because they are always calling on their God to
condemn their souls to perdition. That is what goddam means in
their language. How do you like it?

JOAN. God will be merciful to them; and they will act like His
good children when they go back to the country He made for
them, and made them for. I have heard the tales of the Black
Prince. The moment he touched the soil of our country the devil
entered into him and made him a black fiend. But at home, in the
place made for him by God, he was good. It is always so. If I
went into England against the will of God to conquer England,
and tried to live there and speak its language, the devil would
enter into me; and when I was old I should shudder to remember
the wickednesses I did.

ROBERT. Perhaps. But the more devil you were the better you
might fight. That is why the goddams will take Orleans. And
you cannot stop them, nor ten thousand like you.

JOAN. One thousand like me can stop them. Ten like me can stop
them with God on our side. [She rises impetuously, and goes at him,
unable to sit quiet any longer.] You do not understand, squire. Our
soldiers are always beaten because they are fighting only to save
their skins; and the shortest way to save your skin is to run
away. Our knights are thinking only of the money they will make
in ransoms: it is not kill or be killed with them, but pay or be
paid. But I will teach them all to fight that the will of God may
be done in France; and then they will drive the poor goddams
before them like sheep. You and Polly will live to see the day
when there will not be an English soldier on the soil of France;
and there will be but one king there: not the feudal English
king, but God's French one.

ROBERT. [To Poulengey.] This may be all rot, Polly; but the troops
might swallow it, though nothing that we can say seems able
to put any fight into them. Even the Dauphin might swallow it.
And if she can put fight into him, she can put it into anybody.

POULENGEY. I can see no harm in trying. Can you? And there is
something about the girl——

ROBERT. [Turning to Joan.] Now listen you to me; and [desperately]
dont cut in before I have time to think.

JOAN. [Plumping down on the stool again, like an obedient schoolgirl.]
Yes, squire.

ROBERT. Your orders are, that you are to go to Chinon under the
escort of this gentleman and three of his friends.

JOAN. [Radiant, clasping her hands.] Oh, squire! Your head is all
circled with light, like a saint's.

POULENGEY. How is she to get into the royal presence?

ROBERT. [Who has looked up for his halo rather apprehensively.] I dont know: how did she get into my presence? If the Dauphin can keep her out he is a better man than I take him for. [*Rising.*] I will send her to Chinon; and she can say I sent her. Then let come what may: I can do no more.

JOAN. And the dress? I may have a soldier's dress, maynt I, squire?

ROBERT. Have what you please. I wash my hands of it.

JOAN. [*Wildly excited by her success.*] Come, Polly.

[*She dashes out.*

ROBERT. [*Shaking Poulengey's hand.*] Goodbye, old man, I am taking a big chance. Few other men would have done it. But as you say, there is something about her.

POULENGEY. Yes: there is something about her. Goodbye.

[*He goes out.*

[*Robert, still very doubtful whether he has not been made a fool of by a crazy female, and a social inferior to boot, scratches his head and slowly comes back from the door.*

The steward runs in with a basket.

STEWARD. Sir, sir——

ROBERT. What now?

STEWARD. The hens are laying like mad, sir. Five dozen eggs!

ROBERT. [*Stiffens convulsively; crosses himself; and forms with his pale lips the words*] Christ in heaven! [*Aloud but breathless.*] She did come from God.

Chinon, in Touraine. An end of the throne room in the castle, curtained off to make an antechamber. The Archbishop of Rheims, close on fifty, a full-fed political prelate with nothing of the ecclesiastic about him except his imposing bearing, and the Lord Chamberlain, Monseigneur de la Trémouille, a monstrous arrogant wineskin of a man, are waiting for the Dauphin. There is a door in the wall to the right of the two men. It is late in the afternoon on the 8th of March, 1429. The Archbishop stands with dignity whilst the Chamberlain, on his left, fumes about in the worst of tempers.

LA TRÉMOUILLE. What the devil does the Dauphin mean by keeping us waiting like this? I dont know how you have the patience to stand there like a stone idol.

THE ARCHBISHOP. You see, I am an archbishop; and an archbishop is a sort of idol. At any rate he has to learn to keep still and suffer fools patiently. Besides, my dear Lord Chamberlain, it is the Dauphin's royal privilege to keep you waiting, is it not?

LA TRÉMOUILLE. Dauphin be damned! saving your reverence. Do you know how much money he owes me?

THE ARCHBISHOP. Much more than he owes me, I have no doubt, because you are a much richer man. But I take it he owes you all you can afford to lend him. That is what he owes me.

LA TRÉMOUILLE. Twenty-seven thousand: that was his last haul. A cool twenty-seven thousand!

THE ARCHBISHOP. What becomes of it all? He never has a suit of clothes that I would throw to a curate.

LA TRÉMOUILLE. He dines on a chicken or a scrap of mutton. He borrows my last penny; and there is nothing to shew for it. [*A page appears in the doorway.*] At last!

THE PAGE. No, my lord: it is not His Majesty. Monsieur de Rais is approaching.

LA TRÉMOUILLE. Young Bluebeard! Why announce him?

THE PAGE. Captain La Hire is with him. Something has happened, I think.

[Gilles de Rais, a young man of twenty-five, very smart and self-possessed, and sporting the extravagance of a little curled beard dyed blue at a clean-shaven court, comes in. He is determined to make himself agreeable, but lacks natural joyousness, and is not

156

really pleasant. In fact when he defies the Church some eleven years later he is accused of trying to extract pleasure from horrible cruelties, and hanged. So far, however, there is no shadow of the gallows on him. He advances gaily to the Archbishop. The page withdraws.

BLUEBEARD. Your faithful lamb, Archbishop. Good day, my lord. Do you know what has happened to La Hire?

LA TRÉMOUILLE. He has sworn himself into a fit, perhaps.

BLUEBEARD. No: just the opposite. Foul Mouthed Frank, the only man in Touraine who could beat him at swearing, was told by a soldier that he shouldnt use such language when he was at the point of death.

THE ARCHBISHOP. Nor at any other point. But was Foul Mouthed Frank on the point of death?

BLUEBEARD. Yes: he has just fallen into a well and been drowned. La Hire is frightened out of his wits.

[*Captain La Hire comes in; a war dog with no court manners and pronounced camp ones.*

BLUEBEARD. I have just been telling the Chamberlain and the Archbishop. The Archbishop says you are a lost man.

LA HIRE. [*Striding past Bluebeard, and planting himself between the Archbishop and La Trémouille.*] This is nothing to joke about. It is worse than we thought. It was not a soldier, but an angel dressed as a soldier.

THE ARCHBISHOP. ⎫
THE CHAMBERLAIN. ⎬ [*Exclaiming all together.*] An angel!
BLUEBEARD.   ⎭

LA HIRE. Yes, an angel. She has made her way from Champagne with half a dozen men through the thick of everything: Burgundians, goddams, deserters, robbers, and Lord knows who; and they never met a soul except the country folk. I know one of them: de Poulengey. He says she's an angel. If ever I utter an oath again may my soul be blasted to eternal damnation!

THE ARCHBISHOP. A very pious beginning, Captain.

[*Bluebeard and La Trémouille laugh at him. The page returns.*

THE PAGE. His Majesty.

[*They stand perfunctorily at court attention. The Dauphin, aged twenty-six, really King Charles the Seventh since the death of his father, but as yet uncrowned, comes in through the curtains with a paper in his hands. He is a poor creature physically; and the current fashion of shaving closely, and hiding every scrap of hair under the head-covering or headdress, both by women and men, makes the worst of his appearance. He has little narrow eyes, near together, a long pendulous nose that droops over his thick short upper lip, and the expression of a young dog accustomed to be kicked, yet incorrigible*

*and irrepressible. But he is neither vulgar nor stupid; and he has a
cheeky humor which enables him to hold his own in conversation.
Just at present he is excited, like a child with a new toy. He comes
to the Archbishop's left hand. Bluebeard and La Hire retire
towards the curtains.*

CHARLES. Oh, Archbishop, do you know what Robert de Baudricourt is sending me from Vaucouleurs?

THE ARCHBISHOP. [*Contemptuously.*] I am not interested in the
newest toys.

CHARLES. [*Indignantly.*] It isnt a toy. [*Sulkily.*] However, I can get
on very well without your interest.

THE ARCHBISHOP. Your Highness is taking offence very un-
necessarily.

CHARLES. Thank you. You are always ready with a lecture, arnt you?

LA TRÉMOUILLE. [*Roughly.*] Enough grumbling. What have you
got there?

CHARLES. What is that to you?

LA TRÉMOUILLE. It is my business to know what is passing between
you and the garrison at Vaucouleurs.

[*He snatches the paper from the Dauphin's hand, and begins reading
it with some difficulty, following the words with his finger and
spelling them out syllable by syllable.*

CHARLES. [*Mortified.*] You all think you can treat me as you please
because I owe you money, and because I am no good at fighting.
But I have the blood royal in my veins.

THE ARCHBISHOP. Even that has been questioned, your Highness.
One hardly recognizes in you the grandson of Charles the Wise.

CHARLES. I want to hear no more of my grandfather. He was so
wise that he used up the whole family stock of wisdom for five
generations, and left me the poor fool I am, bullied and insulted
by all of you.

THE ARCHBISHOP. Control yourself, sir. These outbursts of petu-
lance are not seemly.

CHARLES. Another lecture! Thank you. What a pity it is that
though you are an archbishop saints and angels dont come to
see you!

THE ARCHBISHOP. What do you mean?

CHARLES. Aha! Ask that bully there.   [*Pointing to La Trémouille.*

LA TRÉMOUILLE. [*Furious.*] Hold your tongue. Do you hear?

CHARLES. Oh, I hear. You neednt shout. The whole castle can
hear. Why dont you go and shout at the English, and beat them
for me?

LA TRÉMOUILLE. [*Raising his fist.*] You young——

CHARLES. [*Running behind the Archbishop.*] Dont you raise your hand
to me. It's high treason.

LA HIRE. Steady, Duke! Steady!

THE ARCHBISHOP. [*Resolutely.*] Come, come! this will not do. My Lord Chamberlain: please! please! we must keep some sort of order. [*To the Dauphin.*] And you, sir: if you cannot rule your kingdom, at least try to rule yourself.

CHARLES. Another lecture! Thank you.

LA TRÉMOUILLE. [*Handing the paper to the Archbishop.*] Here: read the accursed thing for me. He has sent the blood boiling into my head: I cant distinguish the letters.

CHARLES. [*Coming back and peering round La Trémouille's left shoulder.*] I will read it for you if you like. I can read, you know.

LA TRÉMOUILLE. [*With intense contempt, not at all stung by the taunt.*] Yes: reading is about all you are fit for. Can you make it out, Archbishop?

THE ARCHBISHOP. I should have expected more commonsense from De Baudricourt. He is sending some cracked country lass here——

CHARLES. [*Interrupting.*] No: he is sending a saint: an angel. And she is coming to me: to me, the king, and not to you, Archbishop, holy as you are. She knows the blood royal if you dont.

    [*He struts up to the curtains between Bluebeard and La Hire.*

THE ARCHBISHOP. You cannot be allowed to see this crazy wench.

CHARLES. [*Turning.*] But I am the king; and I will.

LA TRÉMOUILLE. [*Brutally.*] Then she cannot be allowed to see you. Now!

CHARLES. I tell you I will. I am going to put my foot down——

BLUEBEARD. [*Laughing at him.*] Naughty! What would your wise grandfather say?

CHARLES. That just shews your ignorance, Bluebeard. My grandfather had a saint who used to float in the air when she was praying, and told him everything he wanted to know. My poor father had two saints, Marie de Maillé and the Gasque of Avignon. It is in our family; and I dont care what you say: I will have my saint too.

THE ARCHBISHOP. This creature is not a saint. She is not even a respectable woman. She does not wear women's clothes. She is dressed like a soldier, and rides round the country with soldiers. Do you suppose such a person can be admitted to your Highness's court?

LA HIRE. Stop. [*Going to the Archbishop.*] Did you say a girl in armor, like a soldier?

THE ARCHBISHOP. So De Baudricourt describes her.

LA HIRE. But by all the devils of hell—Oh, God forgive me, what am I saying?—by Our Lady and all the saints, this must be the angel that struck Foul Mouthed Frank dead for swearing.

CHARLES. [*Triumphant.*] You see! A miracle!

LA HIRE. She may strike the lot of us dead if we cross her. For Heaven's sake, Archbishop, be careful what you are doing.

THE ARCHBISHOP. [*Severely.*] Rubbish! Nobody has been struck dead. A drunken blackguard who has been rebuked a hundred times for swearing has fallen into a well, and been drowned. A mere coincidence.

LA HIRE. I do not know what a coincidence is. I do know that the man is dead, and that she told him he was going to die.

THE ARCHBISHOP. We are all going to die, Captain.

LA HIRE. [*Crossing himself.*] I hope not.

[*He backs out of the conversation.*

BLUEBEARD. We can easily find out whether she is an angel or not. Let us arrange when she comes that I shall be the Dauphin, and see whether she will find me out.

CHARLES. Yes: I agree to that. If she cannot find the blood royal I will have nothing to do with her.

THE ARCHBISHOP. It is for the Church to make saints: let De Baudricourt mind his own business, and not dare usurp the function of his priest. I say the girl shall not be admitted.

BLUEBEARD. But, Archbishop——

THE ARCHBISHOP. [*Sternly.*] I speak in the Church's name. [*To the Dauphin.*] Do you dare say she shall?

CHARLES. [*Intimidated but sulky.*] Oh, if you make it an excommunication matter, I have nothing more to say, of course. But you havnt read the end of the letter. De Baudricourt says she will raise the siege of Orleans, and beat the English for us.

LA TRÉMOUILLE. Rot!

CHARLES. Well, will you save Orleans for us, with all your bullying?

LA TRÉMOUILLE. [*Savagely.*] Do not throw that in my face again: do you hear? I have done more fighting than you ever did or ever will. But I cannot be everywhere.

THE DAUPHIN. Well, thats something.

BLUEBEARD. [*Coming between the Archbishop and Charles.*] You have Jack Dunois at the head of your troops in Orleans: the brave Dunois, the handsome Dunois, the wonderful invincible Dunois, the darling of all the ladies, the beautiful bastard. Is it likely that the country lass can do what he cannot do?

CHARLES. Why doesn't he raise the siege, then?

LA HIRE. The wind is against him.

BLUEBEARD. How can the wind hurt him at Orleans? It is not on the Channel.

LA HIRE. It is on the River Loire; and the English hold the bridgehead. He must ship his men across the river and upstream, if he is to take them in the rear. Well, he cannot, because there is

a devil of a wind blowing the other way. He is tired of paying
the priests to pray for a west wind. What he needs is a miracle.
You tell me that what the girl did to Foul Mouthed Frank was
no miracle. No matter: it finished Frank. If she changes the wind
for Dunois, that may not be a miracle either; but it may finish the
English. What harm is there in trying?

THE ARCHBISHOP. [*Who has read the end of the letter and become more
thoughtful.*] It is true that De Baudricourt seems extraordinarily
impressed.

LA HIRE. De Baudricourt is a blazing ass; but he is a soldier; and
if he thinks she can beat the English, all the rest of the army
will think so too.

LA TRÉMOUILLE. [*To the Archbishop, who is hesitating.*] Oh, let
them have their way. Dunois' men will give up the town in
spite of him if somebody does not put some fresh spunk into
them.

THE ARCHBISHOP. The Church must examine the girl before anything decisive is done about her. However, since his Highness
desires it, let her attend the Court.

LA HIRE. I will find her and tell her.   [*He goes out.*

CHARLES. Come with me, Bluebeard; and let us arrange so that
she will not know who I am. You will pretend to be me.

[*He goes out through the curtains.*

BLUEBEARD. Pretend to be that thing! Holy Michael!

[*He follows the Dauphin.*

LA TRÉMOUILLE. I wonder will she pick him out!

THE ARCHBISHOP. Of course she will.

LA TRÉMOUILLE. Why? How is she to know?

THE ARCHBISHOP. She will know what everybody in Chinon
knows: that the Dauphin is the meanest-looking and worst-
dressed figure in the Court, and that the man with the blue
beard is Gilles de Rais.

LA TRÉMOUILLE. I never thought of that.

THE ARCHBISHOP. You are not so accustomed to miracles as I am.
It is part of my profession.

LA TRÉMOUILLE. [*Puzzled and a little scandalized.*] But that would not
be a miracle at all.

THE ARCHBISHOP. [*Calmly.*] Why not?

LA TRÉMOUILLE. Well, come! what is a miracle?

THE ARCHBISHOP. A miracle, my friend, is an event which creates
faith. That is the purpose and nature of miracles. They may seem
very wonderful to the people who witness them, and very simple
to those who perform them. That does not matter: if they con-
firm or create faith they are true miracles.

LA TRÉMOUILLE. Even when they are frauds, do you mean?

THE ARCHBISHOP. Frauds deceive. An event which creates faith does not deceive: therefore it is not a fraud, but a miracle.

LA TRÉMOUILLE. [*Scratching his neck in his perplexity.*] Well, I suppose as you are an archbishop you must be right. It seems a bit fishy to me. But I am no churchman, and dont understand these matters.

THE ARCHBISHOP. You are not a churchman; but you are a diplomatist and a soldier. Could you make our citizens pay war taxes, or our soldiers sacrifice their lives, if they knew what is really happening instead of what seems to them to be happening?

LA TRÉMOUILLE. No, by Saint Dennis: the fat would be in the fire before sundown.

THE ARCHBISHOP. Would it not be quite easy to tell them the truth?

LA TRÉMOUILLE. Man alive, they wouldnt believe it.

THE ARCHBISHOP. Just so. Well, the Church has to rule men for the good of their souls as you have to rule them for the good of their bodies. To do that, the Church must do as you do: nourish their faith by poetry.

LA TRÉMOUILLE. Poetry! I should call it humbug.

THE ARCHBISHOP. You would be wrong, my friend. Parables are not lies because they describe events that have never happened. Miracles are not frauds because they are often—I do not say always—very simple and innocent contrivances by which the priest fortifies the faith of his flock. When this girl picks out the Dauphin among his courtiers, it will not be a miracle for me, because I shall know how it has been done, and my faith will not be increased. But as for the others, if they feel the thrill of the supernatural, and forget their sinful clay in a sudden sense of the glory of God, it will be a miracle and a blessed one. And you will find that the girl herself will be more affected than anyone else. She will forget how she really picked him out. So, perhaps, will you.

LA TRÉMOUILLE. Well, I wish I were clever enough to know how much of you is God's archbishop and how much the most artful fox in Touraine. Come on, or we shall be late for the fun; and I want to see it, miracle or no miracle.

THE ARCHBISHOP. [*Detaining him a moment.*] Do not think that I am a lover of crooked ways. There is a new spirit rising in men: we are at the dawning of a wider epoch. If I were a simple monk, and had not to rule men, I should seek peace for my spirit with Aristotle and Pythagoras rather than with the saints and their miracles.

LA TRÉMOUILLE. And who the deuce was Pythagoras?

THE ARCHBISHOP. A sage who held that the earth is round, and that it moves round the sun.

LA TRÉMOUILLE. What an utter fool! Couldnt he use his eyes?

[*They go out together through the curtains, which are presently with-drawn, revealing the full depth of the throne room with the Court assembled. On the right are two Chairs of State on a dais. Bluebeard is standing theatrically on the dais, playing the king, and, like the courtiers, enjoying the joke rather obviously. There is a curtained arch in the wall behind the dais; but the main door, guarded by men-at-arms, is at the other side of the room; and a clear path across is kept and lined by the courtiers. Charles is in this path in the middle of the room. La Hire is on his right. The Archbishop, on his left, has taken his place by the dais; La Trémouille at the other side of it. The Duchess de la Trémouille, pretending to be the Queen, sits in the Consort's chair, with a group of ladies in waiting close by, behind the Archbishop.*

The chatter of the courtiers makes such a noise that nobody notices the appearance of the page at the door.]

THE PAGE. The Duke of—— [*Nobody listens.*] The Duke of——

[*The chatter continues. Indignant at his failure to command a hearing, he snatches the halberd of the nearest man-at-arms, and thumps the floor with it. The chatter ceases; and everybody looks at him in silence.*] Attention! [*He restores the halberd to the man-at-arms.*] The Duke of Vendôme presents Joan the Maid to his Majesty.

CHARLES. [*Putting his finger on his lip.*] Ssh!

[*He hides behind the nearest courtier, peering out to see what happens.*]

BLUEBEARD. [*Majestically.*] Let her approach the throne.

[*Joan, dressed as a soldier, with her hair bobbed and hanging thickly round her face, is led in by a bashful and speechless nobleman, from whom she detaches herself to stop and look round eagerly for the Dauphin.*]

THE DUCHESS. [*To the nearest lady in waiting.*] My dear! Her hair!

[*All the ladies explode in uncontrollable laughter.*]

BLUEBEARD. [*Trying not to laugh, and waving his hand in deprecation of their merriment.*] Ssh—ssh! Ladies! Ladies!!

JOAN. [*Not at all embarrassed.*] I wear it like this because I am a soldier. Where be Dauphin?

[*A titter runs through the Court as she walks to the dais.*]

BLUEBEARD. [*Condescendingly.*] You are in the presence of the Dauphin.

[*Joan looks at him sceptically for a moment, scanning him hard up and down to make sure. Dead silence, all watching her. Fun dawns in her face.*]

JOAN. Coom, Bluebeard! Thou canst not fool me. Where be Dauphin?

[*A roar of laughter breaks out as Gilles, with a gesture of surrender, joins in the laugh, and jumps down from the dais beside La*

Trémouille. Joan, also on the broad grin, turns back, searching along the row of courtiers, and presently makes a dive, and drags out Charles by the arm.

JOAN. [*Releasing him and bobbing him a little curtsy.*] Gentle little Dauphin, I am sent to you to drive the English away from Orleans and from France, and to crown you king in the cathedral at Rheims, where all true kings of France are crowned.

CHARLES. [*Triumphant, to the Court.*] You see, all of you: she knew the blood royal. Who dare say now that I am not my father's son? [*To Joan.*] But if you want me to be crowned at Rheims you must talk to the Archbishop, not to me. There he is!

[*He is standing behind her.*

JOAN. [*Turning quickly, overwhelmed with emotion.*] Oh, my lord! [*She falls on both knees before him, with bowed head, not daring to look up.*] My lord: I am only a poor country girl; and you are filled with the blessedness and glory of God Himself; but you will touch me with your hands, and give me your blessing, wont you?

BLUEBEARD. [*Whispering to La Trémouille.*] The old fox blushes.

LA TRÉMOUILLE. Another miracle!

THE ARCHBISHOP. [*Touched, putting his hand on her head.*] Child: you are in love with religion.

JOAN. [*Startled; looking up at him.*] Am I? I never thought of that. Is there any harm in it?

THE ARCHBISHOP. There is no harm in it, my child. But there is danger.

JOAN. [*Rising, with a sunflush of reckless happiness irradiating her face.*] There is always danger, except in heaven. Oh, my lord, you have given me such strength, such courage. It must be a most wonderful thing to be Archbishop.

[*The Court smiles broadly; even titters a little.*

THE ARCHBISHOP. [*Drawing himself up sensitively.*] Gentlemen: your levity is rebuked by this maid's faith. I am, God help me, all unworthy; but your mirth is a deadly sin.

[*Their faces fall. Dead silence.*

BLUEBEARD. My lord, we were laughing at her, not at you.

THE ARCHBISHOP. What? Not at my unworthiness but at her faith! Gilles de Rais: this maid prophesied that the blasphemer should be drowned in his sin——

JOAN. [*Distressed.*] No!

THE ARCHBISHOP. [*Silencing her by a gesture.*] I prophesy now that you will be hanged in yours if you do not learn when to laugh and when to pray.

BLUEBEARD. My lord: I stand rebuked. I am sorry: I can say no more. But if you prophesy that I shall be hanged, I shall never

be able to resist temptation, because I shall always be telling myself that I may as well be hanged for a sheep as a lamb.

   [*The courtiers take heart at this. There is more tittering.*

JOAN. [*Scandalized.*] You are an idle fellow, Bluebeard; and you
 have great impudence to answer the Archbishop.

LA HIRE. [*With a huge chuckle.*] Well said, lass! Well said!

JOAN. [*Impatiently to the Archbishop.*] Oh, my lord, will you send
 all these silly folks away so that I may speak to the Dauphin
 alone?

LA HIRE. [*Goodhumoredly.*] I can take a hint.

   [*He salutes; turns on his heel; and goes out.*

THE ARCHBISHOP. Come, gentlemen. The maid comes with God's
 blessing, and must be obeyed.

  [*The courtiers withdraw, some through the arch, others at the opposite
 side. The Archbishop marches across to the door, followed by the
 Duchess and La Trémouille. As the Archbishop passes Joan, she
 falls on her knees, and kisses the hem of his robe fervently. He
 shakes his head in instinctive remonstrance; gathers the robe from
 her; and goes out. She is left kneeling directly in the Duchess's way.*

THE DUCHESS. [*Coldly.*] Will you allow me to pass, please?

JOAN. [*Hastily rising, and standing back.*] Beg pardon, maam, I am sure.

  [*The Duchess passes on. Joan stares after her; then whispers to the
 Dauphin.*

JOAN. Be that Queen?

CHARLES. No. She thinks she is.

JOAN. [*Again staring after the Duchess.*] Oo-oo-ooh!

  [*Her awestruck amazement at the figure cut by the magnificently
 dressed lady is not wholly complimentary.*

LA TRÉMOUILLE. [*Very surly.*] I'll trouble your Highness not to
 gibe at my wife.   [*He goes out. The others have already gone.*

JOAN. [*To the Dauphin.*] Who be old Gruff-and-Grum?

CHARLES. He is the Duke de la Trémouille.

JOAN. What be his job?

CHARLES. He pretends to command the army. And whenever I
 find a friend I can care for, he kills him.

JOAN. Why dost let him?

CHARLES. [*Petulantly moving to the throne side of the room to escape
 from her magnetic field.*] How can I prevent him? He bullies me.
 They all bully me.

JOAN. Art afraid?

CHARLES. Yes: I am afraid. It's no use preaching to me about it.
 It's all very well for these big men with their armor that is too
 heavy for me, and their swords that I can hardly lift, and their
 muscle and their shouting and their bad tempers. They like fighting: most of them are making fools of themselves all the time

they are not fighting; but I am quiet and sensible; and I dont
want to kill people: I only want to be left alone to enjoy myself
in my own way. I never asked to be a king: it was pushed on me.
So if you are going to say, 'Son of St Louis: gird on the sword
of your ancestors, and lead us to victory', you may spare your
breath to cool your porridge; for I cannot do it. I am not built
that way; and there is an end of it.

JOAN. [*Trenchant and masterful.*] Blethers! We are all like that to
begin with. I shall put courage into thee.

CHARLES. But I dont want to have courage put into me. I want
to sleep in a comfortable bed, and not live in continual terror of
being killed or wounded. Put courage into the others, and let
them have their bellyful of fighting; but let me alone.

JOAN. It's no use, Charlie: thou must face what God puts on thee.
If thou fail to make thyself king, thoult be a beggar: what else
art fit for? Come! Let me see thee sitting on the throne. I have
looked forward to that.

CHARLES. What is the good of sitting on the throne when the
other fellows give all the orders? However! [*He sits enthroned, a
piteous figure.*] Here is the king for you! Look your fill at the poor
devil.

JOAN. Thourt not king yet, lad: thourt but Dauphin. Be not led
away by them around thee. Dressing up dont fill empty noddle.
I know the people: the real people that make thy bread for thee;
and I tell thee they count no man king of France until the holy
oil has been poured on his hair, and himself consecrated and
crowned in Rheims Cathedral. And thou needs new clothes,
Charlie. Why does not Queen look after thee properly?

CHARLES. We're too poor. She wants all the money we can spare
to put on her own back. Besides, I like to see her beautifully
dressed; and I dont care what I wear myself: I should look ugly
anyhow.

JOAN. There is some good in thee, Charlie; but it is not yet a
king's good.

CHARLES. We shall see. I am not such a fool as I look. I have my
eyes open; and I can tell you that one good treaty is worth ten
good fights. These fighting fellows lose all on the treaties that
they gain on the fights. If we can only have a treaty, the English
are sure to have the worst of it, because they are better at fighting
than at thinking.

JOAN. If the English win, it is they that will make the treaty; and
then God help poor France! Thou must fight, Charlie, whether
thou will or no. I will go first to hearten thee. We must take our
courage in both hands: aye, and pray for it with both hands too.

CHARLES. [*Descending from his throne and again crossing the room to escape from her dominating urgency.*] Oh, do stop talking about God and praying. I cant bear people who are always praying. Isnt it bad enough to have to do it at the proper times?

JOAN. [*Pitying him.*] Thou poor child, thou hast never prayed in thy life. I must teach thee from the beginning.

CHARLES. I am not a child: I am a grown man and a father; and I will not be taught any more.

JOAN. Aye, you have a little son. He that will be Louis the Eleventh when you die. Would you not fight for him?

CHARLES. No: a horrid boy. He hates me. He hates everybody, selfish little beast! I dont want to be bothered with children. I dont want to be a father; and I dont want to be a son: especially a son of St Louis. I don't want to be any of these fine things you all have your heads full of: I want to be just what I am. Why cant you mind your own business, and let me mind mine?

JOAN. [*Again contemptuous.*] Minding your own business is like minding your own body: it's the shortest way to make yourself sick. What is my business? Helping mother at home. What is thine? Petting lapdogs and sucking sugar-sticks. I call that muck. I tell thee it is God's business we are here to do: not our own. I have a message to thee from God; and thou must listen to it, though thy heart break with the terror of it.

CHARLES. I dont want a message; but can you tell me any secrets? Can you do any cures? Can you turn lead into gold, or anything of that sort?

JOAN. I can turn thee into a king, in Rheims Cathedral; and that is a miracle that will take some doing, it seems.

CHARLES. If we go to Rheims, and have a coronation, Anne will want new dresses. We cant afford them. I am all right as I am.

JOAN. As you are! And what is that? Less than my father's poorest shepherd. Thourt not lawful owner of thy own land of France till thou be consecrated.

CHARLES. But I shall not be lawful owner of my own land anyhow. Will the consecration pay off my mortgages? I have pledged my last acre to the Archbishop and that fat bully. I owe money even to Bluebeard.

JOAN. [*Earnestly.*] Charlie: I come from the land, and have gotten my strength working on the land; and I tell thee that the land is thine to rule righteously and keep God's peace in, and not to pledge at the pawnshop as a drunken woman pledges her children's clothes. And I come from God to tell thee to kneel in the cathedral and solemnly give thy kingdom to Him for ever and ever, and become the greatest king in the world as His steward and His bailiff, His soldier and His servant. The very clay of France will become holy: her soldiers will be the soldiers of God:

the rebel dukes will be rebels against God: the English will fall
on their knees and beg thee let them return to their lawful homes
in peace. Wilt be a poor little Judas, and betray me and Him that
sent me?

CHARLES. [*Tempted at last.*] Oh, if I only dare!

JOAN. I shall dare, dare, and dare again, in God's name! Art for
or against me?

CHARLES. [*Excited.*] I'll risk it, I warn you I shant be able to keep
it up; but I'll risk it. You shall see. [*Running to the main door and
shouting.*] Hallo! Come back, everybody. [*To Joan, as he runs
back to the arch opposite.*] Mind you stand by and dont let me be
bullied. [*Through the arch.*] Come along, will you—the whole
Court. [*He sits down in the royal chair as they all hurry in to their
former places, chattering and wondering.*] Now I'm in for it; but
no matter: here goes! [*To the page.*] Call for silence, you little
beast, will you?

THE PAGE. [*Snatching a halberd as before and thumping with it repeatedly.*]
Silence for His Majesty the King. The King speaks. [*Peremptorily.*]
Will you be silent there? [*Silence.*

CHARLES. [*Rising.*] I have given the command of the army to The
Maid. The Maid is to do as she likes with it.

[*He descends from the dais.*

[*General amazement. La Hire, delighted, slaps his steel thigh-piece
with his gauntlet.*]

LA TRÉMOUILLE. [*Turning threateningly towards Charles.*] What is this?
I command the army.

[*Joan quickly puts her hand on Charles's shoulder as he instinctively
recoils. Charles, with a grotesque effort culminating in an extravagant gesture, snaps his fingers in the Chamberlain's face.*]

JOAN. Thourt answered, old Gruff-and-Grum. [*Suddenly flashing
out her sword as she divines that her moment has come.*] Who is for God
and His Maid? Who is for Orleans with me?

LA HIRE. [*Carried away, drawing also.*] For God and His Maid! To
Orleans!

ALL THE KNIGHTS. [*Following his lead with enthusiasm.*] To Orleans!

[*Joan, radiant, falls on her knees in thanksgiving to God. They all
kneel, except the Archbishop, who gives his benediction with a sign,
and La Trémouille, who collapses, cursing.*

Orleans, 29th April 1429. Dunois, aged twenty-six, is pacing up and down a patch of ground on the south bank of the silver Loire, commanding a long view of the river in both directions. He has had his lance stuck up with a pennon, which streams in a strong east wind. His shield with its bend sinister lies beside it. He has his commander's baton in his hand. He is well built, carrying his armor easily. His broad brow and chin give him an equilaterally triangular face, already marked by active service and responsibility, with the expression of a goodnatured and capable man who has no affectations and no foolish illusions. His page is sitting on the ground, elbows on knees, cheeks on fists, idly watching the water. It is evening; and both man and boy are affected by the loveliness of the Loire.

DUNOIS. [*Halting for a moment to glance up at the streaming pennon and shake his head wearily before he resumes his pacing.*] West wind, west wind, west wind. Strumpet: steadfast when you should be wanton, wanton when you should be steadfast. West wind on the silver Loire: what rhymes to Loire? [*He looks again at the pennon, and shakes his fist at it.*] Change, curse you, change. English harlot of a wind, change. West, west, I tell you. [*With a growl he resumes his march in silence, but soon begins again.*] West wind, wanton wind, wilful wind, womanish wind, false wind from over the water, will you never blow again?

THE PAGE. [*Bounding to his feet.*] See! There! There she goes!

DUNOIS. [*Startled from his reverie; eagerly.*] Where? Who? The Maid?

THE PAGE. No: the kingfisher. Like blue lightning. She went into that bush.

DUNOIS. [*Furiously disappointed.*] Is that all? You infernal young idiot: I have a mind to pitch you into the river.

THE PAGE. [*Not afraid, knowing his man.*] It looked frightfully jolly, that flash of blue. Look! There goes the other!

DUNOIS. [*Running eagerly to the river brim.*] Where? Where?

THE PAGE. [*Pointing.*] Passing the reeds.

DUNOIS. [*Delighted.*] I see.

[*They follow the flight till the bird takes cover.*

THE PAGE. You blew me up because you were not in time to see them yesterday.

DUNOIS. You knew I was expecting The Maid when you set up your yelping. I will give you something to yelp for next time.

THE PAGE. Arnt they lovely? I wish I could catch them.

DUNOIS. Let me catch you trying to trap them, and I will put you in the iron cage for a month to teach you what a cage feels like. You are an abominable boy.

> [*The Page laughs, and squats down as before.*

DUNOIS. [*Pacing.*] Blue bird, blue bird, since I am friend to thee, change thou the wind for me. No: it does not rhyme. He who has sinned for thee: thats better. No sense in it, though. [*He finds himself close to the page.*] You abominable boy! [*He turns away from him.*] Mary in the blue snood, kingfisher color: will you grudge me a west wind?

A SENTRY'S VOICE WESTWARD. Halt! Who goes there?

JOAN'S VOICE. The Maid.

DUNOIS. Let her pass. Hither, Maid! To me!

> *Joan, in splendid armor, rushes in in a blazing rage. The wind drops; and the pennon flaps idly down the lance; but Dunois is too much occupied with Joan to notice it.*

JOAN. [*Bluntly.*] Be you Bastard of Orleans?

DUNOIS. [*Cool and stern, pointing to his shield.*] You see the bend sinister. Are you Joan the Maid?

JOAN. Sure.

DUNOIS. Where are your troops?

JOAN. Miles behind. They have cheated me. They have brought me to the wrong side of the river.

DUNOIS. I told them to.

JOAN. Why did you? The English are on the other side!

DUNOIS. The English are on both sides.

JOAN. But Orleans is on the other side. We must fight the English there. How can we cross the river?

DUNOIS. [*Grimly.*] There is a bridge.

JOAN. In God's name, then, let us cross the bridge, and fall on them.

DUNOIS. It seems simple; but it cannot be done.

JOAN. Who says so?

DUNOIS. I say so; and older and wiser heads than mine are of the same opinion.

JOAN. [*Roundly.*] Then your older and wiser heads are fatheads: they have made a fool of you; and now they want to make a fool of me too, bringing me to the wrong side of the river. Do you not know that I bring you better help than ever came to any general or any town?

DUNOIS. [*Smiling patiently.*] Your own?

JOAN. No: the help and counsel of the King of Heaven. Which is the way to the bridge?

DUNOIS. You are impatient, Maid.

JOAN. Is this a time for patience? Our enemy is at our gates; and here we stand doing nothing. Oh, why are you not fighting? Listen to me: I will deliver you from fear. I——

DUNOIS. [*Laughing heartily, and waving her off.*] No, no, my girl: if you delivered me from fear I should be a good knight for a story book, but a very bad commander of the army. Come! let me begin to make a soldier of you. [*He takes her to the water's edge.*] Do you see those two forts at this end of the bridge? the big ones?

JOAN. Yes. Are they ours or the goddams'?

DUNOIS. Be quiet, and listen to me. If I were in either of those forts with only ten men I could hold it against an army. The English have more than ten times ten goddams in those forts to hold them against us.

JOAN. They cannot hold them against God. God did not give them the land under those forts: they stole it from Him. He gave it to us. I will take those forts.

DUNOIS. Single-handed?

JOAN. Our men will take them. I will lead them.

DUNOIS. Not a man will follow you.

JOAN. I will not look back to see whether anyone is following me.

DUNOIS. [*Recognizing her mettle, and clapping her heartily on the shoulder.*] Good. You have the makings of a soldier in you. You are in love with war.

JOAN. [*Startled.*] Oh! And the Archbishop said I was in love with religion.

DUNOIS. I, God forgive me, am a little in love with war myself, the ugly devil! I am like a man with two wives. Do you want to be like a woman with two husbands?

JOAN. [*Matter-of-fact.*] I will never take a husband. A man in Toul took an action against me for breach of promise; but I never promised him. I am a soldier: I do not want to be thought of as a woman. I will not dress as a woman. I do not care for the things women care for. They dream of lovers, and of money. I dream of leading a charge, and of placing the big guns. You soldiers do not know how to use the big guns: you think you can win battles with a great noise and smoke.

DUNOIS. [*With a shrug.*] True. Half the time the artillery is more trouble than it is worth.

JOAN. Aye, lad; but you cannot fight stone walls with horses: you must have guns, and much bigger guns too.

DUNOIS. [*Grinning at her familiarity, and echoing it.*] Aye, lass; but a good heart and a stout ladder will get over the stoniest wall.

JOAN. I will be first up the ladder when we reach the fort, Bastard. I dare you to follow me.

DUNOIS. You must not dare a staff officer, Joan: only company
   officers are allowed to indulge in displays of personal courage.
   Besides, you must know that I welcome you as a saint, not as a
   soldier. I have daredevils enough at my call, if they could help me.

JOAN. I am not a daredevil: I am a servant of God. My sword is
   sacred: I found it behind the altar in the church of St Catherine,
   where God hid it for me; and I may not strike a blow with it.
   My heart is full of courage, not of anger. I will lead; and your
   men will follow: that is all I can do. But I must do it: you shall
   not stop me.

DUNOIS. All in good time. Our men cannot take those forts by a
   sally across the bridge. They must come by water, and take the
   English in the rear on this side.

JOAN. [Her military sense asserting itself.] Then make rafts and put
   big guns on them; and let your men cross to us.

DUNOIS. The rafts are ready; and the men are embarked. But they
   must wait for God.

JOAN. What do you mean? God is waiting for them.

DUNOIS. Let Him send us a wind then. My boats are downstream:
   they cannot come up against both wind and current. We must
   wait until God changes the wind. Come: let me take you to the
   church.

JOAN. No. I love church; but the English will not yield to prayers:
   they understand nothing but hard knocks and slashes. I will not
   go to church until we have beaten them.

DUNOIS. You must: I have business for you there.

JOAN. What business?

DUNOIS. To pray for a west wind. I have prayed; and I have given
   two silver candlesticks; but my prayers are not answered. Yours
   may be: you are young and innocent.

JOAN. Oh yes: you are right. I will pray: I will tell St Catherine:
   she will make God give me a west wind. Quick: shew me the
   way to the church.

THE PAGE. [Sneezes violently.] At-cha!!!

JOAN. God bless you, child! Coom, Bastard.

   [They go out. The page rises to follow. He picks up the shield, and
      is taking the spear as well when he notices the pennon, which is now
      streaming eastward.

THE PAGE. [Dropping the shield and calling excitedly after them.]
   Siegneur! Seigneur! Mademoiselle!

DUNOIS. [Running back.] What is it? The kingfisher?
                           [He looks eagerly for it up the river.

JOAN. [Joining them.] Oh, a kingfisher! Where?

THE PAGE. No: the wind, the wind, the wind [pointing to the pennon]
   —that is what made me sneeze.

DUNOIS. [*Looking at the pennon.*] The wind has changed. [*He crosses himself.*] God has spoken. [*Kneeling and handing his baton to Joan.*] You command the king's army. I am your soldier.

THE PAGE. [*Looking down the river.*] The boats have put off. They are ripping upstream like anything.

DUNOIS. [*Rising.*] Now for the forts. You dared me to follow. Dare you lead?

JOAN. [*Bursting into tears and flinging her arms round Dunois, kissing him on both cheeks.*] Dunois, dear comrade in arms, help me. My eyes are blinded with tears. Set my foot on the ladder, and say, 'Up Joan.'

DUNOIS. [*Dragging her out.*] Never mind the tears: make for the flash of the guns.

JOAN. [*In a blaze of courage.*] Ah!

DUNOIS. [*Dragging her along with him.*] For God and Saint Dennis!

THE PAGE. [*Shrilly.*] The Maid! The Maid! God and The Maid! Hurray-ay-ay!

[*He snatches up the shield and lance, and capers out after them, mad with excitement.*

*A tent in the English camp. A bullnecked English chaplain of fifty is
sitting on a stool at a table, hard at work writing. At the other side of
the table an imposing nobleman, aged forty-six, is seated in a handsome
chair turning over the leaves of an illuminated Book of Hours. The
nobleman is enjoying himself: the chaplain is struggling with suppressed
wrath. There is an unoccupied leather stool on the nobleman's left. The
table is on his right.*

THE NOBLEMAN. Now this is what I call workmanship. There is
nothing on earth more exquisite than a bonny book, with well-
placed columns of rich black writing in beautiful borders, and
illuminated pictures cunningly inset. But nowadays, instead of
looking at books, people read them. A book might as well be one
of those orders for bacon and bran that you are scribbling.

THE CHAPLAIN. I must say, my lord, you take our situation very
coolly. Very coolly indeed.

THE NOBLEMAN. [*Supercilious.*] What is the matter?

THE CHAPLAIN. The matter, my lord, is that we English have been
defeated.

THE NOBLEMAN. That happens, you know. It is only in history
books and ballads that the enemy is always defeated.

THE CHAPLAIN. But we are being defeated over and over again.
First, Orleans——

THE NOBLEMAN. [*Poohpoohing.*] Oh, Orleans!

THE CHAPLAIN. I know what you are going to say, my lord: that
was a clear case of witchcraft and sorcery. But we are still being
defeated. Jargeau, Meung, Beaugency, just like Orleans. And
now we have been butchered at Patay, and Sir John Talbot
taken prisoner. [*He throws down his pen, almost in tears.*] I feel it,
my lord: I feel it very deeply. I cannot bear to see my countrymen
defeated by a parcel of foreigners.

THE NOBLEMAN. Oh, you are an Englishman, are you?

THE CHAPLAIN. Certainly not, my lord: I am a gentleman. Still,
like your lordship, I was born in England; and it makes a
difference.

THE NOBLEMAN. You are attached to the soil, eh?

THE CHAPLAIN. It pleases your lordship to be satirical at my
expense: your greatness privileges you to be so with impunity.

But your lordship knows very well that I am not attached to the soil in a vulgar manner, like a serf. Still, I have a feeling about it; [*with growing agitation*] and I am not ashamed of it; and [*rising wildly*] by God, if this goes on any longer I will fling my cassock to the devil, and take arms myself, and strangle the accursed witch with my own hands.

THE NOBLEMAN. [*Laughing at him goodnaturedly.*] So you shall, chaplain: so you shall, if we can do nothing better. But not yet, not quite yet.

[*The Chaplain resumes his seat very sulkily.*

THE NOBLEMAN. [*Airily.*] I should not care very much about the witch—you see, I have made my pilgrimage to the Holy Land; and the Heavenly Powers, for their own credit, can hardly allow me to be worsted by a village sorceress—but the Bastard of Orleans is a harder nut to crack; and as he has been to the Holy Land too, honors are easy between us as far as that goes.

THE CHAPLAIN. He is only a Frenchman, my lord.

THE NOBLEMAN. A Frenchman! Where did you pick up that expression? Are these Burgundians and Bretons and Picards and Gascons beginning to call themselves Frenchman, just as our fellows are beginning to call themselves Englishmen? They actually talk of France and England as their countries. Theirs, if you please! What is to become of me and you if that way of thinking comes into fashion?

THE CHAPLAIN. Why, my lord? Can it hurt us?

THE NOBLEMAN. Men cannot serve two masters. If this cant of serving their country once takes hold of them, goodbye to the authority of their feudal lords, and goodbye to the authority of the Church. That is, goodbye to you and me.

THE CHAPLAIN. I hope I am a faithful servant of the Church; and there are only six cousins between me and the barony of Stogumber, which was created by the Conqueror. But is that any reason why I should stand by and see Englishmen beaten by a French bastard and a witch from Lousy Champagne?

THE NOBLEMAN. Easy, man, easy: we shall burn the witch and beat the bastard all in good time. Indeed I am waiting at present for the Bishop of Beauvais, to arrange the burning with him. He has been turned out of his diocese by her faction.

THE CHAPLAIN. You have first to catch her, my lord.

THE NOBLEMAN. Or buy her. I will offer a king's ransom.

THE CHAPLAIN. A king's ransom! For that slut!

THE NOBLEMAN. One has to leave a margin. Some of Charles's people will sell her to the Burgundians; the Burgundians will sell her to us; and there will probably be three or four middlemen who will expect their little commissions.

THE CHAPLAIN. Monstrous. It is all those scoundrels of Jews:
they get in every time money changes hands. I would not leave a
Jew alive in Christendom if I had my way.

THE NOBLEMAN. Why not? The Jews generally give value. They
make you pay; but they deliver the goods. In my experience the
men who want something for nothing are invariably Christians.

[*A page appears.*

THE PAGE. The Right Reverend the Bishop of Beauvais: Monseigneur Cauchon.

[*Cauchon, aged about sixty, comes in. The page withdraws. The two
Englishmen rise.*

THE NOBLEMAN. [*With effusive courtesy.*] My dear Bishop, how good
of you to come! Allow me to introduce myself: Richard de
Beauchamp, Earl of Warwick, at your service.

CAUCHON. Your lordship's fame is well known to me.

WARWICK. This reverend cleric is Master John de Stogumber.

THE CHAPLAIN. [*Glibly.*] John Bowyer Spenser Neville de Sto-
gumber, at your service, my lord: Bachelor of Theology, and
Keeper of the Private Seal to His Eminence the Cardinal of
Winchester.

WARWICK. [*To Cauchon.*] You call him the Cardinal of England, I
believe. Our king's uncle.

CAUCHON. Messire John de Stogumber: I am always the very good
friend of His Eminence.

[*He extends his hand to the chaplain, who kisses his ring.*

WARWICK. Do me the honor to be seated.

[*He gives Cauchon his chair, placing it at the head of the table.*
[*Cauchon accepts the place of honor with a grave inclination. Warwick
fetches the leather stool carelessly, and sits in his former place. The
chaplain goes back to his chair.*
*Though Warwick has taken second place in calculated deference to
the Bishop, he assumes the lead in opening the proceedings as a
matter of course. He is still cordial and expansive; but there is a
new note in his voice which means that he is coming to business.*

WARWICK. Well, my Lord Bishop, you find us in one of our
unlucky moments. Charles is to be crowned at Rheims, practically
by the young woman from Lorraine; and—I must not deceive
you, nor flatter your hopes—we cannot prevent it. I suppose it
will make a great difference to Charles's position.

CAUCHON. Undoubtedly. It is a masterstroke of The Maid's.

THE CHAPLAIN. [*Again agitated.*] We were not fairly beaten, my
lord. No Englishman is ever fairly beaten.

[*Cauchon raises his eyebrows slightly, then quickly composes his face.*

WARWICK. Our friend here takes the view that the young woman
is a sorceress. It would, I presume, be the duty of your reverend

lordship to denounce her to the Inquisition, and have her burnt for that offence.

CAUCHON. If she were captured in my diocese: yes.

WARWICK. [*Feeling that they are getting on capitally.*] Just so. Now I suppose there can be no reasonable doubt that she is a sorceress.

THE CHAPLAIN. Not the least. An arrant witch.

WARWICK. [*Gently reproving the interruption.*] We are asking for the Bishop's opinion, Messire John.

CAUCHON. We shall have to consider not merely our own opinions here, but the opinions—the prejudices, if you like—of a French court.

WARWICK. [*Correcting.*] A Catholic court, my lord.

CAUCHON. Catholic courts are composed of mortal men, like other courts, however sacred their function and inspiration may be. And if the men are Frenchmen, as the modern fashion calls them, I am afraid the bare fact that an English army has been defeated by a French one will not convince them that there is any sorcery in the matter.

THE CHAPLAIN. What! Not when the famous Sir John Talbot himself has been defeated and actually taken prisoner by a drab from the ditches of Lorraine!

CAUCHON. Sir John Talbot, we all know, is a fierce and formidable soldier, Messire; but I have yet to learn that he is an able general. And though it pleases you to say that he has been defeated by this girl, some of us may be disposed to give a little of the credit to Dunois.

THE CHAPLAIN. [*Contemptuously.*] The Bastard of Orleans!

CAUCHON. Let me remind——

WARWICK. [*Interposing.*] I know what you are going to say, my Lord. Dunois defeated me at Montargis.

CAUCHON. [*Bowing.*] I take that as evidence that the Seigneur Dunois is a very able commander indeed.

WARWICK. Your lordship is the flower of courtesy. I admit, on our side, that Talbot is a mere fighting animal, and that it probably served him right to be taken at Patay.

THE CHAPLAIN. [*Chafing.*] My lord: at Orleans this woman had her throat pierced by an English arrow, and was seen to cry like a child from the pain of it. It was a death wound; yet she fought all day; and when our men had repulsed all her attacks like true Englishmen, she walked alone to the wall of our fort with a white banner in her hand; and our men were paralysed, and could neither shoot nor strike whilst the French fell on them and drove them on to the bridge, which immediately burst into flames and crumbled under them, letting them down into the river, where they were drowned in heaps. Was this your bastard's general-ship? Or were those flames the flames of hell, conjured up by witchcraft?

WARWICK. You will forgive Messire John's vehemence, my lord; but he has put our case. Dunois is a great captain, we admit; but why could he do nothing until the witch came?

CAUCHON. I do not say that there were no supernatural powers on her side. But the names on that white banner were not the names of Satan and Beelzebub, but the blessed names of our Lord and His holy mother. And your commander who was drowned—Clahz-da I think you call him——

WARWICK. Glasdale. Sir William Glasdale.

CAUCHON. Glass-dell, thank you. He was no saint; and many of our people think that he was drowned for his blasphemies against The Maid.

WARWICK. [*Beginning to look very dubious.*] Well, what are we to infer from all this, my lord? Has The Maid converted you?

CAUCHON. If she had, my lord, I should have known better than to have trusted myself here within your grasp.

WARWICK. [*Blandly deprecating.*] Oh! Oh! My lord!

CAUCHON. If the devil is making use of this girl—and I believe he is——

WARWICK. [*Reassured.*] Ah! You hear, Messire John? I knew your lordship would not fail us. Pardon my interruption. Proceed.

CAUCHON. If it be so, the devil has longer views than you give him credit for.

WARWICK. Indeed? In what way? Listen to this, Messire John.

CAUCHON. If the devil wanted to damn a country girl, do you think so easy a task would cost him the winning of half a dozen battles? No, my lord: any trumpery imp could do that much if the girl could be damned at all. The Prince of Darkness does not condescend to such cheap drudgery. When he strikes, he strikes at the Catholic Church, whose realm is the whole spiritual world. When he damns, he damns the souls of the entire human race. Against that dreadful design The Church stands ever on guard. And it is as one of the instruments of that design that I see this girl. She is inspired, but diabolically inspired.

THE CHAPLAIN. I told you she was a witch.

CAUCHON. [*Fiercely.*] She is not a witch. She is a heretic.

THE CHAPLAIN. What difference does that make?

CAUCHON. You, a priest, ask me that! You English are strangely blunt in the mind. All these things that you call witchcraft are capable of a natural explanation. The woman's miracles would not impose on a rabbit: she does not claim them as miracles her-self. What do her victories prove but that she has a better head on her shoulders than your swearing Glass-dells and mad bull Talbots, and that the courage of faith, even though it be a false faith, will always outstay the courage of wrath?

THE CHAPLAIN. [*Hardly able to believe his ears.*] Does your lordship compare Sir John Talbot, three times Governor of Ireland, to a mad bull?!!!

WARWICK. It would not be seemly for you to do so, Messire John, as you are still six removes from a barony. But as I am an earl, and Talbot is only a knight, I may make bold to accept the comparison. [*To the Bishop.*] My lord: I wipe the slate as far as the witchcraft goes. None the less, we must burn the woman.

CAUCHON. I cannot burn her. The Church cannot take life. And my first duty is to seek this girl's salvation.

WARWICK. No doubt. But you do burn people occasionally.

CAUCHON. No. When The Church cuts off an obstinate heretic as a dead branch from the tree of life, the heretic is handed over to the secular arm. The Church has no part in what the secular arm may see fit to do.

WARWICK. Precisely. And I shall be the secular arm in this case. Well, my lord, hand over your dead branch; and I will see that the fire is ready for it. If you will answer for The Church's part, I will answer for the secular part.

CAUCHON. [*With smouldering anger.*] I can answer for nothing. You great lords are too prone to treat The Church as a mere political convenience.

WARWICK. [*Smiling and propitiatory.*] Not in England, I assure you.

CAUCHON. In England more than anywhere else. No, my lord: the soul of this village girl is of equal value with yours or your king's before the throne of God; and my first duty is to save it. I will not suffer your lordship to smile at me as if I were repeating a meaningless form of words, and it were well understood between us that I should betray the girl to you. I am no mere political bishop: my faith is to me what your honor is to you; and if there be a loophole through which the baptized child of God can creep to her salvation, I shall guide her to it.

THE CHAPLAIN. [*Rising in a fury.*] You are a traitor.

CAUCHON. [*Springing up.*] You lie, priest. [*Trembling with rage.*] If you dare do what this woman has done—set your country above the holy Catholic Church—you shall go to the fire with her.

THE CHAPLAIN. My lord: I—I went too far. I——

[*He sits down with a submissive gesture.*

WARWICK. [*Who has risen apprehensively.*] My lord: I apologize to you for the word used by Messire John de Stogumber. It does not mean in England what it does in France. In your language

traitor means betrayer: one who is perfidious, treacherous, un-
faithful, disloyal. In our country it means simply one who is not
wholly devoted to our English interests.

CAUCHON. I am sorry: I did not understand.

[*He subsides into his chair with dignity.*

WARWICK. [*Resuming his seat, much relieved.*] I must apologize on
my own account if I have seemed to take the burning of this
poor girl too lightly. When one has seen whole countrysides
burnt over and over again as mere items in military routine, one
has to grow a very thick skin. Otherwise one might go mad: at
all events, I should. May I venture to assume that your lordship
also, having to see so many heretics burned from time to time, is
compelled to take—shall I say—a professional view of what
would otherwise be a very horrible incident?

CAUCHON. Yes: it is a painful duty: even, as you say, a horrible one.
But in comparison with the horror of heresy it is less than
nothing. I am not thinking of this girl's body, which will suffer
for a few moments only, and which must in any event die in
some more or less painful manner, but of her soul, which may
suffer to all eternity.

WARWICK. Just so; and God grant that her soul may be saved! But
the practical problem would seem to be how to save her soul
without saving her body. For we must face it, my lord: if this
cult of The Maid goes on, our cause is lost.

THE CHAPLAIN. [*His voice broken like that of a man who has been
crying.*] May I speak, my lord?

WARWICK. Really, Messire John, I had rather you did not, unless
you can keep your temper.

THE CHAPLAIN. It is only this. I speak under correction; but The
Maid is full of deceit: she pretends to be devout. Her prayers and
confessions are endless. How can she be accused of heresy when
she neglects no observance of a faithful daughter of The Church?

CAUCHON. [*Flaming up.*] A faithful daughter of The Church! The
Pope himself at his proudest dare not presume as this woman
presumes. She acts as if she herself were The Church. She brings
the message of God to Charles; and The Church must stand
aside. She will crown him in the cathedral of Rheims: she, not
The Church! She sends letters to the king of England giving him
God's command through her to return to his island on pain of
God's vengeance, which she will execute. Let me tell you that
the writing of such letters was the practice of the accursed
Mahomet, the anti-Christ. Has she ever in all her utterances said
one word of The Church? Never. It is always God and herself.

WARWICK. What can you expect? A beggar on horseback! Her
head is turned.

CAUCHON. Who has turned it? The devil. And for a mighty purpose. He is spreading this heresy everywhere. The man Hus,
burnt only thirteen years ago at Constance, infected all Bohemia
with it. A man named WcLeef, himself an anointed priest, spread
the pestilence in England; and to your shame you let him die in
his bed. We have such people here in France too: I know the
breed. It is cancerous: if it be not cut out, stamped out, burnt out,
it will not stop until it has brought the whole body of human
society into sin and corruption, into waste and ruin. By it an
Arab camel driver drove Christ and His Church out of Jerusalem,
and ravaged his way west like a wild beast until at last there stood
only the Pyrenees and God's mercy between France and damnation. Yet what did the camel driver do at the beginning more
than this shepherd girl is doing? He had his voices from the angel
Gabriel: she has her voices from St Catherine and St Margaret
and the Blessed Michael. He declared himself the messenger of
God, and wrote in God's name to the kings of the earth. Her
letters to them are going forth daily. It is not the Mother of God
now to whom we must look for intercession, but to Joan the
Maid. What will the world be like when The Church's accumu-
lated wisdom and knowledge and experience, its councils of
learned, venerable pious men, are thrust into the kennel by every
ignorant laborer or dairymaid whom the devil can puff up with
the monstrous self-conceit of being directly inspired from heaven?
It will be a world of blood, of fury, of devastation, of each man
striving for his own hand: in the end a world wrecked back into
barbarism. For now you have only Mahomet and his dupes, and
the Maid and her dupes; but what will it be when every girl
thinks herself a Joan and every man a Mahomet? I shudder to
the very marrow of my bones when I think of it. I have fought
it all my life; and I will fight it to the end. Let all this woman's
sins be forgiven her except only this sin; for it is the sin against
the Holy Ghost; and if she does not recant in the dust before
the world, and submit herself to the last inch of her soul to her
Church, to the fire she shall go if she once falls into my hand.

WARWICK. [*Unimpressed.*] You feel strongly about it, naturally.

CAUCHON. Do not you?

WARWICK. I am a soldier, not a churchman. As a pilgrim I saw
something of the Mahometans. They were not so ill-bred as I
had been led to believe. In some respects their conduct compared
favorably with ours.

CAUCHON. [*Displeased.*] I have noticed this before. Men go to the
East to convert the infidels. And the infidels pervert them. The
Crusader comes back more than half a Saracen. Not to mention
that all Englishmen are born heretics.

THE CHAPLAIN. Englishmen heretics!!! [*Appealing to Warwick.*]
My lord: must we endure this? His lordship is beside himself.
How can what an Englishman believes be heresy? It is a contra-
diction in terms.

CAUCHON. I absolve you, Messire de Stogumber, on the ground
of invincible ignorance. The thick air of your country does not
breed theologians.

WARWICK. You would not say so if you heard us quarrelling about
religion, my lord! I am sorry you think I must be either a heretic
or a blockhead because, as a travelled man, I know that the
followers of Mahomet profess great respect for our Lord, and
are more ready to forgive St Peter for being a fisherman than your
lordship is to forgive Mahomet for being a camel driver. But at
least we can proceed in this matter without bigotry.

CAUCHON. When men call the zeal of the Christian Church bigotry
I know what to think.

WARWICK. They are only east and west views of the same
thing.

CAUCHON. [*Bitterly ironical.*] Only east and west! Only!!

WARWICK. Oh, my Lord Bishop, I am not gainsaying you. You
will carry The Church with you; but you have to carry the
nobles also. To my mind there is a stronger case against The
Maid than the one you have so forcibly put. Frankly, I am not
afraid of this girl becoming another Mahomet, and superseding
The Church by a great heresy. I think you exaggerate that risk.
But have you noticed that, in these letters of hers, she proposed
to all the kings of Europe, as she has already pressed on Charles,
a transaction which would wreck the whole social structure of
Christendom?

CAUCHON. Wreck The Church. I tell you so.

WARWICK. [*Whose patience is wearing out.*] My lord: pray get The
Church out of your head for a moment; and remember that there
are temporal institutions in the world as well as spiritual ones.
I and my peers represent the feudal aristocracy as you represent
The Church. We are the temporal power. Well, do you not see
how this girl's idea strikes at us?

CAUCHON. How does her idea strike at you, except as it strikes at
all of us, through The Church?

WARWICK. Her idea is that the kings should give their realms to
God, and then reign as God's bailiffs.

CAUCHON. [*Not interested.*] Quite sound theologically, my lord.
But the king will hardly care, provided he reign. It is an abstract
idea: a mere form of words.

WARWICK. By no means. It is a cunning device to supersede the
aristocracy, and make the king sole and absolute autocrat.

Instead of the king being merely the first among his peers, he becomes their master. That we cannot suffer: we call no man master. Nominally we hold our lands and dignities from the king, because there must be a keystone to the arch of human society; but we hold our lands in our own hands, and defend them with our own swords and those of our own tenants. Now by The Maid's doctrine the king will take our lands—our lands! —and make them a present to God; and God will then vest them wholly in the king.

CAUCHON. Need you fear that? You are the makers of kings after all. York or Lancaster in England, Lancaster or Valois in France: they reign according to your pleasure.

WARWICK. Yes; but only as long as the people follow their feudal lords, and know the king only as a travelling show, owning nothing but the highway that belongs to everybody. If the people's thoughts and hearts were turned to the king, and their lords became only the king's servants in their eyes, the king could break us across his knee one by one; and then what should we be but liveried courtiers in his halls?

CAUCHON. Still you need not fear, my lord. Some men are born kings; and some are born statesmen. The two are seldom the same. Where would the king find counsellors to plan and carry out such a policy for him?

WARWICK. [*With a not too friendly smile.*] Perhaps in the Church, my lord.

[*Cauchon, with an equally sour smile, shrugs his shoulders, and does not contradict him.*

WARWICK. Strike down the barons; and the cardinals will have it all their own way.

CAUCHON. [*Conciliatory, dropping his polemical tone.*] My lord: we shall not defeat The Maid if we strive against one another. I know well that there is a Will to Power in the world. I know that while it lasts there will be a struggle between the Emperor and the Pope, between the dukes and the political cardinals, between the barons and the kings. The devil divides us and governs. I see you are no friend to The Church: you are an earl first and last, as I am a churchman first and last. But can we not sink our differences in the face of a common enemy? I see now that what is in your mind is not that this girl has never once mentioned The Church, and thinks only of God and herself, but that she has never once mentioned the peerage, and thinks only of the king and herself.

WARWICK. Quite so. These two ideas of hers are the same idea at bottom. It goes deep, my lord. It is the protest of the individual soul against the interference of priest or peer between the private

man and his God. I should call it Protestantism if I had to find a
name for it.

CAUCHON. [*Looking hard at him.*] You understand it wonderfully
well, my lord. Scratch an Englishman, and find a Protestant.

WARWICK. [*Playing the pink of courtesy.*] I think you are not entirely
void of sympathy with The Maid's secular heresy, my lord. I
leave you to find a name for it.

CAUCHON. You mistake me, my lord. I have no sympathy with her
political presumptions. But as a priest I have gained a knowledge
of the minds of the common people; and there you will find yet
another most dangerous idea. I can express it only by such
phrases as France for the French, England for the English, Italy
for the Italians, Spain for the Spanish, and so forth. It is sometimes so narrow and bitter in country folk that it surprises me
that this country girl can rise above the idea of her village for its
villagers. But she can. She does. When she threatens to drive
the English from the soil of France she is undoubtedly thinking
of the whole extent of country in which French is spoken. To
her the French-speaking people are what the Holy Scriptures
describe as a nation. Call this side of her heresy Nationalism if
you will: I can find you no better name for it. I can only tell you
that it is essentially anti-Catholic and anti-Christian; for the
Catholic Church knows only one realm, and that is the realm of
Christ's kingdom. Divide that kingdom into nations, and you
dethrone Christ. Dethrone Christ, and who will stand between our
throats and the sword? The world will perish in a welter of war.

WARWICK. Well, if you will burn the Protestant, I will burn the
Nationalist, though perhaps I shall not carry Messire John with
me there. England for the English will appeal to him.

THE CHAPLAIN. Certainly England for the English goes without
saying: it is the simple law of nature. But this woman denies
to England her legitimate conquests, given her by God because
of her peculiar fitness to rule over less civilized races for their
own good. I do not understand what your lordships mean by
Protestant and Nationalist: you are too learned and subtle for a
poor clerk like myself. But I know as a matter of plain common
sense that the woman is a rebel; and that is enough for me. She
rebels against Nature by wearing man's clothes, and fighting. She
rebels against The Church by usurping the divine authority of
the Pope. She rebels against God by her damnable league with
Satan and his evil spirits against our army. And all these rebellions
are only excuses for her great rebellion against England. That is
not to be endured. Let her perish. Let her burn. Let her not infect
the whole flock. It is expedient that one woman die for the
people.

WARWICK. [*Rising.*] My lord: we seem to be agreed.

CAUCHON. [*Rising also, but in protest.*] I will not imperil my soul. I will uphold the justice of the Church. I will strive to the utmost for this woman's salvation.

WARWICK. I am sorry for the poor girl. I hate these severities. I will spare her if I can.

THE CHAPLAIN. [*Implacably.*] I would burn her with my own hands.

CAUCHON. [*Blessing him.*] Sancta simplicitas!

The ambulatory in the cathedral of Rheims, near the door of the vestry. A pillar bears one of the stations of the cross. The organ is playing the people out of the nave after the coronation. Joan is kneeling in prayer before the station. She is beautifully dressed, but still in male attire. The organ ceases as Dunois, also splendidly arrayed, comes into the ambulatory from the vestry.

DUNOIS. Come, Joan! You have had enough praying. After that fit of crying you will catch a chill if you stay here any longer. It is all over: the cathedral is empty; and the streets are full. They are calling for The Maid. We have told them you are staying here alone to pray; but they want to see you again.

JOAN. No: let the king have all the glory.

DUNOIS. He only spoils the show, poor devil. No, Joan: you have crowned him; and you must go through with it.

[Joan shakes her head reluctantly.

DUNOIS. [*Raising her.*] Come come! it will be over in a couple of hours. It's better than the bridge at Orleans: eh?

JOAN. Oh, dear Dunois, how I wish it were the bridge at Orleans again! We lived at that bridge.

DUNOIS. Yes, faith, and died too: some of us.

JOAN. Isnt it strange, Jack? I am such a coward: I am frightened beyond words before a battle; but it is so dull afterwards when there is no danger: oh, so dull! dull! dull!

DUNOIS. You must learn to be abstemious in war, just as you are in your food and drink, my little saint.

JOAN. Dear Jack: I think you like me as a soldier likes his comrade.

DUNOIS. You need it, poor innocent child of God. You have not many friends at court.

JOAN. Why do all these courtiers and knights and churchmen hate me? What have I done to them? I have asked nothing for myself except that my village shall not be taxed; for we cannot afford war taxes. I have brought them luck and victory: I have set them right when they were doing all sorts of stupid things: I have crowned Charles and made him a real king; and all the honors he is handing out have gone to them. Then why do they not love me?

DUNOIS. [*Rallying her.*] Sim-ple-ton! Do you expect stupid people to love you for shewing them up? Do blundering old military dug-outs love the successful young captains who supersede them?

Do ambitious politicians love the climbers who take the front
seats from them? Do archbishops enjoy being played off their
own altars, even by saints? Why, I should be jealous of you myself if I were ambitious enough.

JOAN. You are the pick of the basket here, Jack: the only friend
I have among all these nobles. I'll wager your mother was from
the country. I will go back to the farm when I have taken Paris.

DUNOIS. I am not so sure that they will let you take Paris.

JOAN. [Startled.] What!

DUNOIS. I should have taken it myself before this if they had all
been sound about it. Some of them would rather Paris took you,
I think. So take care.

JOAN. Jack: the world is too wicked for me. If the goddams and
the Burgundians do not make an end of me, the French will.
Only for my voices I should lose all heart. That is why I had to
steal away to pray here alone after the coronation. I'll tell you
something, Jack. It is in the bells I hear my voices. Not today,
when they all rang: that was nothing but jangling. But here in
this corner, where the bells come down from heaven, and the
echoes linger, or in the fields, where they come from a distance
through the quiet of the countryside, my voices are in them. [The
cathedral clock chimes the quarter.] Hark! [She becomes rapt.] Do
you hear? 'Dear-child-of-God': just what you said. At the half-
hour they will say 'Be-brave-go-on'. At the three-quarters they
will say 'I-am-the-Help'. But it is at the hour, when the great
bell goes after 'God-will-save-France': it is then that St Margaret
and St Catherine and sometimes even the blessed Michael will
say things that I cannot tell beforehand. Then, oh then——

DUNOIS. [Interrupting her kindly but not sympathetically.] Then, Joan,
we shall hear whatever we fancy in the booming of the bell.
You make me uneasy when you talk about your voices: I should
think you were a bit cracked if I hadnt noticed that you give me
very sensible reasons for what you do, though I hear you telling
others you are only obeying Madame Saint Catherine.

JOAN. [Crossly.] Well, I have to find reasons for you, because you
do not believe in my voices. But the voices come first; and I find
the reasons after: whatever you may choose to believe.

DUNOIS. Are you angry, Joan?

JOAN. Yes. [Smiling.] No, not with you. I wish you were one of the
village babies.

DUNOIS. Why?

JOAN. I could nurse you for awhile.

DUNOIS. You are a bit of a woman after all.

JOAN. No; not a bit; I am a soldier and nothing else. Soldiers
always nurse children when they get a chance.

DUNOIS. That is true.   [*He laughs.*

[*King Charles, with Bluebeard on his left and La Hire on his right, comes from the vestry, where he has been disrobing. Joan shrinks away behind the pillar. Dunois is left between Charles and La Hire.*

DUNOIS. Well, Your Majesty is an anointed king at last. How do you like it?

CHARLES. I would not go through it again to be emperor of the sun and moon. The weight of those robes! I thought I should have dropped when they loaded that crown on to me. And the famous holy oil they talked so much about was rancid—phew! The Archbishop must be nearly dead: his robes must have weighed a ton: they are stripping him still in the vestry.

DUNOIS. [*Drily.*] Your Majesty should wear armor oftener. That would accustom you to heavy dressing.

CHARLES. Yes; the old jibe! Well, I am not going to wear armor: fighting is not my job. Where is The Maid?

JOAN. [*Coming forward between Charles and Bluebeard, and falling on her knee.*] Sire; I have made you king; my work is done. I am going back to my father's farm.

CHARLES. [*Surprised, but relieved.*] Oh, are you? Well, that will be very nice.   [*Joan rises, deeply discouraged.*

CHARLES. [*Continuing heedlessly.*] A healthy life, you know.

DUNOIS. But a dull one.

BLUEBEARD. You will find the petticoats tripping you up after leaving them off for so long.

LA HIRE. You will miss the fighting. It's a bad habit, but a grand one, and the hardest of all to break yourself of.

CHARLES. [*Anxiously.*] Still, we dont want you to stay if you would really rather go home.

JOAN. [*Bitterly.*] I know well that none of you will be sorry to see me go.

[*She turns her shoulder to Charles and walks past him to the more congenial neighborhood of Dunois and La Hire.*

LA HIRE. Well, I shall be able to swear when I want to. But I shall miss you at times.

JOAN. La Hire: in spite of all your sins and swears we shall meet in heaven; for I love you as I love Pitou, my old sheep dog. Pitou could kill a wolf. You will kill the English wolves until they go back to their country and become good dogs of God, will you not?

LA HIRE. You and I together: yes.

JOAN. No: I shall last only a year from the beginning.

ALL THE OTHERS. What!

JOAN. I know it somehow.

DUNOIS. Nonsense!

JOAN. Jack: do you think you will be able to drive them out?

DUNOIS. [*With quiet conviction.*] Yes: I shall drive them out. They beat us because we thought battles were tournaments and ransom markets. We played the fool while the goddams took war seriously. But I have learnt my lesson, and taken their measure. They have no roots here. I have beaten them before; and I shall beat them again.

JOAN. You will not be cruel to them, Jack?

DUNOIS. The goddams will not yield to tender handling. We did not begin it.

JOAN. [*Suddenly.*] Jack: before I go home, let us take Paris.

CHARLES. [*Terrified.*] Oh no, no. We shall lose everything we have gained. Oh, dont let us have any more fighting. We can make a very good treaty with the Duke of Burgundy.

JOAN. Treaty!   [*She stamps with impatience.*

CHARLES. Well, why not, now that I am crowned and anointed? Oh, that oil!

[*The Archbishop comes from the vestry, and joins the group between Charles and Bluebeard.*

CHARLES. Archbishop; The Maid wants to start fighting again.

THE ARCHBISHOP. Have we ceased fighting, then? Are we at peace?

CHARLES. No: I suppose not; but let us be content with what we have done. Let us make a treaty. Our luck is too good to last; and now is our chance to stop before it turns.

JOAN. Luck! God has fought for us; and you call it luck! And you would stop while there are still Englishmen on this holy earth of dear France!

THE ARCHBISHOP. [*Sternly.*] Maid: the king addressed himself to me, not to you. You forget yourself. You very often forget yourself.

JOAN. [*Unabashed, and rather roughly.*] Then speak, you; and tell him that it is not God's will that he should take his hand from the plough.

THE ARCHBISHOP. If I am not so glib with the name of God as you are, it is because I interpret His will with the authority of the Church and of my sacred office. When you first came you respected it, and would not have dared to speak as you are now speaking. You came clothed with the virtue of humility; and because God blessed your enterprises accordingly, you have stained yourself with the sin of pride. The old Greek tragedy is rising among us. It is the chastisement of *hubris*.

CHARLES. Yes: she thinks she knows better than everyone else.

JOAN. [*Distressed, but naïvely incapable of seeing the effect she is producing.*] But I do know better than any of you seem to. And I am not proud: I never speak unless I know I am right.

BLUEBEARD.   ⎫ *[Exclaiming together]* ⎰ Ha ha!
CHARLES.   ⎬   ⎱ Just so.

THE ARCHBISHOP. How do you know you are right?

JOAN. I always know. My voices——

CHARLES. Oh, your voices, your voices. Why dont the voices come to me? I am king, not you.

JOAN. They do come to you; but you do not hear them. You have not sat in the field in the evening listening for them. When the angelus rings you cross yourself and have done with it; but if you prayed from your heart, and listened to the thrilling of the bells in the air after they stop ringing, you would hear the voices as well as I do. [*Turning brusquely from him.*] But what voices do you need to tell you what the blacksmith can tell you: that you must strike while the iron is hot? I tell you we must make a dash at Compiègne and relieve it as we relieved Orleans. Then Paris will open its gates; or if not, we will break through them. What is your crown worth without your capital?

LA HIRE. That is what I say too. We shall go through them like a red hot shot through a pound of butter. What do you say, Bastard?

DUNOIS. If our cannon balls were all as hot as your head, and we had enough of them, we should conquer the earth, no doubt. Pluck and impetuosity are good servants in war, but bad masters: they have delivered us into the hands of the English every time we have trusted to them. We never know when we are beaten: that is our great fault.

JOAN. You never know when you are victorious: that is a worse fault. I shall have to make you carry looking-glasses in battle to convince you that the English have not cut off all your noses. You would have been besieged in Orleans still, you and your councils of war, if I had not made you attack. You should always attack; and if you only hold on long enough the enemy will stop first. You dont know how to begin a battle; and you dont know how to use your cannons. And I do.

       [*She squats down on the flags with crossed ankles, pouting.*

DUNOIS. I know what you think of us, General Joan.

JOAN. Never mind that, Jack. Tell them what you think of me.

DUNOIS. I think that God was on your side; for I have not forgotten how the wind changed, and how our hearts changed when you came; and by my faith I shall never deny that it was in your sign that we conquered. But I tell you as a soldier that God is no man's daily drudge, and no maid's either. If you are worthy of it He will sometimes snatch you out of the jaws of death and set you on your feet again; but that is all: once on your feet you must fight with all your might and all your craft. For

He has to be fair to your enemy too: dont forget that. Well, He set us on our feet through you at Orleans; and the glory of it has carried us through a few good battles here to the coronation. But if we presume on it further, and trust to God to do the work we should do ourselves, we shall be defeated; and serve us right!

JOAN. But——

DUNOIS. Sh! I have not finished. Do not think, any of you, that these victories of ours were won without generalship. King Charles: you have said no word in your proclamations of my part in this campaign; and I make no complaint of that; for the people will run after The Maid and her miracles and not after the Bastard's hard work finding troops for her and feeding them. But I know exactly how much God did for us through The Maid, and how much He left me to do by my own wits; and I tell you that your little hour of miracles is over, and that from this time on he who plays the war game best will win—if the luck is on his side.

JOAN. Ah! if, if, if, if! If ifs and ans were pots and pans there'd be no need of tinkers. [*Rising impetuously*.] I tell you, Bastard, your art of war is no use, because your knights are no good for real fighting. War is only a game to them, like tennis and all their other games: they make rules as to what is fair and what is not fair, and heap armor on themselves and on their poor horses to keep out the arrows; and when they fall they cant get up, and have to wait for their squires to come and lift them to arrange about the ransom with the man that has poked them off their horse. Cant you see that all the like of that is gone by and done with? What use is armor against gunpowder? And if it was, do you think men that are fighting for France and for God will stop to bargain about ransoms, as half your knights live by doing? No: they will fight to win; and they will give up their lives out of their own hand into the hand of God when they go into battle, as I do. Common folks understand this. They cannot afford armor and cannot pay ransoms; but they followed me half naked into the moat and up the ladder and over the wall. With them it is my life or thine, and God defend the right! You may shake your head, Jack; and Bluebeard may twirl his billygoat's beard and cock his nose at me; but remember the day your knights and captains refused to follow me to attack the English at Orleans! You locked the gates to keep me in; and it was the townsfolk and the common people that followed me, and forced the gate, and shewed you the way to fight in earnest.

BLUEBEARD. [*Offended*.] Not content with being Pope Joan, you must be Caesar and Alexander as well.

THE ARCHBISHOP. Pride will have a fall, Joan.

JOAN. Oh, never mind whether it is pride or not. Is it true? Is it common sense?

LA HIRE. It is true. Half of us are afraid of having our handsome noses broken; and the other half are out for paying off their mortgages. Let her have her way, Dunois: she does not know everything; but she has got hold of the right end of the stick. Fighting is not what it was; and those who know least about it often make the best job of it.

DUNOIS. I know all that. I do not fight in the old way: I have learnt the lesson of Agincourt, of Poitiers and Crecy. I know how many lives any move of mine will cost; and if the move is worth the cost I make it and pay the cost. But Joan never counts the cost at all: she goes ahead and trusts to God: she thinks she has God in her pocket. Up to now she has had the numbers on her side; and she has won. But I know Joan; and I see that some day she will go ahead when she has only ten men to do the work of a hundred. And then she will find that God is on the side of the big battalions. She will be taken by the enemy. And the lucky man that makes the capture will receive sixteen thousand pounds from the Earl of Ouareek.

JOAN. [*Flattered.*] Sixteen thousand pounds! Eh, laddie, have they offered that for me? There cannot be so much money in the world.

DUNOIS. There is, in England. And now tell me, all of you, which of you will lift a finger to save Joan once the English have got her? I speak first, for the army. The day after she has been dragged from her horse by a goddam or a Burgundian, and he is not struck dead: the day after she is locked in a dungeon, and the bars and bolts do not fly open at the touch of St Peter's angel: the day when the enemy finds out that she is as vulnerable as I am and not a bit more invincible, she will not be worth the life of a single soldier to us; and I will not risk that life, much as I cherish her as a companion-in-arms.

JOAN. I dont blame you, Jack: you are right. I am not worth one soldier's life if God lets me be beaten; but France may think me worth my ransom after what God has done for her through me.

CHARLES. I tell you I have no money; and this coronation, which is all your fault, has cost me the last farthing I can borrow.

JOAN. The Church is richer than you. I put my trust in the Church.

THE ARCHBISHOP. Woman: they will drag you through the streets, and burn you as a witch.

JOAN. [*Running to him.*] Oh, my lord, do not say that. It is impossible. I a witch!

THE ARCHBISHOP. Peter Cauchon knows his business. The University of Paris has burnt a woman for saying that what you have done was well done, and according to God.

JOAN. [*Bewildered.*] But why? What sense is there in it? What I have done is according to God. They could not burn a woman for speaking the truth.

THE ARCHBISHOP. They did.

JOAN. But you know that she was speaking the truth. You would not let them burn me.

THE ARCHBISHOP. How could I prevent them?

JOAN. You would speak in the name of the Church. You are a great prince of the Church. I would go anywhere with your blessing to protect me.

THE ARCHBISHOP. I have no blessing for you while you are proud and disobedient.

JOAN. Oh, why will you go on saying things like that? I am not proud and disobedient. I am a poor girl, and so ignorant that I do not know A from B. How could I be proud? And how can you say that I am disobedient when I always obey my voices, because they come from God.

THE ARCHBISHOP. The voice of God on earth is the voice of the Church Militant; and all the voices that come to you are the echoes of your own wilfulness.

JOAN. It is not true.

THE ARCHBISHOP. [*Flushing angrily.*] You tell the Archbishop in his cathedral that he lies; and yet you say you are not proud and disobedient.

JOAN. I never said you lied. It was you that as good as said my voices lied. When have they ever lied? If you will not believe in them: even if they are only the echoes of my own common sense, are they not always right? and are not your earthly counsels always wrong?

THE ARCHBISHOP. [*Indignantly.*] It is waste of time admonishing you.

CHARLES. It always comes back to the same thing. She is right; and everyone else is wrong.

THE ARCHBISHOP. Take this as your last warning. If you perish through setting your private judgment above the instructions of your spiritual directors, the Church disowns you, and leaves you to whatever fate your presumption may bring upon you. The Bastard has told you that if you persist in setting up your military conceit above the counsels of your commanders——

DUNOIS. [*Interposing.*] To put it quite exactly, if you attempt to relieve the garrison in Compiègne without the same superiority in numbers you had at Orleans——

THE ARCHBISHOP. The army will disown you, and will not rescue you. And His Majesty the King has told you that the throne has not the means of ransoming you.

CHARLES. Not a penny.

THE ARCHBISHOP. You stand alone: absolutely alone, trusting to your own conceit, your own ignorance, your own headstrong presumption, your own impiety in hiding all these sins under the cloak of a trust in God. When you pass through these doors into the sunlight, the crowd will cheer you. They will bring you their little children and their invalids to heal: they will kiss your hands and feet, and do what they can, poor simple souls, to turn your head, and madden you with the self-confidence that is leading you to your destruction. But you will be none the less alone: they cannot save you. We and we only can stand between you and the stake at which our enemies have burnt that wretched woman in Paris.

JOAN. [Her eyes skyward.] I have better friends and better counsel than yours.

THE ARCHBISHOP. I see that I am speaking in vain to a hardened heart. You reject our protection, and are determined to turn us all against you. In future, then, fend for yourself; and if you fail, God have mercy on your soul.

DUNOIS. That is the truth, Joan. Heed it.

JOAN. Where would you all have been now if I had heeded that sort of truth? There is no help, no counsel, in any of you. Yes: I am alone on earth: I have always been alone. My father told my brothers to drown me if I would not stay to mind his sheep while France was bleeding to death: France might perish if only our lambs were safe. I thought France would have friends at the court of the king of France; and I find only wolves fighting for pieces of her poor torn body. I thought God would have friends everywhere, because He is the friend of everyone; and in my innocence I believed that you who now cast me out would be like strong towers to keep harm from me. But I am wiser now; and nobody is any the worse for being wiser. Do not think you can frighten me by telling me that I am alone. France is alone; and God is alone; and what is my loneliness before the loneliness of my country and my God? I see now that the loneliness of God is His strength: what would He be if He listened to your jealous little counsels? Well, my loneliness shall be my strength too; it is better to be alone with God: His friendship will not fail me, nor His counsel, nor His love. In His strength I will dare, and dare, and dare, until I die. I will go out now to the common people, and let the love in their eyes comfort me for the hate in yours. You will all be glad to see me burnt; but if I go through the fire I shall go through it to their hearts for ever and ever. And so, God be with me!

[She goes from them. They stare after her in glum silence for a moment. Then Gilles de Rais twirls his beard.

BLUEBEARD. You know, the woman is quite impossible. I dont
dislike her, really; but what are you to do with such a character?

DUNOIS. As God is my judge, if she fell into the Loire I would
jump in in full armor to fish her out. But if she plays the fool at
Compiègne, and gets caught, I must leave her to her doom.

LA HIRE. Then you had better chain me up; for I could follow her
to hell when the spirit rises in her like that.

THE ARCHBISHOP. She disturbs my judgment too: there is a
dangerous power in her outbursts. But the pit is open at her
feet; and for good or evil we cannot turn her from it.

CHARLES. If only she would keep quiet, or go home!

[*They follow her dispiritedly.*

Rouen, 30th May 1431. A great stone hall in the castle, arranged for a trial-at-law, but not a trial-by-jury, the court being the Bishop's court with the Inquisition participating: hence there are two raised chairs side by side for the Bishop and the Inquisitor as judges. Rows of chairs radiating from them at an obtuse angle are for the canons, the doctors of law and theology, and the Dominican monks, who act as assessors. In the angle is a table for the scribes, with stools. There is also a heavy rough wooden stool for the prisoner. All these are at the inner end of the hall. The further end is open to the courtyard through a row of arches. The court is shielded from the weather by screens and curtains.

Looking down the great hall from the middle of the inner end, the judicial chairs and scribes' table are to the right. The prisoner's stool is to the left. There are arched doors right and left. It is a fine sunshiny May morning.

Warwick comes in through the arched doorway on the judges' side, followed by his page.

THE PAGE. [*Pertly.*] I suppose your lordship is aware that we have no business here. This is an ecclesiastical court; and we are only the secular arm.

WARWICK. I am aware of that fact. Will it please your impudence to find the Bishop of Beauvais for me, and give him a hint that he can have a word with me here before the trial, if he wishes?

THE PAGE. [*Going.*] Yes, my lord.

WARWICK. And mind you behave yourself. Do not address him as Pious Peter.

THE PAGE. No, my lord. I shall be kind to him, because, when The Maid is brought in, Pious Peter will have to pick a peck of pickled pepper.

[*Cauchon enters through the same door with a Dominican monk and a canon, the latter carrying a brief.*

THE PAGE. The Right Reverend his lordship the Bishop of Beauvais. And two other reverend gentlemen.

WARWICK. Get out; and see that we are not interrupted.

THE PAGE. Right, my lord. [*He vanishes airily.*

CAUCHON. I wish your lordship good morrow.

WARWICK. Good morrow to your lordship. Have I had the pleasure of meeting your friends before? I think not.

CAUCHON. [*Introducing the monk, who is on his right.*] This, my lord, is Brother John Lemaître, of the order of St Dominic. He is acting as deputy for the Chief Inquisitor into the evil of heresy in France. Brother John: the Earl of Warwick.

WARWICK. Your Reverence is most welcome. We have no Inquisitor in England, unfortunately; though we miss him greatly, especially on occasions like the present.

[*The Inquisitor smiles patiently, and bows. He is a mild elderly gentleman, but has evident reserves of authority and firmness.*

CAUCHON. [*Introducing the Canon, who is on his left.*] This gentleman is Canon John D'Estivet, of the Chapter of Bayeux. He is acting as Promoter.

WARWICK. Promoter?

CAUCHON. Prosecutor, you would call him in civil law.

WARWICK. Ah! Prosecutor. Quite, quite. I am very glad to make your acquaintance, Canon D'Estivet.

[*D'Estivet bows. He is on the young side of middle age, well mannered, but vulpine beneath his veneer.*

WARWICK. May I ask what stage the proceedings have reached? It is now more than nine months since The Maid was captured at Compiègne by the Burgundians. It is fully four months since I bought her from the Burgundians for a very handsome sum, solely that she might be brought to justice. It is very nearly three months since I delivered her up to you, my Lord Bishop, as a person suspected of heresy. May I suggest that you are taking a rather unconscionable time to make up your minds about a very plain case? Is this trial never going to end?

THE INQUISITOR. [*Smiling.*] It has not yet begun, my lord.

WARWICK. Not yet begun! Why, you have been at it eleven weeks!

CAUCHON. We have not been idle, my lord. We have held fifteen examinations of The Maid: six public and nine private.

THE INQUISITOR. [*Always patiently smiling.*] You see, my lord, I have been present at only two of these examinations. They were proceedings of the Bishop's court solely, and not of the Holy Office. I have only just decided to associate myself—that is, to associate the Holy Inquisition—with the Bishop's court. I did not at first think that this was a case of heresy at all. I regarded it as a political case, and The Maid as a prisoner of war. But having now been present at two of the examinations, I must admit that this seems to be one of the gravest cases of heresy within my experience. Therefore everything is now in order, and we proceed to trial this morning.

[*He moves towards the judicial chairs.*

CAUCHON. This moment, if your lordship's convenience allows.

WARWICK. [*Graciously.*] Well, that is good news, gentlemen. I will not attempt to conceal from you that our patience was becoming strained.

CAUCHON. So I gathered from the threats of your soldiers to drown those of our people who favor The Maid.

WARWICK. Dear me! At all events their intentions were friendly to you, my lord.

CAUCHON. [*Sternly.*] I hope not. I am determined that the woman shall have a fair hearing. The justice of the Church is not a mockery, my lord.

THE INQUISITOR. [*Returning.*] Never has there been a fairer examination within my experience, my lord. The Maid needs no lawyers to take her part: she will be tried by her most faithful friends, all ardently desirous to save her soul from perdition.

D'ESTIVET. Sir: I am the Promoter; and it has been my painful duty to present the case against the girl; but believe me, I would throw up my case today and hasten to her defence if I did not know that men far my superiors in learning and piety, in eloquence and persuasiveness, have been sent to reason with her, to explain to her the danger she is running, and the ease with which she may avoid it. [*Suddenly bursting into forensic eloquence, to the disgust of Cauchon and the Inquisitor, who have listened to him so far with patronizing approval.*] Men have dared to say that we are acting from hate; but God is our witness that they lie. Have we tortured her? No. Have we ceased to exhort her; to implore her to have pity on herself; to come to the bosom of her Church as an erring but beloved child? Have we——

CAUCHON. [*Interrupting drily.*] Take care, Canon. All that you say is true; but if you make his lordship believe it I will not answer for your life, and hardly for my own.

WARWICK. [*Deprecating, but by no means denying.*] Oh, my lord, you are very hard on us poor English. But we certainly do not share your pious desire to save The Maid: in fact I tell you now plainly that her death is a political necessity which I regret but cannot help. If the Church lets her go——

CAUCHON. [*With fierce and menacing pride.*] If the Church lets her go, woe to the man, were he the Emperor himself, who dares lay a finger on her! The Church is not subject to political necessity, my lord.

THE INQUISITOR. [*Interposing smoothly.*] You need have no anxiety about the result, my lord. You have an invincible ally in the matter: one who is far more determined than you that she shall burn.

WARWICK. And who is this very convenient partisan, may I ask?

THE INQUISITOR. The Maid herself. Unless you put a gag in her mouth you cannot prevent her from convicting herself ten times over every time she opens it.

D'ESTIVET. That is perfectly true, my lord. My hair bristles on my head when I hear so young a creature utter such blasphemies.

WARWICK. Well, by all means do your best for her if you are quite sure it will be of no avail. [*Looking hard at Cauchon.*] I should be sorry to have to act without the blessing of the Church.

CAUCHON. [*With a mixture of cynical admiration and contempt.*] And yet they say Englishmen are hypocrites! You play for your side, my lord, even at the peril of your soul. I cannot but admire such devotion; but I dare not go so far myself. I fear damnation.

WARWICK. If we feared anything we could never govern England, my lord. Shall I send your people in to you?

CAUCHON. Yes: it will be very good of your lordship to withdraw and allow the court to assemble.

[*Warwick turns on his heel, and goes out through the courtyard. Cauchon takes one of the judicial seats; and D'Estivet sits at the scribes' table, studying his brief.*

CAUCHON. [*Casually, as he makes himself comfortable.*] What scoundrels these English nobles are!

THE INQUISITOR. [*Taking the other judicial chair on Cauchon's left.*] All secular power makes men scoundrels. They are not trained for the work; and they have not the Apostolic Succession. Our own nobles are just as bad.

[*The Bishop's assessors hurry into the hall, headed by Chaplain de Stogumber and Canon de Courcelles, a young priest of thirty. The scribes sit at the table, leaving a chair vacant opposite D'Estivet. Some of the assessors take their seats: others stand chatting, waiting for the proceedings to begin formally. De Stogumber, aggrieved and obstinate, will not take his seat: neither will the Canon, who stands on his right.*

CAUCHON. Good morning, Master de Stogumber. [*To the Inquisitor.*] Chaplain to the Cardinal of England.

THE CHAPLAIN. [*Correcting him.*] Of Winchester, my lord. I have to make a protest, my lord.

CAUCHON. You make a great many.

THE CHAPLAIN. I am not without support, my lord. Here is Master de Courcelles, Canon of Paris, who associates himself with me in my protest.

CAUCHON. Well, what is the matter?

THE CHAPLAIN. [*Sulkily.*] Speak you, Master de Courcelles, since I do not seem to enjoy his lordship's confidence.

[*He sits down in dudgeon next to Cauchon, on his right.*

COURCELLES. My lord: we have been at great pains to draw up an indictment of The Maid on sixty-four counts. We are now told that they have been reduced, without consulting us.

THE INQUISITOR. Master de Courcelles: I am the culprit. I am

overwhelmed with admiration for the zeal displayed in your
sixty-four counts; but in accusing a heretic, as in other things,
enough is enough. Also you must remember that all the members
of the court are not so subtle and profound as you, and that some
of your very great learning might appear to them to be very
great nonsense. Therefore I have thought it well to have your
sixty-four articles cut down to twelve——

COURCELLES. [*Thunderstruck.*] Twelve !!!

THE INQUISITOR. Twelve will, believe me, be quite enough for
your purpose.

THE CHAPLAIN. But some of the most important points have been
reduced almost to nothing. For instance, The Maid has actually
declared that the blessed saints Margaret and Catherine, and the
holy Archangel Michael, spoke to her in French. That is a vital
point.

THE INQUISITOR. You think, doubtless, that they should have
spoken in Latin?

CAUCHON. No: he thinks they should have spoken in English.

THE CHAPLAIN. Naturally, my lord.

THE INQUISITOR. Well, as we are all here agreed, I think, that these
voices of The Maid are the voices of evil spirits tempting her to
her damnation, it would not be very courteous to you, Master
de Stogumber, or to the King of England, to assume that English
is the devil's native language. So let it pass. The matter is not
wholly omitted from the twelve articles. Pray take your places,
gentlemen; and let us proceed to business.

> [*All who have not taken their seats, do so.*

THE CHAPLAIN. Well, I protest. That is all.

COURCELLES. I think it hard that all our work should go for
nothing. It is only another example of the diabolical influence
which this woman exercises over the court.

> [*He takes his chair, which is on the Chaplain's right.*

CAUCHON. Do you suggest that I am under diabolical influence?

COURCELLES. I suggest nothing, my lord. But it seems to me that
there is a conspiracy here to hush up the fact that The Maid
stole the Bishop of Senlis's horse.

CAUCHON. [*Keeping his temper with difficulty.*] This is not a police
court. Are we to waste our time on such rubbish?

COURCELLES. [*Rising, shocked.*] My lord: do you call the Bishop's
horse rubbish?

THE INQUISITOR. [*Blandly.*] Master de Courcelles: The Maid alleges
that she paid handsomely for the Bishop's horse, and that if he
did not get the money the fault was not hers. As that may
be true, the point is one on which The Maid may well be
acquitted.

COURCELLES. Yes, if it were an ordinary horse. But the Bishop's horse! How can she be acquitted for that?

[*He sits down again, bewildered and discouraged.*

THE INQUISITOR. I submit to you, with great respect, that if we persist in trying The Maid on trumpery issues on which we may have to declare her innocent, she may escape us on the great main issue of heresy, on which she seems so far to insist on her own guilt. I will ask you, therefore, to say nothing, when The Maid is brought before us, of these stealings of horses, and dancings round fairy trees with the village children, and prayings at haunted wells, and a dozen other things which you were diligently inquiring into until my arrival. There is not a village girl in France against whom you could not prove such things: they all dance round haunted trees, and pray at magic wells. Some of them would steal the Pope's horse if they got the chance. Heresy, gentlemen, heresy is the charge we have to try. The detection and suppression of heresy is my peculiar business: I am here as an inquisitor, not as an ordinary magistrate. Stick to the heresy, gentlemen; and leave the other matters alone.

CAUCHON. I may say that we have sent to the girl's village to make inquiries about her, and there is practically nothing serious against her.

| THE CHAPLAIN. | [*Rising and clamoring together.*] | Nothing serious, my lord—— |
| COURCELLES. | | What! The fairy tree not—— |

CAUCHON. [*Out of patience.*] Be silent, gentlemen; or speak one at a time.

[*Courcelles collapses into his chair, intimidated.*

THE CHAPLAIN. [*Sulkily resuming his seat.*] That is what The Maid said to us last Friday.

CAUCHON. I wish you had followed her counsel, sir. When I say nothing serious, I mean nothing that men of sufficiently large mind to conduct an inquiry like this would consider serious. I agree with my colleague the Inquisitor that it is on the count of heresy that we must proceed.

LADVENU. [*A young but ascetically fine-drawn Dominican who is sitting next Courcelles, on his right.*] But is there any great harm in the girl's heresy? Is it not merely her simplicity? Many saints have said as much as Joan.

THE INQUISITOR. [*Dropping his blandness and speaking very gravely.*] Brother Martin: if you had seen what I have seen of heresy, you would not think it a light thing even in its most apparently harmless and even lovable and pious origins. Heresy begins with people who are to all appearance better than their neighbors.

A gentle and pious girl, or a young man who has obeyed the command of our Lord by giving all his riches to the poor, and putting on the garb of poverty, the life of austerity, and the rule of humility and charity, may be the founder of a heresy that will wreck both Church and Empire if not ruthlessly stamped out in time. The records of the holy Inquisition are full of histories we dare not give to the world, because they are beyond the belief of honest men and innocent women; yet they all began with saintly simpletons. I have seen this again and again. Mark what I say: the woman who quarrels with her clothes, and puts on the dress of a man, is like the man who throws off his fur gown and dresses like John the Baptist: they are followed, as surely as the night follows the day, by bands of wild women and men who refuse to wear any clothes at all. When maids will neither marry nor take regular vows, and men reject marriage and exalt their lusts into divine inspirations, then, as surely as the summer follows the spring, they begin with polygamy, and end by incest. Heresy at first seems innocent and even laudable; but it ends in such a monstrous horror of unnatural wickedness that the most tender-hearted among you, if you saw it at work as I have seen it, would clamor against the mercy of the Church in dealing with it. For two hundred years the Holy Office has striven with these diabolical madnesses; and it knows that they begin always in vain and ignorant persons setting up their own judgment against the Church, and taking it upon themselves to be the interpreters of God's will. You must not fall into the common error of mistaking these simpletons for liars and hypocrites. They believe honestly and sincerely that their diabolical inspiration is divine. Therefore you must be on your guard against your natural compassion. You are all, I hope, merciful men: how else could you have devoted your lives to the service of our gentle Savior? You are going to see before you a young girl, pious and chaste; for I must tell you, gentlemen, that the things said of her by our English friends are supported by no evidence, whilst there is abundant testimony that her excesses have been excesses of religion and charity and not of worldliness and wantonness. This girl is not one of those whose hard features are the sign of hard hearts, and whose brazen looks and lewd demeanor condemn them before they are accused. The devilish pride that has led her into her present peril has left no mark on her countenance. Strange as it may seem to you, it has even left no mark on her character outside those special matters in which she is proud; so that you will see a diabolical pride and a natural humility seated side by side in the selfsame soul. Therefore be on your guard. God forbid that I should tell you to harden your hearts; for her punishment if we condemn her will be so cruel that we should forfeit our own hope of divine mercy were there one grain of malice against her in our hearts. But if you hate cruelty—and if any man here does not hate it I command him on his soul's salvation to quit this holy court—I say, if you hate cruelty, remember that nothing is so cruel in its consequences as the toleration of heresy. Remember also that no court of law can be so cruel as the common people are to those whom they suspect of heresy. The heretic in the hands of the Holy Office is safe from violence, is assured of a fair trial, and cannot suffer death, even when guilty, if repentance follows sin. Innumerable lives of heretics have been saved because the Holy Office has taken them out of the hands of the people, and because the people have yielded them up, knowing that the Holy Office would deal with them. Before the Holy Inquisition existed, and even now when its officers are not within reach, the unfortunate wretch suspected of heresy, perhaps quite ignorantly and unjustly, is stoned, torn in pieces, drowned, burned in his house with all his innocent children, without a trial, unshriven, unburied save as a dog is buried: all of them deeds hateful to God and most cruel to man. Gentlemen: I am compassionate by nature as well as by my profession; and though the work I have to do may seem cruel to those who do not know how much more cruel it would be to leave it undone, I would go to the stake myself sooner than do it if I did not know its righteousness, its necessity, its essential mercy. I ask you to address yourself to this trial in that conviction. Anger is a bad counsellor: cast out anger. Pity is sometimes worse: cast out pity. But do not cast out mercy. Remember only that justice comes first. Have you anything to say, my lord, before we proceed to trial?

CAUCHON. You have spoken for me, and spoken better than I could. I do not see how any sane man could disagree with a word that has fallen from you. But this I will add. The crude heresies of which you have told us are horrible; but their horror is like that of the black death: they rage for a while and then die out, because sound and sensible men will not under any incitement be reconciled to nakedness and incest and polygamy and the like. But we are confronted today throughout Europe with a heresy that is spreading among men not weak in mind nor diseased in brain: nay, the stronger the mind, the more obstinate the heretic. It is neither discredited by fantastic extremes nor corrupted by the common lusts of the flesh; but it, too, sets up the private judgment of the single erring mortal against the considered wisdom and experience of the Church. The mighty structure of Catholic Christendom will never be shaken by naked madmen or by the sins of Moab and Ammon. But it may be betrayed from within, and brought to barbarous ruin and desolation, by this arch heresy which the English Commander calls Protestantism.

THE ASSESSORS. [*Whispering.*] Protestantism! What was that? What does the Bishop mean? Is it a new heresy? The English Commander, he said. Did you ever hear of Protestantism, etc. etc.?

CAUCHON. [*Continuing.*] And that reminds me. What provision has the Earl of Warwick made for the defence of the secular arm should The Maid prove obdurate, and the people be moved to pity her?

THE CHAPLAIN. Have no fear on that score, my lord. The noble earl has eight hundred men-at-arms at the gates. She will not slip through our English fingers even if the whole city be on her side.

CAUCHON. [*Revolted.*] Will you not add, God grant that she repent and purge her sin?

THE CHAPLAIN. That does not seem to me to be consistent; but of course I agree with your lordship.

CAUCHON. [*Giving him up with a shrug of contempt.*] The court sits.

THE INQUISITOR. Let the accused be brought in.

LADVENU. [*Calling.*] The accused. Let her be brought in.

[*Joan, chained by the ankles, is brought in through the arched door behind the prisoner's stool by a guard of English soldiers. With them is the Executioner and his assistants. They lead her to the prisoner's stool, and place themselves behind it after taking off her chain. She wears a page's black suit. Her long imprisonment and the strain of the examinations which have preceded the trial have left their mark on her; but her vitality still holds: she confronts the court unabashed, without a trace of the awe which their formal solemnity seems to require for the complete success of its impressiveness.*]

THE INQUISITOR. [*Kindly.*] Sit down, Joan. [*She sits on the prisoner's stool.*] You look very pale today. Are you not well?

JOAN. Thank you kindly: I am well enough. But the Bishop sent me some carp; and it made me ill.

CAUCHON. I am sorry. I told them to see that it was fresh.

JOAN. You meant to be good to me, I know; but it is a fish that does not agree with me. The English thought you were trying to poison me——

CAUCHON. } [*Together.*] { What!
THE CHAPLAIN. }   { No, my lord.

JOAN. [*Continuing.*] They are determined that I shall be burnt as a witch; and they sent their doctor to cure me; but he was forbidden to bleed me because the silly people believed that a witch's witchery leaves her if she is bled; so he only called me filthy names. Why do you leave me in the hands of the English? I should be in the hands of the Church. And why must I be chained by the feet to a log of wood? Are you afraid I will fly away?

D'ESTIVET. [*Harshly.*] Woman: it is not for you to question the court: it is for us to question you.

COURCELLES. When you were left unchained, did you not try to escape by jumping from a tower sixty feet high? If you cannot fly like a witch, how is it that you are still alive?

JOAN. I suppose because the tower was not so high then. It has grown higher every day since you began asking me questions about it.

D'ESTIVET. Why did you jump from the tower?

JOAN. How do you know that I jumped?

D'ESTIVET. You were found lying in the moat. Why did you leave the tower?

JOAN. Why would anybody leave a prison if they could get out?

D'ESTIVET. You tried to escape?

JOAN. Of course I did; and not for the first time either. If you leave the door of the cage open the bird will fly out.

D'ESTIVET [*Rising.*] That is a confession of heresy. I call the attention of the court to it.

JOAN. Heresy, he calls it? Am I a heretic because I try to escape from prison?

D'ESTIVET. Assuredly, if you are in the hands of the Church, and you wilfully take yourself out of its hands, you are deserting the Church; and that is heresy.

JOAN. It is great nonsense. Nobody could be such a fool as to think that.

D'ESTIVET. You hear, my lord, how I am reviled in the execution of my duty by this woman.   [*He sits down indignantly.*

CAUCHON. I have warned you before, Joan, that you are doing yourself no good by these pert answers.

JOAN. But you will not talk sense to me. I am reasonable if you will be reasonable.

THE INQUISITOR. [*Interposing.*] This is not yet in order. You forget, Master Promoter, that the proceedings have not been formally opened. The time for questions is after she has sworn on the Gospels to tell us the whole truth.

JOAN. You say this to me every time. I have said again and again that I will tell you all that concerns this trial. But I cannot tell you the whole truth: God does not allow the whole truth to be told. You do not understand it when I tell it. It is an old saying that he who tells too much truth is sure to be hanged. I am weary of this argument: we have been over it nine times already. I have sworn as much as I will swear; and I will swear no more.

COURCELLES. My lord: she should be put to the torture.

THE INQUISITOR. You hear, Joan? That is what happens to the obdurate. Think before you answer. Has she been shewn the instruments?

THE EXECUTIONER. They are ready, my lord. She has seen them.

JOAN. If you tear me limb from limb until you separate my soul from my body you will get nothing out of me beyond what I have told you. What more is there to tell that you could understand? Besides, I cannot bear to be hurt; and if you hurt me I will say anything you like to stop the pain. But I will take it all back afterwards; so what is the use of it?

LADVENU. There is much in that. We should proceed mercifully.

COURCELLES. But the torture is customary.

THE INQUISITOR. It must not be applied wantonly. If the accused will confess voluntarily, then its use cannot be justified.

COURCELLES. But this is unusual and irregular. She refuses to take the oath.

LADVENU. [*Disgusted.*] Do you want to torture the girl for the mere pleasure of it?

COURCELLES. [*Bewildered.*] But it is not a pleasure. It is the law. It is customary. It is always done.

THE INQUISITOR. That is not so, Master, except when the inquiries are carried on by people who do not know their legal business.

COURCELLES. But the woman is a heretic. I assure you it is always done.

CAUCHON. [*Decisively.*] It will not be done today if it is not necessary. Let there be an end of this. I will not have it said that we proceeded on forced confessions. We have sent our best preachers and doctors to this woman to exhort and implore her to save her soul and body from the fire: we shall not now send the executioner to thrust her into it.

COURCELLES. Your lordship is merciful, of course. But it is a great responsibility to depart from the usual practice.

JOAN. Thou art a rare noodle, Master. Do what was done last time is thy rule, eh?

COURCELLES. [*Rising.*] Thou wanton: dost thou dare call me noodle?

THE INQUISITOR. Patience, Master, patience; I fear you will soon be only too terribly avenged.

COURCELLES. [*Mutters.*] Noodle indeed!

[*He sits down, much discontented.*

THE INQUISITOR. Meanwhile, let us not be moved by the rough side of a shepherd lass's tongue.

JOAN. Nay: I am no shepherd lass, though I have helped with the sheep like anyone else. I will do a lady's work in the house—spin or weave—against any woman in Rouen.

THE INQUISITOR. This is not a time for vanity, Joan. You stand in great peril.

JOAN. I know it. Have I not been punished for my vanity? If I had not worn my cloth of gold surcoat in battle like a fool, that Burgundian soldier would never have pulled me backwards off my horse; and I should not have been here.

THE CHAPLAIN. If you are so clever at woman's work why do you not stay at home and do it?

JOAN. There are plenty of other women to do it; but there is nobody to do my work.

CAUCHON. Come! we are wasting time on trifles. Joan: I am going to put a most solemn question to you. Take care how you answer; for your life and salvation are at stake on it. Will you for all you have said and done, be it good or bad, accept the judgment of God's Church on earth? More especially as to the acts and words that are imputed to you in this trial by the Promoter here, will you submit your case to the inspired interpretation of the Church Militant?

JOAN. I am a faithful child of the Church. I will obey the Church——

CAUCHON. [Hopefully leaning forward.] You will?

JOAN. —[provided it does not command anything impossible. [Cauchon sinks back in his chair with a heavy sigh. The Inquisitor purses his lips and frowns. Ladvenu shakes his head pitifully.

D'ESTIVET. She imputes to the Church the error and folly of commanding the impossible.

JOAN. If you command me to declare that all that I have done and said, and all the visions and revelations I have had, were not from God, then that is impossible: I will not declare it for anything in the world. What God made me do I will never go back on; and what He commanded or shall command I will not fail to do in spite of any man alive. That is what I mean by impossible. And in case the Church should bid me do anything contrary to the command I have from God, I will not consent to it, no matter what it may be.

THE ASSESSORS. [Shocked and indignant.] Oh! The Church contrary to God! What do you say now? Flat heresy. This is beyond everything, etc. etc.

D'ESTIVET. [Throwing down his brief.] My lord: do you need anything more than this?

CAUCHON. Woman: you have said enough to burn ten heretics. Will you not be warned? Will you not understand?

THE INQUISITOR. If the Church Militant tells you that your revelations and visions are sent by the devil to tempt you to your damnation, will you not believe that the Church is wiser than you?

JOAN. I believe that God is wiser than I; and it is His commands that I will do. All the things that you call my crimes have come to me by the command of God. I say that I have done them by the order of God: it is impossible for me to say anything else. If any Churchman says the contrary I shall not mind him: I shall mind God alone, whose command I always follow.

LADVENU. [*Pleading with her urgently.*] You do not know what you are saying, child. Do you want to kill yourself? Listen. Do you not believe that you are subject to the Church of God on earth?

JOAN. Yes. When have I ever denied it?

LADVENU. Good. That means, does it not, that you are subject to our Lord the Pope, to the cardinals, the archbishops, and the bishops for whom his lordship stands here today?

JOAN. God must be served first.

D'ESTIVET. Then your voices command you not to submit yourself to the Church Militant?

JOAN. My voices do not tell me to disobey the Church; but God must be served first.

CAUCHON. And you, and not the Church, are to be the judge?

JOAN. What other judgment can I judge by but my own?

THE ASSESSORS. [*Scandalized.*] Oh!   [*They cannot find words.*

CAUCHON. Out of your own mouth you have condemned yourself. We have striven for your salvation to the verge of sinning ourselves: we have opened the door to you again and again; and you have shut it in our faces and in the face of God. Dare you pretend, after what you have said, that you are in a state of grace?

JOAN. If I am not, may God bring me to it: if I am, may God keep me in it!

LADVENU. That is a very good reply, my lord.

COURCELLES. Were you in a state of grace when you stole the Bishop's horse?

CAUCHON. [*Rising in a fury.*] Oh, devil take the Bishop's horse and you too! We are here to try a case of heresy; and no sooner do we come to the root of the matter than we are thrown back by idiots who understand nothing but horses.

                    [*Trembling with rage, he forces himself to sit down.*

THE INQUISITOR. Gentlemen, gentlemen. In clinging to these small issues you are The Maid's best advocates. I am not surprised that his lordship has lost patience with you. What does the Promoter say? Does he press these trumpery matters?

D'ESTIVET. I am bound by my office to press everything; but when the woman confesses a heresy that must bring upon her the doom of excommunication, of what consequence is it that she has been guilty also of offences which expose her to minor penances? I share the impatience of his lordship as to these minor charges. Only, with great respect, I must emphasize the gravity of two very horrible and blasphemous crimes which she does not deny. First, she has intercourse with evil spirits, and is therefore a sorceress. Second, she wears men's clothes, which is indecent, unnatural and abominable; and in spite of our most earnest remonstrances and entreaties, she will not change them even to receive the sacrament.

JOAN. Is the blessed St Catherine an evil spirit? Is St Margaret? Is Michael the Archangel?

COURCELLES. How do you know that the spirit which appears to you is an archangel? Does he not appear to you as a naked man?

JOAN. Do you think God cannot afford clothes for him?

[*The assessors cannot help smiling, especially as the joke is against Courcelles.*]

LADVENU. Well answered, Joan.

THE INQUISITOR. It is, in effect, well answered. But no evil spirit would be so simple as to appear to a young girl in a guise that would scandalize her when he meant her to take him for a messenger from the Most High? Joan: the Church instructs you that these apparitions are demons seeking your soul's perdition. Do you accept the instruction of the Church?

JOAN. I accept the messenger of God. How could any faithful believer in the Church refuse him?

CAUCHON. Wretched woman. Again I ask you, do you know what you are saying?

THE INQUISITOR. You wrestle in vain with the devil for her soul, my lord; she will not be saved. Now as to this matter of the man's dress. For the last time, will you put off that impudent attire, and dress as becomes your sex?

JOAN. I will not.

D'ESTIVET. [*Pouncing.*] The sin of disobedience, my lord.

JOAN. [*Distressed.*] But my voices tell me I must dress as a soldier.

LADVENU. Joan, Joan: does not that prove to you that the voices are the voices of evil spirits? Can you suggest to us one good reason why an angel of God should give you such shameless advice?

JOAN. Why, yes: what can be plainer common sense? I was a soldier living among soldiers. I am a prisoner guarded by soldiers. If I were to dress as a woman they would think of me as a woman; and then what would become of me? If I dress as a soldier they think of me as a soldier, and I can live with them as I do at home with my brothers. That is why St Catherine tells me I must not dress as a woman until she gives me leave.

COURCELLES. When will she give you leave?

JOAN. When you take me out of the hands of the English soldiers. I have told you that I should be in the hands of the Church, and not left night and day with four soldiers of the Earl of Warwick. Do you want me to live with them in petticoats?

LADVENU. My lord: what she says is, God knows, very wrong and shocking; but there is a grain of worldly sense in it such as might impose on a simple village maiden.

JOAN. If we were as simple in the village as you are in your courts and palaces, there would soon be no wheat to make bread for you.

CAUCHON. That is the thanks you get for trying to save her, Brother Martin.

LADVENU. Joan: we are all trying to save you. His lordship is trying to save you. The Inquisitor could not be more just to you if you were his own daughter. But you are blinded by a terrible pride and self-sufficiency.

JOAN. Why do you say that? I have said nothing wrong. I cannot understand.

THE INQUISITOR. The blessed St Athanasius has laid it down in his creed that those who cannot understand are damned. It is not enough to be simple. It is not enough even to be what simple people call good. The simplicity of a darkened mind is no better than the simplicity of a beast.

JOAN. There is great wisdom in the simplicity of a beast, let me tell you; and sometimes great foolishness in the wisdom of scholars.

LADVENU. We know that, Joan: we are not so foolish as you think us. Try to resist the temptation to make pert replies to us. Do you see that man who stands behind you?

[He indicates the Executioner.

JOAN. [Turning and looking at the man.] Your torturer? But the Bishop said I was not to be tortured.

LADVENU. You are not to be tortured because you have confessed everything that is necessary to your condemnation. That man is not only the torturer: he is also the Executioner. Executioner, let The Maid hear your answers to my questions. Are you prepared for the burning of a heretic this day?

THE EXECUTIONER. Yes, Master.

LADVENU. Is the stake ready?

THE EXECUTIONER. It is. In the market-place. The English have built it too high for me to get near her and make the death easier. It will be a cruel death.

JOAN. [Horrified.] But you are not going to burn me now?

THE INQUISITOR. You realize it at last.

LADVENU. There are eight hundred English soldiers waiting to take you to the market-place the moment the sentence of excommunication has passed the lips of your judges. You are within a few short moments of that doom.

JOAN. [Looking round desperately for rescue.] Oh, God!

LADVENU. Do not despair, Joan. The Church is merciful. You can save yourself.

JOAN. [*Hopefully*.] Yes: my voices promised me I should not be burnt. St Catherine bade me be bold.

CAUCHON. Woman: are you quite mad? Do you not yet see that your voices have deceived you?

JOAN. Oh no: that is impossible.

CAUCHON. Impossible! They have led you straight to your excommunication, and to the stake which is there waiting for you.

LADVENU. [*Pressing the point hard*.] Have they kept a single promise to you since you were taken at Compiègne? The devil has betrayed you. The Church holds out its arms to you.

JOAN. [*Despairing*.] Oh, it is true: it is true: my voices have deceived me. I have been mocked by devils; my faith is broken. I have dared and dared; but only a fool will walk into a fire. God, who gave me my common sense, cannot will me to do that.

LADVENU. Now God be praised that He has saved you at the eleventh hour!

[*He hurries to the vacant seat at the scribes' table, and snatches a sheet of paper, on which he sets to work writing eagerly.*

CAUCHON. Amen!

JOAN. What must I do?

CAUCHON. You must sign a solemn recantation of your heresy.

JOAN. Sign? That means to write my name. I cannot write.

CAUCHON. You have signed many letters before.

JOAN. Yes; but someone held my hand and guided the pen. I can make my mark.

THE CHAPLAIN. [*Who has been listening with growing alarm and indignation*.] My lord: do you mean that you are going to allow this woman to escape us?

THE INQUISITOR. The law must take its course, Master de Stogumber. And you know the law.

THE CHAPLAIN. [*Rising, purple with fury*.] I know that there is no faith in a Frenchman. [*Tumult, which he shouts down*.] I know what my lord the Cardinal of Winchester will say when he hears of this. I know what the Earl of Warwick will do when he learns that you intend to betray him. There are eight hundred men at the gate who will see that this abominable witch is burnt in spite of your teeth.

THE ASSESSORS. [*Meanwhile*.] What is this? What did he say? He accuses us of treachery! This is past bearing. No faith in a Frenchman! Did you hear that? This is an intolerable fellow. Who is he? Is this what English Churchmen are like? He must be mad or drunk, etc. etc.

THE INQUISITOR. [*Rising*.] Silence, pray! Gentlemen, pray silence! Master Chaplain, bethink you a moment of your holy office—of what you are, and where you are. I direct you to sit down.

THE CHAPLAIN. [*Folding his arms doggedly, his face working convulsively.*] I will NOT sit down.

CAUCHON. Master Inquisitor: this man has called me a traitor to my face before now.

THE CHAPLAIN. So you are a traitor. You are all traitors. You have been doing nothing but begging this damnable witch on your knees to recant all through this trial.

THE INQUISITOR. [*Placidly resuming his seat.*] If you will not sit, you must stand: that is all.

THE CHAPLAIN. I will NOT stand.

[*He flings himself back into his chair.*

LADVENUE. [*Rising with the paper in his hand.*] My lord, here is the form of recantation for The Maid to sign.

CAUCHON. Read it to her.

JOAN. Do not trouble. I will sign it.

THE INQUISITOR. Woman, you must know what you are putting your hand to. Read it to her, Brother Martin. And let all be silent.

LADVENU. [*Reading quietly.*] 'I, Joan, commonly called The Maid, a miserable sinner, do confess that I have most grievously sinned in the following articles: I have pretended to have revelations from God and the angels and the blessed saints, and perversely rejected the Church's warnings that these were temptations by demons. I have blasphemed abominably by wearing an immodest dress, contrary to the Holy Scripture and the canons of the Church. Also I have clipped my hair in the style of a man, and, against all the duties which have made my sex specially acceptable in heaven, have taken up the sword, even to the shedding of human blood, inciting men to slay each other, invoking evil spirits to delude them, and stubbornly and most blasphemously imputing these sins to Almighty God. I confess to the sin of sedition, to the sin of idolatry, to the sin of disobedience, to the sin of pride, and to the sin of heresy. All of which sins I now renounce and abjure and depart from, humbly thanking you Doctors and Masters who have brought me back to the truth and into the grace of our Lord. And I will never return to my errors, but will remain in communion with our Holy Church and in obedience to our Holy Father the Pope of Rome. All this I swear by God Almighty and the Holy Gospels, in witness whereto I sign my name to this recantation.'

THE INQUISITOR. You understand this, Joan?

JOAN. [*Listless.*] It is plain enough, sir.

THE INQUISITOR. And it is true?

JOAN. It may be true. If it were not true, the fire would not be ready for me in the market-place.

LADVENU. [*Taking up his pen and a book, and going to her quickly lest she should compromise herself again.*] Come, child; let me guide your hand. Take the pen. [*She does so; and they begin to write, using the book as a desk.*] JEHANE. So. Now make your mark by yourself.

JOAN. [*Makes her mark and gives him back the pen, tormented by the rebellion of her soul against her mind and body.*] There!

LADVENU. [*Replacing the pen on the table and handing the recantation to Cauchon with a reverence.*] Praise be to God, my brothers, the lamb has returned to the flock; and the shepherd rejoices in her more than in ninety and nine just persons.   [*He returns to his seat.*

THE INQUISITOR. [*Taking the paper from Cauchon.*] We declare thee by this act set free from the danger of excommunication in which thou stoodest.   [*He throws the paper down to the table.*

JOAN. I thank you.

THE INQUISITOR. But because thou hast sinned most presumptuously against God and the Holy Church, and that thou mayst repent thy errors in solitary contemplation, and be shielded from all temptation to return to them, we, for the good of thy soul, and for a penance that may wipe out thy sins and bring thee finally unspotted to the throne of grace, do condemn thee to eat the bread of sorrow and drink the water of affliction to the end of thy earthly days in perpetual imprisonment.

JOAN. [*Rising in consternation and terrible anger.*] Perpetual imprisonment! Am I not then to be set free?

LADVENU. [*Mildly shocked.*] Set free, child, after such wickedness as yours! What are you dreaming of?

JOAN. Give me that writing. [*She rushes to the table, snatches up the paper and tears it into fragments.*] Light your fire: do you think I dread it as much as the life of a rat in a hole? My voices were right.

LADVENU. Joan! Joan!

JOAN. Yes: they told me you were fools [*the word gives great offence*], and that I was not to listen to your fine words nor trust to your charity. You promised me my life; but you lied. [*Indignant exclamations.*] You think that life is nothing but not being stone dead. It is not the bread and water I fear: I can live on bread: when have I asked for more? It is no hardship to drink water if the water be clean. Bread has no sorrow for me, and water no affliction. But to shut me from the light of the sky and the sight of the fields and flowers; to chain my feet so that I can never again ride with the soldiers nor climb the hills; to make me breathe foul damp darkness, and keep from me everything that brings me back to the love of God when your wickedness and foolishness tempt me to hate Him: all this is worse than the furnace in the Bible that was heated seven times. I could do without

my warhorse; I could drag about in a skirt; I could let the
banners and the trumpets and the knights and soldiers pass me
and leave me behind as they leave the other women, if only I
could still hear the wind in the trees, the larks in the sunshine,
the young lambs crying through the healthy frost, and the blessed
blessed church bells that send my angel voices floating to me on
the wind. But without these things I cannot live; and by your
wanting to take them away from me, or from any human creature,
I know that your counsel is of the devil, and that mine is of God.

THE ASSESSORS. [*In great commotion.*] Blasphemy! Blasphemy! She
is possessed. She said our counsel was of the devil. And hers of
God. Monstrous! The devil is in our midst, etc. etc.

D'ESTIVET. [*Shouting above the din.*] She is a relapsed heretic, obstinate,
incorrigible, and altogether unworthy of the mercy we have
shewn her. I call for her excommunication.

THE CHAPLAIN. [*To the Executioner.*] Light your fire, man. To the
stake with her.

[*The Executioner and his assistants hurry out through the courtyard.*

LADVENU. You wicked girl: if your counsel were of God would He
not deliver you?

JOAN. His ways are not your ways. He wills that I go through the
fire to His bosom; for I am His child, and you are not fit that I
should live among you. That is my last word to you.

[*The soldiers seize her.*

CAUCHON. [*Rising.*] Not yet.

[*They wait. There is a dead silence. Cauchon turns to the Inquisitor
with an inquiring look. The Inquisitor nods affirmatively. They rise
solemnly, and intone the sentence antiphonally.*

CAUCHON. We decree that thou art a relapsed heretic.

THE INQUISITOR. Cast out from the unity of the Church.

CAUCHON. Sundered from her body.

THE INQUISITOR. Infected with the leprosy of heresy.

CAUCHON. A member of Satan.

THE INQUISITOR. We declare that thou must be excommunicate.

CAUCHON. And now we do cast thee out, segregate thee, and
abandon thee to the secular power.

THE INQUISITOR. Admonishing the same secular power that it
moderate its judgment of thee in respect of death and division of
the limbs.   [*He resumes his seat.*

CAUCHON. And if any true sign of penitence appear in thee, to
permit our Brother Martin to administer to thee the sacrament of
penance.

THE CHAPLAIN. Into the fire with the witch!

[*He rushes at her, and helps the soldiers to push her out.*
[*Joan is taken away through the courtyard. The assessors rise in*

disorder and follow the soldiers, except Ladvenu, who has hidden his face in his hands.

CAUCHON. [*Rising again in the act of sitting down.*] No, no: this is irregular. The representative of the secular arm should be here to receive her from us.

THE INQUISITOR. [*Also on his feet again.*] That man is an incorrigible fool.

CAUCHON. Brother Martin: see that everything is done in order.

LADVENU. My place is at her side, my lord. You must exercise your own authority.   [*He hurries out.*

CAUCHON. These English are impossible: they will thrust her straight into the fire. Look!

> *He points to the courtyard, in which the glow and flicker of fire can now be seen reddening the May daylight. Only the Bishop and the Inquisitor are left in the court.*

CAUCHON. [*Turning to go.*] We must stop that.

THE INQUISITOR. [*Calmly.*] Yes; but not too fast, my lord.

CAUCHON. [*Halting.*] But there is not a moment to lose.

THE INQUISITOR. We have proceeded in perfect order. If the English choose to put themselves in the wrong, it is not our business to put them in the right. A flaw in the procedure may be useful later on: one never knows. And the sooner it is over, the better for that poor girl.

CAUCHON. [*Relaxing.*] That is true. But I suppose we must see this dreadful thing through.

THE INQUISITOR. One gets used to it. Habit is everything. I am accustomed to the fire: it is soon over. But it is a terrible thing to see a young and innocent creature crushed between these mighty forces, the Church and the Law.

CAUCHON. You call her innocent!

THE INQUISITOR. Oh, quite innocent. What does she know of the Church and the Law? She did not understand a word we were saying. It is the ignorant who suffer. Come, or we shall be late for the end.

CAUCHON. [*Going with him.*] I shall not be sorry if we are: I am not so accustomed as you.

> [*They are going out when Warwick comes in, meeting them.*

WARWICK. Oh, I am intruding. I thought it was all over.

> [*He makes a feint of retiring.*

CAUCHON. Do not go, my lord. It is all over.

THE INQUISITOR. The execution is not in our hands, my lord; but it is desirable that we should witness the end. So by your leave——   [*He bows, and goes out through the courtyard.*

CAUCHON. There is some doubt whether your people have observed the forms of law, my lord.

WARWICK. I am told that there is some doubt whether your authority runs in this city, my lord. It is not in your diocese. However, if you will answer for that I will answer for the rest.

CAUCHON. It is to God that we both must answer. Good morning, my lord.

WARWICK. My lord: good morning.

[*They look at one another for a moment with unconcealed hostility. Then Cauchon follows the Inquisitor out. Warwick looks round. Finding himself alone, he calls for attendance.*]

WARWICK. Hallo: some attendance here! [*Silence.*] Hallo, there! [*Silence.*] Hallo! Brian, you young blackguard, where are you? [*Silence.*] Guard! [*Silence.*] They have all gone to see the burning: even that child.

[*The silence is broken by someone frantically howling and sobbing.*]

WARWICK. What in the devil's name——?

[*The Chaplain staggers in from the courtyard like a demented creature, his face streaming with tears, making the piteous sounds that Warwick has heard. He stumbles to the prisoner's stool, and throws himself upon it with heartrending sobs.*]

WARWICK. [*Going to him and patting him on the shoulder.*] What is it, Master John? What is the matter?

THE CHAPLAIN. [*Clutching at his hands.*] My lord, my lord: for Christ's sake pray for my wretched guilty soul.

WARWICK. [*Soothing him.*] Yes, yes: of course I will. Calmly, gently——

THE CHAPLAIN. [*Blubbering miserably.*] I am not a bad man, my lord.

WARWICK. No, no: not at all.

THE CHAPLAIN. I meant no harm. I did not know what it would be like.

WARWICK. [*Hardening.*] Oh! You saw it, then?

THE CHAPLAIN. I did not know what I was doing. I am a hot-headed fool; and I shall be damned to all eternity for it.

WARWICK. Nonsense! Very distressing, no doubt; but it was not your doing.

THE CHAPLAIN. [*Lamentably.*] I let them do it. If I had known, I would have torn her from their hands. You dont know; you havnt seen; it is so easy to talk when you dont know. You madden yourself with words; you damn yourself because it feels grand to throw oil on the flaming hell of your own temper. But when it is brought home to you; when you see the thing you have done; when it is blinding your eyes, stifling your nostrils, tearing your heart, then—then—— [*Falling on his knees.*] O God, take away this sight from me! O Christ, deliver me from this fire that is consuming me! She cried to Thee in the midst of it. Jesus! Jesus! Jesus! She is in Thy bosom; and I am in hell for evermore.

WARWICK. [*Summarily hauling him to his feet.*] Come come, man!
You must pull yourself together. We shall have the whole town
talking of this. [*He throws him not too gently into a chair at the table.*]
If you have not the nerve to see these things, why do you not
do as I do, and stay away?

THE CHAPLAIN. [*Bewildered and submissive.*] She asked for a cross. A
soldier gave her two sticks tied together. Thank God he was an
Englishman! I might have done it; but I did not: I am a coward,
a mad dog, a fool. But he was an Englishman too.

WARWICK. The fool! They will burn him too if the priests get
hold of him.

THE CHAPLAIN. [*Shaken with a convulsion.*] Some of the people
laughed at her. They would have laughed at Christ. They were
French people, my lord: I know they were French.

WARWICK. Hush—someone is coming. Control yourself.

[*Ladvenu comes back through the courtyard to Warwick's right hand,
carrying a bishop's cross which he has taken from a church. He is
very grave and composed.*]

WARWICK. I am informed that it is all over, Brother Martin.

LADVENU. [*Enigmatically.*] We do not know, my lord. It may have
only just begun.

WARWICK. What does that mean, exactly?

LADVENU. I took this cross from the church for her that she might
see it to the last; she had only two sticks that she put into her
bosom. When the fire crept round us, and she saw that if I held
the cross before her I should be burnt myself, she warned me to
get down and save myself. My lord: a girl who could think of
another's danger in such a moment was not inspired by the
devil. When I had to snatch the cross from her sight, she looked
up to heaven. And I do not believe that the heavens were empty.
I firmly believe that her Savior appeared to her then in His ten-
derest glory. She called to Him and died. This is not the end for
her, but the beginning.

WARWICK. I am afraid it will have a bad effect on the people.

LADVENU. It had, my lord, on some of them. I heard laughter.
Forgive me for saying that I hope and believe it was English
laughter.

THE CHAPLAIN. [*Rising frantically.*] No: it was not. There was only
one Englishman there that disgraced his country: and that was
the mad dog, de Stogumber. [*He rushes wildly out, shrieking.*] Let
them torture him. Let them burn him. I will go pray among her
ashes. I am no better than Judas: I will hang myself.

WARWICK. Quick, Brother Martin: follow him; he will do himself
some mischief. After him, quick.

[*Ladvenu hurries out, Warwick urging him. The Executioner comes*] *in by the door behind the judges' chairs; and Warwick, returning, finds himself face to face with him.*

WARWICK. Well, fellow: who are you?

THE EXECUTIONER. [*With dignity.*] I am not addressed as fellow, my lord. I am the Master Executioner of Rouen; it is a highly skilled mystery. I am come to tell your lordship that your orders have been obeyed.

WARWICK. I crave your pardon, Master Executioner; and I will see that you lose nothing by having no relics to sell. I have your word, have I, that nothing remains, not a bone, not a nail, not a hair?

THE EXECUTIONER. Her heart would not burn, my lord; but everything that was left is at the bottom of the river. You have heard the last of her.

WARWICK. [*With a wry smile, thinking of what Ladvenu said.*] The last of her? Hm! I wonder!

EPILOGUE

*A restless fitfully windy night in June 1456, full of summer lightning after
many days of heat. King Charles the Seventh of France, formerly Joan's
Dauphin, now Charles the Victorious, aged fifty-one, is in bed in one
of his royal chateaux. The bed, raised on a dais of two steps, is towards
the side of the room so as to avoid blocking a tall lancet window in the
middle. Its canopy bears the royal arms in embroidery. Except for the
canopy and the huge down pillows there is nothing to distinguish it from
a broad settee with bed-clothes and a valance. Thus its occupant is in full
view from the foot.*

*Charles is not asleep: he is reading in bed, or rather looking at the pictures
in Fouquet's 'Boccaccio' with his knees doubled up to make a reading desk.
Beside the bed on his left is a little table with a picture of the Virgin,
lighted by candles of painted wax. The walls are hung from ceiling to
floor with painted curtains which stir at times in the draughts. At first
glance the prevailing yellow and red in these hanging pictures is somewhat
flamelike when the folds breathe in the wind.*

*The door is on Charles's left, but in front of him close to the corner farthest
from him. A large watchman's rattle, handsomely designed and gaily
painted, is in the bed under his hand.*

*Charles turns a leaf. A distant clock strikes the half-hour softly. Charles
shuts the book with a clap; throws it aside; snatches up the rattle; and
whirls it energetically, making a deafening clatter. Ladvenu enters,
twenty-five years older, strange and stark in bearing, and still carrying the
cross from Rouen. Charles evidently does not expect him; for he springs
out of bed on the farther side from the door.*

CHARLES. Who are you? Where is my gentleman of the bed-
chamber? What do you want?

LADVENU. [*Solemnly.*] I bring you glad tidings of great joy. Rejoice,
O king; for the taint is removed from your blood, and the stain
from your crown. Justice, long delayed, is at last triumphant.

CHARLES. What are you talking about? Who are you?

LADVENU. I am Brother Martin.

CHARLES. And who, saving your reverence, may Brother Martin be?

LADVENU. I held this cross when The Maid perished in the fire.
Twenty-five years have passed since then: nearly ten thousand
days. And on every one of those days I have prayed God to
justify His daughter on earth as she is justified in heaven.

219

CHARLES. [*Reassured, sitting down on the foot of the bed.*] Oh, I remember now. I have heard of you. You have a bee in your
bonnet about The Maid. Have you been at the inquiry?

LADVENU. I have given my testimony.

CHARLES. Is it over?

LADVENU. It is over.

CHARLES. Satisfactorily?

LADVENU. The ways of God are very strange.

CHARLES. How so?

LADVENU. At the trial which sent a saint to the stake as a heretic
and a sorceress, the truth was told; the law was upheld; mercy
was shewn beyond all custom; no wrong was done but the final
and dreadful wrong of the lying sentence and the pitiless fire.
At this inquiry from which I have just come, there was shameless perjury, courtly corruption, calumny of the dead who did
their duty according to their lights, cowardly evasion of the issue,
testimony made of idle tales that could not impose on a plough-
boy. Yet out of this insult to justice, this defamation of the
Church, this orgy of lying and foolishness, the truth is set in the
noonday sun on the hilltop; the white robe of innocence is
cleansed from the smirch of the burning faggots; the holy life is
sanctified; the true heart that lived through the flame is consecrated; a great lie is silenced for ever; and a great wrong is set
right before all men.

CHARLES. My friend: provided they can no longer say that I was
crowned by a witch and a heretic, I shall not fuss about how
the trick has been done. Joan would not have fussed about it if
it came all right in the end: she was not that sort: I knew her. Is
her rehabilitation complete? I made it pretty clear that there was
to be no nonsense about it.

LADVENU. It is solemnly declared that her judges were full of
corruption, cozenage, fraud and malice. Four falsehoods.

CHARLES. Never mind the falsehoods: her judges are dead.

LADVENU. The sentence on her is broken, annulled, annihilated,
set aside as non-existent, without value or effect.

CHARLES. Good. Nobody can challenge my consecration now, can
they?

LADVENU. Not Charlemagne nor King David himself was more
sacredly crowned.

CHARLES. [*Rising.*] Excellent. Think of what that means to me!

LADVENU. I think of what it means to her!

CHARLES. You cannot. None of us ever knew what anything
meant to her. She was like nobody else; and she must take care
of herself wherever she is; for *I* cannot take care of her; and
neither can you, whatever you may think: you are not big

enough. But I will tell you this about her. If you could bring her back to life, they would burn her again within six months, for all their present adoration of her. And you would hold up the cross, too, just the same. So [*crossing himself*] let her rest; and let you and I mind our own business, and not meddle with hers.

LADVENU. God forbid that I should have no share in her, nor she in me! [*He turns and strides out as he came, saying*] Henceforth my path will not lie through palaces, nor my conversation be with kings.

CHARLES. [*Following him towards the door, and shouting after him.*] Much good may it do you, holy man! [*He returns to the middle of the chamber, where he halts, and says quizzically to himself*] That was a funny chap. How did he get in? Where are my people? [*He goes impatiently to the bed, and swings the rattle. A rush of wind through the open door sets the walls swaying agitatedly. The candles go out. He calls in the darkness.*] Hallo! Someone come and shut the windows: everything is being blown all over the place. [*A flash of summer lightning shews up the lancet window. A figure is seen in silhouette against it.*] Who is there? Who is that? Help! Murder!

[*Thunder. He jumps into bed, and hides under the clothes.*

JOAN'S VOICE. Easy, Charlie, easy. What art making all that noise for? No one can hear thee. Thourt asleep.

[*She is dimly seen in a pallid greenish light by the bedside.*

CHARLES. [*Peeping out.*] Joan! Are you a ghost, Joan?

JOAN. Hardly even that, lad. Can a poor burnt-up lass have a ghost? I am but a dream that thourt dreaming. [*The light increases: they become plainly visible as he sits up.*] Thou looks older, lad.

CHARLES. I am older. Am I really asleep?

JOAN. Fallen asleep over thy silly book.

CHARLES. That's funny.

JOAN. Not so funny as that I am dead, is it?

CHARLES. Are you really dead?

JOAN. As dead as anybody ever is, laddie. I am out of the body.

CHARLES. Just fancy! Did it hurt much?

JOAN. Did what hurt much?

CHARLES. Being burnt.

JOAN. Oh, that! I cannot remember very well. I think it did at first; but then it all got mixed up; and I was not in my right mind until I was free of the body. But do not thou go handling fire and thinking it will not hurt thee. How hast been ever since?

CHARLES. Oh, not so bad. Do you know, I actually lead my army out and win battles? Down into the moat up to my waist in mud and blood. Up the ladders with the stones and hot pitch raining down. Like you.

JOAN. No! Did I make a man of thee after all, Charlie?

CHARLES. I am Charles the Victorious now. I had to be brave because you were. Agnes put a little pluck into me too.

JOAN. Agnes! Who was Agnes?

CHARLES. Agnes Sorel. A woman I fell in love with. I dream of her often. I never dreamed of you before.

JOAN. Is she dead, like me?

CHARLES. Yes. But she was not like you. She was very beautiful.

JOAN. [*Laughing heartily.*] Ha, ha! I was no beauty: I was always a rough one: a regular soldier. I might almost as well have been a man. Pity I wasnt: I should not have bothered you all so much then. But my head was in the skies; and the glory of God was upon me; and, man or woman, I should have bothered you as long as your noses were in the mud. Now tell me what has happened since you wise men knew no better than to make a heap of cinders of me?

CHARLES. Your mother and brothers have sued the courts to have your case tried over again. And the courts have declared that your judges were full of corruption and cozenage, fraud and malice.

JOAN. Not they. They were as honest a lot of poor fools as ever burned their betters.

CHARLES. The sentence on you is broken, annihilated, annulled: null, non-existent, without value or effect.

JOAN. I was burned, all the same. Can they unburn me?

CHARLES. If they could, they would think twice before they did it. But they have decreed that a beautiful cross be placed where the stake stood, for your perpetual memory and for your salvation.

JOAN. It is the memory and the salvation that sanctify the cross, not the cross that sanctifies the memory and the salvation. [*She turns away, forgetting him.*] I shall outlast that cross. I shall be remembered when men will have forgotten where Rouen stood.

CHARLES. There you go with your self-conceit, the same as ever! I think you might say a word of thanks to me for having had justice done at last.

CAUCHON. [*Appearing at the window between them.*] Liar!

CHARLES. Thank you.

JOAN. Why, if it isnt Peter Cauchon! How are you, Peter? What luck have you had since you burned me?

CAUCHON. None. I arraign the justice of Man. It is not the justice of God.

JOAN. Still dreaming of justice, Peter? See what justice came to with me! But what has happened to thee? Art dead or alive?

CAUCHON. Dead. Dishonored. They pursued me beyond the grave. They excommunicated my dead body: they dug it up and flung it into the common sewer.

JOAN. Your dead body did not feel the spade and the sewer as my live body felt the fire.

CAUCHON. But this thing that they have done against me hurts justice; destroys faith; saps the foundation of the Church. The solid earth sways like the treacherous sea beneath the feet of men and spirits alike when the innocent are slain in the name of law, and their wrongs are undone by slandering the pure of heart.

JOAN. Well, well, Peter, I hope men will be the better for remembering me; and they would not remember me so well if you had not burned me.

CAUCHON. They will be the worse for remembering me: they will see in me evil triumphing over good, falsehood over truth, cruelty over mercy, hell over heaven. Their courage will rise as they think of you, only to faint as they think of me. Yet God is my witness I was just: I was merciful: I was faithful to my light: I could do no other than I did.

CHARLES. [*Scrambling out of the sheets and enthroning himself on the side of the bed.*] Yes: it is always you good men that do the big mischiefs. Look at me! I am not Charles the Good, nor Charles the Wise, nor Charles the Bold. Joan's worshippers may even call me Charles the Coward because I did not pull her out of the fire. But I have done less harm than any of you. You people with your heads in the sky spend all your time trying to turn the world upside down; but I take the world as it is, and say that top-side-up is right-side-up; and I keep my nose pretty close to the ground. And I ask you, what king of France has done better, or been a better fellow in his little way?

JOAN. Art really king of France, Charlie? Be the English gone?

DUNOIS. [*Coming through the tapestry on Joan's left, the candles relighting themselves at the same moment, and illuminating his armor and surcoat cheerfully.*] I have kept my word: the English are gone.

JOAN. Praised be God! Now is fair France a province in heaven. Tell me all about the fighting, Jack. Was it thou that led them? Wert thou God's captain to thy death?

DUNOIS. I am not dead. My body is very comfortably asleep in my bed at Chateaudun; but my spirit is called here by yours.

JOAN. And you fought them my way, Jack: eh? Not the old way, chaffering for ransoms; but The Maid's way: staking life against death, with the heart high and humble and void of malice, and nothing counting under God but France free and French. Was it my way, Jack?

DUNOIS. Faith, it was any way that would win. But the way that won was always your way. I give you best, lassie. I wrote a fine letter to set you right at the new trial. Perhaps I should never have let the priests burn you; but I was busy fighting; and it was the Church's business, not mine. There was no use in both of us being burned, was there?

CAUCHON. Ay; put the blame on the priests! But I, who am beyond praise and blame, tell you that the world is saved neither by its priest nor its soldiers, but by God and His Saints. The Church Militant sent this woman to the fire; but even as she burned, the flames whitened into the radiance of the Church Triumphant.

[*The clock strikes the third quarter. A rough male voice is heard trolling an improvised tune.*

Rum tum trumpledum,
Bacon fat and rumpledum,
Old Saint mumpledum,
Pull his tail and stumpledum
O my Ma—ry Ann!

[*A ruffianly English soldier comes through the curtains and marches between Dunois and Joan.*

DUNOIS. What villainous troubadour taught you that doggerel?

THE SOLDIER. No troubadour. We made it up ourselves as we marched. We were not gentlefolks and troubadours. Music straight out of the heart of the people, as you might say. Rum tum trumpledum, Bacon fat and rumpledum, Old Saint mumpledum, Pull his tail and stumpledum: that dont mean anything, you know; but it keeps you marching. Your servant, ladies and gentlemen. Who asked for a saint?

JOAN. Be you a saint?

THE SOLDIER. Yes, lady, straight from hell.

DUNOIS. A saint, and from hell!

THE SOLDIER. Yes, noble captain: I have a day off. Every year, you know. Thats my allowance for my one good action.

CAUCHON. Wretch! In all the years of your life did you do only one good action?

THE SOLDIER. I never thought about it: it came natural like. But they scored it up for me.

CHARLES. What was it?

THE SOLDIER. Why, the silliest thing you ever heard of. I——

JOAN. [*Interrupting him by strolling across to the bed, where she sits beside Charles.*] He tied two sticks together, and gave them to a poor lass that was going to be burned.

THE SOLDIER. Right. Who told you that?

JOAN. Never mind. Would you know her if you saw her again?

THE SOLDIER. Not I. There are so many girls! and they all expect you to remember them as if there was only one in the world. This one must have been a prime sort; for I have a day off every year for her; and so, until twelve o'clock punctually, I am a saint, at your service, noble lords and lovely ladies.

CHARLES. And after twelve?

THE SOLDIER. After twelve, back to the only place fit for the likes of me.

JOAN. [*Rising.*] Back there! You that gave the lass the cross!

THE SOLDIER. [*Excusing his unsoldierly conduct.*] Well, she asked for it; and they were going to burn her. She had as good a right to a cross as they had; and they had dozens of them. It was her funeral, not theirs. Where was the harm in it?

JOAN. Man: I am not reproaching you. But I cannot bear to think of you in torment.

THE SOLDIER. [*Cheerfully.*] No great torment, lady. You see I was used to worse.

CHARLES. What—worse than hell?

THE SOLDIER. Fifteen years' service in the French wars. Hell was a treat after that.

[*Joan throws up her arms, and takes refuge from despair of humanity before the picture of the Virgin.*

THE SOLDIER. [*Continuing.*] Suits me somehow. The day off was dull at first, like a wet Sunday. I dont mind it so much now. They tell me I can have as many as I like as soon as I want them.

CHARLES. What is hell like?

THE SOLDIER. You wont find it so bad, sir. Jolly. Like as if you were always drunk without the trouble and expense of drinking. Tip-top company too: emperors and popes and kings and all sorts. They chip me about giving that young judy the cross; but I dont care: I stand up to them proper, and tell them that if she hadnt a better right to it than they, she'd be where they are. That dumbfounds them, that does. All they can do is gnash their teeth, hell fashion; and I must laugh, and go off singing the old chanty: Rum tum trumple—— Hallo! Who's that knocking at the door?

[*They listen. A long gentle knocking is heard.*

CHARLES. Come in.

[*The door opens; and an old priest, white-haired, bent, with a silly but benevolent smile, comes in and trots over to Joan.*

THE NEWCOMER. Excuse me, gentle lords and ladies. Do not let me disturb you. Only a poor old harmless English rector. Formerly chaplain to the cardinal: to my lord of Winchester. John de Stogumber, at your service. [*He looks at them inquiringly.*] Did you say anything? I am a little deaf, unfortunately. Also a little—well, not always in my right mind, perhaps; but still, it is a small village with a few simple people. I suffice: I suffice: they love me there; and I am able to do a little good. I am well connected, you see; and they indulge me.

JOAN. Poor old John! What brought thee to this state?

DE STOGUMBER. I tell my folks they must be very careful. I say to them, 'If you only saw what you think about you would think quite differently about it. It would give you a great shock. Oh, a great shock.' And they all say 'Yes, parson: we all know you are a kind man, and would not harm a fly.' That is a great comfort to me. For I am not cruel by nature, you know.

THE SOLDIER. Who said you were?

DE STOGUMBER. Well, you see, I did a very cruel thing once because I did not know what cruelty was like. I had not seen it, you know. That is the great thing: you must see it. And then you are redeemed and saved.

CAUCHON. Were not the sufferings of our Lord Christ enough for you?

DE STOGUMBER. No. Oh no: not at all. I had seen them in pictures, and read of them in books, and been greatly moved by them, as I thought. But it was no use: it was not our Lord that redeemed me, but a young woman whom I saw actually burned to death. It was dreadful: oh, most dreadful. But it saved me. I have been a different man ever since, though a little astray in my wits sometimes.

CAUCHON. Must then a Christ perish in torment in every age to save those that have no imagination?

JOAN. Well, if I saved all those he would have been cruel to if he had not been cruel to me, I was not burnt for nothing, was I?

DE STOGUMBER. Oh no; it was not you. My sight is bad: I cannot distinguish your features: but you are not she: oh no: she was burned to a cinder: dead and gone, dead and gone.

THE EXECUTIONER. [*Stepping from behind the bed curtains on Charles's right, the bed being between them.*] She is more alive than you, old man. Her heart would not burn; and it would not drown. I was a master at my craft: better than the master of Paris, better than the master of Toulouse; but I could not kill The Maid. She is up and alive everywhere.

THE EARL OF WARWICK. [*Sallying from the bed curtains on the other side, and coming to Joan's left hand.*] Madam: my congratulations on your rehabilitation. I feel that I owe you an apology.

JOAN. Oh, please dont mention it.

WARWICK. [*Pleasantly.*] The burning was purely political. There was no personal feeling against you, I assure you.

JOAN. I bear no malice, my lord.

WARWICK. Just so. Very kind of you to meet me in that way: a touch of true breeding. But I must insist on apologizing very amply. The truth is, these political necessities sometimes turn out to be political mistakes; and this one was a veritable howler;

for your spirit conquered us, madam, in spite of our faggots. History will remember me for your sake, though the incidents of the connection were perhaps a little unfortunate.

JOAN. Ay, perhaps just a little, you funny man.

WARWICK. Still, when they make you a saint, you will owe your halo to me, just as this lucky monarch owes his crown to you.

JOAN. [*Turning from him.*] I shall owe nothing to any man: I owe everything to the spirit of God that was within me. But fancy me a saint! What would St Catherine and St Margaret say if the farm girl was cocked up beside them!

> [*A clerical-looking gentleman in black frock-coat and trousers, and tall hat, in the fashion of the year 1920, suddenly appears before them in the corner on their right. They all stare at him. Then they burst into uncontrollable laughter.*

THE GENTLEMAN. Why this mirth, gentlemen?

WARWICK. I congratulate you on having invented a most extraordinarily comic dress.

THE GENTLEMAN. I do not understand. You are all in fancy dress: I am properly dressed.

DUNOIS. All dress is fancy dress, is it not, except our natural skins?

THE GENTLEMAN. Pardon me: I am here on serious business, and cannot engage in frivolous discussions. [*He takes out a paper, and assumes a dry official manner.*] I am sent to announce to you that Joan of Arc, formerly known as The Maid, having been the subject of an inquiry instituted by the Bishop of Orleans——

JOAN. [*Interrupting.*] Ah! They remember me still in Orleans.

THE GENTLEMAN. [*Emphatically, to mark his indignation at the interruption.*] —by the Bishop of Orleans into the claim of the said Joan of Arc to be canonized as a saint——

JOAN. [*Again interrupting.*] But I never made any such claim.

THE GENTLEMAN [*As before.*] —the Church has examined the claim exhaustively in the usual course, and, having admitted the said Joan successively to the ranks of Venerable and Blessed——

JOAN. [*Chuckling.*] Me venerable!

THE GENTLEMAN. —has finally declared her to have been endowed with heroic virtues and favored with private revelations, and calls the said Venerable and Blessed Joan to the communion of the Church Triumphant as Saint Joan.

JOAN. [*Rapt.*] Saint Joan!

THE GENTLEMAN. On every thirtieth day of May, being the anniversary of the death of the said most blessed daughter of God, there shall in every Catholic church to the end of time be celebrated a special office in commemoration of her; and it shall be lawful to dedicate a special chapel to her, and to place her image

on its altar in every such church. And it shall be lawful and laudable for the faithful to kneel and address their prayers through
her to the Mercy Seat.

JOAN. Oh no. It is for the saint to kneel.

[She falls on her knees, still rapt.

THE GENTLEMAN. [*Putting up his paper, and retiring beside the Executioner.*] In Basilica Vaticana, the sixteenth day of May, nineteen
hundred and twenty.

DUNOIS. [*Raising Joan.*] Half an hour to burn you, dear Saint: and
four centuries to find out the truth about you!

DE STOGUMBER. Sir: I was chaplain to the Cardinal of Winchester
once. They always would call him the Cardinal of England. It
would be a great comfort to me and to my master to see a fair
statue to The Maid in Winchester Cathedral. Will they put one
there, do you think?

THE GENTLEMAN. As the building is temporarily in the hands of
the Anglican heresy, I cannot answer for that.

[*A vision of the statue in Winchester Cathedral is seen through the
window.*

DE STOGUMBER. Oh look! look! That is Winchester.

JOAN. Is that meant to be me! I was stiffer on my feet.

[The vision fades.

THE GENTLEMAN. I have been requested by the temporal authorities
of France to mention that the multiplication of public statues to
The Maid threatens to become an obstruction to traffic. I do so
as a matter of courtesy to the said authorities, but must point out
on behalf of the Church that The Maid's horse is no greater
obstruction to traffic than any other horse.

JOAN. Eh! I am glad they have not forgotten my horse.

[*A vision of the statue before Rheims Cathedral appears.*

JOAN. Is that funny little thing me too?

CHARLES. That is Rheims Cathedral where you had me crowned.
It must be you.

JOAN. Who has broken my sword? My sword was never broken.
It is the sword of France.

DUNOIS. Never mind. Swords can be mended. Your soul is un-
broken; and you are the soul of France.

[*The vision fades. The Archbishop and the Inquisitor are now seen
on the right and left of Cauchon.*

JOAN. My sword shall conquer yet: the sword that never struck a
blow. Though men destroyed my body, yet in my soul I have
seen God.

CAUCHON. [*Kneeling to her.*] The girls in the field praise thee; for
thou hast raised their eyes; and they see that there is nothing
between them and heaven.

DUNOIS. [*Kneeling to her.*] The dying soldiers praise thee, because thou art a shield of glory between them and the judgment.

THE ARCHBISHOP. [*Kneeling to her.*] The princes of the Church praise thee, because thou hast redeemed the faith their worldlinesses have dragged through the mire.

WARWICK. [*Kneeling to her.*] The cunning counsellors praise thee, because thou hast cut the knots in which they have tied their own souls.

DE STOGUMBER. [*Kneeling to her.*] The foolish old men on their deathbeds praise thee, because their sins against thee are turned into blessings.

THE INQUISITOR. [*Kneeling to her.*] The judges in the blindness and bondage of the law praise thee, because thou hast vindicated the vision and the freedom of the living soul.

THE SOLDIER. [*Kneeling to her.*] The wicked out of hell praise thee, because thou hast shewn them that the fire that is not quenched is a holy fire.

THE EXECUTIONER. [*Kneeling to her.*] The tormentors and executioners praise thee, because thou hast shewn that their hands are guiltless of the death of the soul.

CHARLES. [*Kneeling to her.*] The unpretending praise thee, because thou hast taken upon thyself the heroic burdens that are too heavy for them.

JOAN. Woe unto me when all men praise me! I bid you remember that I am a saint, and that saints can work miracles. And now tell me: shall I rise from the dead, and come back to you a living woman?

[*A sudden darkness blots out the walls of the room as they all spring to their feet in consternation. Only the figures and the bed remain visible.*

JOAN. What! Must I burn again? Are none of you ready to receive me?

CAUCHON. The heretic is always better dead. And mortal eyes cannot distinguish the saint from the heretic. Spare them.

[*He goes out as he came.*

DUNOIS. Forgive us, Joan: we are not yet good enough for you. I shall go back to my bed.   [*He also goes.*

WARWICK. We sincerely regret our little mistake; but political necessities, though occasionally erroneous, are still imperative; so if you will be good enough to excuse me——

[*He steals discreetly away.*

THE ARCHBISHOP. Your return would not make me the man you once thought me. The utmost I can say is that though I dare not bless you, I hope I may one day enter your blessedness. Meanwhile, however——   [*He goes.*

THE INQUISITOR. I who am of the dead, testified that day that you were innocent. But I do not see how The Inquisition could possibly be dispensed with under existing circumstances. Therefore—— [*He goes.*

DE STOGUMBER. Oh, do not come back: you must not come back. I must die in peace. Give us peace in our time, O Lord! [*He goes.*

THE GENTLEMAN. The possibility of your resurrection was not contemplated in the recent proceedings for your canonization. I must return to Rome for fresh instructions.

[*He bows formally, and withdraws.*

THE EXECUTIONER. As a master in my profession I have to consider its interests. And, after all, my first duty is to my wife and children. I must have time to think over this. [*He goes.*

CHARLES. Poor old Joan! They have all run away from you except this blackguard who has to go back to hell at twelve o'clock. And what can I do but follow Jack Dunois's example, and go back to bed too? [*He does so.*

JOAN. [*Sadly.*] Good night, Charlie.

CHARLES. [*Mumbling in his pillow.*] Goo ni.

[*He sleeps. The darkness envelops the bed.*

JOAN. [*To the soldier.*] And you, my one faithful? What comfort have you for Saint Joan?

THE SOLDIER. Well, what do they all amount to, these kings and captains and bishops and lawyers and such like? They just leave you in the ditch to bleed to death; and the next thing is, you meet them down there, for all the airs they give themselves. What I say is, you have as good a right to your notions as they have to theirs, and perhaps better. [*Settling himself for a lecture on the subject.*] You see, it's like this. If—— [*The first stroke of midnight is heard softly from a distant bell.*] Excuse me: a pressing appointment—— [*He goes on tiptoe.*

[*The last remaining rays of light gather into a white radiance descending on Joan. The hour continues to strike.*

JOAN. O God that madest this beautiful earth, when will it be ready to receive Thy saints? How long, O Lord, how long?

EVERYMAN'S LIBRARY: A Selected List

BIOGRAPHY

The volumes in the Library are under constant editorial revision, and introducers, editors and translators stated in this list should therefore not be regarded as static. The List is, however, frequently revised.

Baxter, Richard (1615–91).
THE AUTOBIOGRAPHY OF RICHARD BAXTER.   868
Boswell, James (1740–95). *See* Johnson.
Brontë, Charlotte (1816–55).
LIFE, 1857. By *Mrs Gaskell.* Introduction by *May Sinclair.* (*See also* Fiction.) 318
Byron, Lord (1788–1824).
LETTERS. Edited by *R. G. Howarth,* B.LITT., and with an Introduction by *André Maurois.*   (*See also* Poetry and Drama.) 931
Canton, William (1845–1926).
A CHILD'S BOOK OF SAINTS, 1898.   61
Cellini, Benvenuto (1500–71).
THE LIFE OF BENVENUTO CELLINI, written by himself. Translated by *Anne Macdonell.* Introduction by *William Gaunt.*   51
Dickens Charles (1812–70).
LIFE, 1874. By *John Forster* (1812–76). Introduction by *G. K. Chesterton.* 2 vols.   (*See also* Fiction.) 781–2
Evelyn, John (1620–1706).
DIARY. Edited by *William Bray,* 1819. Intro. by *G. W. E. Russell.* 2 vols.   220–1
Fox, George (1624–91).
JOURNAL, 1694. Revised by *Norman Penney.* with Account of Fox's last years. Introduction by *Rufus M. Jones.*   754
Franklin, Benjamin (1706–90).
AUTOBIOGRAPHY, 1817. With Introduction and Account of Franklin's later life by *W. Macdonald.* Reset new edition (1949), with a newly compiled Index.   316
Goethe, Johann Wolfgang von (1749–1832).
LIFE, 1855. By *G. H. Lewes* (1817–78). Introduction by *Havelock Ellis.* Index.   (*See also* Poetry and Drama.) 269
Hudson, William Henry (1841–1922).
FAR AWAY AND LONG AGO, 1918. Intro. by *John Galsworthy.*   956
Johnson, Samuel (1709–84).
LIVES OF THE ENGLISH POETS, 1781. Introduction by *Mrs L. Archer-Hind.* 2 vols.   (*See also* Essays.) 770–1
BOSWELL'S LIFE OF JOHNSON, 1791. A new edition (1949), with Introduction by *S. C. Roberts,* M.A., LL.D., and a 30-page Index by Alan Dent. 2 vols.   1–2
Keats, John (1795–1821).
LIFE AND LETTERS, 1848. By *Lord Houghton* (1809–85). Introduction by *Robert Lynd.* Note on the letters by Lewis Gibbs.   (*See also* Poetry and Drama.) 801
Lamb, Charles (1775–1834).
LETTERS. New edition (1945) arranged from the Complete Annotated Edition of the Letters. 2 vols.   (*See also* Fiction.) 342–3
Napoleon Buonaparte (1769–1821).
HISTORY OF NAPOLEON BUONAPARTE, 1829. By *J. G. Lockhart* (1794–1854).   3
LETTERS. Some 300 of the most interesting of the Emperor's letters, chosen and translated by *J. M. Thompson,* F.B.A., F.R.HIST.S.   995
Nelson, Horatio, Viscount (1758–1805).
LIFE, 1813. By *Robert Southey* (1774–1843).   52
NELSON'S LETTERS. Compiled by *Geoffrey Rawson.*   244
Outram, General Sir James (1803–63), 'the Bayard of India.'
LIFE, 1903. Deals with important passages in the history of India in the nineteenth century. By *L. J. Trotter* (1827–1912).   396
Pepys, Samuel (1633–1703).
DIARY. Newly edited (1953), with modernized spelling, by *John Warrington,* from the edition of Mynors Bright (1875–9). 3 vols.   53–5
Plutarch (46?–120).
LIVES OF THE NOBLE GREEKS AND ROMANS. Dryden's edition, 1683–6. Revised, with Introduction. by *A. H. Clough* (1819–61). 3 vols.   407–9

1

Rousseau, Jean Jacques (1712–78).
    CONFESSIONS, 1782. 2 vols. Complete and unabridged English translation.
    Introduction by *Prof. R. Niklaus*, B.A., PH.D., of Exeter University.   859–60
                                      (*See also* Essays, Science.)
Scott, Sir Walter (1771–1832).
    LOCKHART'S LIFE OF SCOTT. An abridgement by *J. G. Lockhart* himself from the
    original 7 volumes. New Introduction by *W. M. Parker*, M.A.   39
Swift, Jonathan (1667–1745).
    JOURNAL TO STELLA, 1710–13. Deciphered by *J. K. Moorhead*.   757
                                  (*See also* Essays, Fiction.)
Vasari, Giorgio, (1511–74). LIVES OF THE PAINTERS, SCULPTORS AND ARCHITECTS.
    Newly edited by William Gaunt. 4 vols.   784–7
Walpole, Horace (1717–97).
    SELECTED LETTERS. Edited, with Introduction, by *W. Hadley*, M.A.   775
Wellington, Arthur Wellesley, Duke of (1769–1852).
    LIFE, 1862. By *G. R. Gleig* (1796–1888).   341

ESSAYS AND CRITICISM

Anthology of English Prose, from Bede to Stevenson.   675
Bacon, Francis, Lord Verulam (1561–1626).
    ESSAYS, 1597–1626. Introduction by *Oliphant Smeaton*. Index of Quotations and
    Foreign Phrases and Glossary.   (*See also* Religion and Philosophy.) 10
Bagehot, Walter (1826–77).
    LITERARY STUDIES, 1879. Introduction by *George Sampson*. 2 vols.   520–1
Belloc, Hilaire (1870–1953).
    STORIES, ESSAYS AND POEMS. Edited with Introduction by *J. B. Morton*, C.B.E.,
    the volume now contains a new selection from the *Sonnets, Verses* and celebrated
    Epigrams.   948
Burke, Edmund (1729–97).
    REFLECTIONS ON THE REVOLUTION IN FRANCE (1790) AND OTHER ESSAYS. Intro-
    duction and Notes by *A. J. Grieve*, M.A.   (*See also* History.) 460
Carlyle, Thomas (1795–1881).
    ESSAYS. Introduction by *J. R. Lowell*. Essays on men and affairs. 2 vols.   703–4
    PAST AND PRESENT, 1843. Introduction by *Douglas Jerrold*.   608
    SARTOR RESARTUS, 1838; and HEROES AND HERO-WORSHIP, 1841.   278
                                       (*See also* History.) 278
Castiglione, Baldassare (1478–1529).
    THE BOOK OF THE COURTIER, 1528. *Sir Thomas Hoby's* Translation, 1561. Intro-
    duction by *W. H. D. Rouse* and Notes by *Prof. W. B. Drayton Henderson*.   807
Century. A CENTURY OF ENGLISH ESSAYS, FROM CAXTON TO BELLOC.   653
Chesterfield, Philip Dormer Stanhope, Earl of (1694–1773).
    LETTERS TO HIS SON; AND OTHERS. Introduction by *Prof. R. K. Root*.   823
Chesterton, Gilbert Keith (1874–1936).
    STORIES, ESSAYS AND POEMS. Introduction by *Maisie Ward*. An 'omnibus' volume
    including four 'Father Brown' stories.   913
Coleridge, Samuel Taylor (1772–1834).
    BIOGRAPHIA LITERARIA, 1817. Edited with a new Introduction by *George Watson*,
    M.A. Coleridge described the work as 'sketches of my literary life and opinions.'   11
    SHAKESPEAREAN CRITICISM, 1849. Edited with a long Introduction by *Prof.*
    T. M. Raysor (1960), 2 vols.   (*See also* Poetry and Drama.) 162, 318
De la Mare, Walter (1873–1956).
    STORIES, ESSAYS AND POEMS. An anthology arranged by *Mildred Bozman*.   940
De Quincey, Thomas (1785–1859).
    CONFESSIONS OF AN ENGLISH OPIUM-EATER, 1822.   223
    THE ENGLISH MAIL-COACH, etc. (1849).   609
    REMINISCENCES OF ENGLISH LAKE POETS.   163
    All volumes introduced by *Professor J. E. Jordan*.
Dryden, John (1631–1700).
    OF DRAMATIC POESY, etc. Introduction by *George Watson*. The whole of Dryden's
    critical writings. 2 vols.   568–9
Eckermann, Johann Peter (1792–1854).
    CONVERSATIONS WITH GOETHE, 1836–8. Translated by *John Oxenford*, 1850.
    Edited by *J. K. Moorhead*, with Introduction by *Havelock Ellis*.   851
                   (*See also* Poetry and Drama, Biography.)
Ellis, Havelock (1859–1939).
    SELECTED ESSAYS. Sixteen essays, with an Introduction by *J. S. Collis*.   930
Elyot, Sir Thomas (1480?–1546).
    THE GOVERNOR. Edited with Introduction by *Stanford E. Lehmberg*.   227
Emerson, Ralph Waldo (1803–82).
    ESSAYS, 1841–4. New Introduction by *Prof. Sherman Paul*.   12

Gray, Thomas (1716–71).
    ESSAYS. (*See* Poetry.)
Hamilton, Alexander (1757–1804), and Others.
    THE FEDERALIST, OR THE NEW CONSTITUTION, 1787–8. Introduction by *William R. Brock*, M.A., PH.D.   519
Hazlitt, William (1778–1830).
    LECTURES ON THE ENGLISH COMIC WRITERS, 1819; and FUGITIVE WRITINGS. Introduction by *Arthur Johnston*, M.A., D.PHIL.   411
    LECTURES ON THE ENGLISH POETS, 1818; and THE SPIRIT OF THE AGE, 1825. Introduction by *Catherine Macdonald Maclean*, M.A., D.LITT., F.R.S.L.   459
    THE ROUND TABLE and CHARACTERS OF SHAKESPEAR'S PLAYS, 1817–18. New Introduction by *Catherine Macdonald Maclean*.   65
    TABLE TALK, 1821–2, 1824. New Introduction by *Catherine Macdonald Maclean*.   321
Holmes, Oliver Wendell (1809–94).
    THE AUTOCRAT OF THE BREAKFAST-TABLE, 1858. Introduction by *Van Wyck Brooks*.   66
Hunt, Leigh (1784–1859).
    SELECTED ESSAYS. 78 essays with Introduction by *J. B. Priestley*.   829
Huxley, Aldous Leonard (*b.* 1894).
    STORIES, ESSAYS AND POEMS.   935
Johnson, Samuel (1709–84).
    THE RAMBLER. Introduction by *S. C. Roberts*.   (*See also* Biography.) 994
Landor, Walter Savage (1775–1864).
    IMAGINARY CONVERSATIONS, AND POEMS, 1824–9, 1853. Edited, with Introduction, by *Havelock Ellis*.   890
Lawrence, David Herbert (1885–1930).
    STORIES, ESSAYS AND POEMS. Selected by *Desmond Hawkins*. Poetry, Essays, Travel Sketches and Letters.   958
    (*See also* Fiction.)
Lynd, Robert (1879–1949).
    ESSAYS ON LIFE AND LITERATURE. Introduction by *Desmond MacCarthy*.   990
Macaulay, Thomas Babington, Lord (1800–59).
    CRITICAL AND HISTORICAL ESSAYS, 1843. New Introduction by *Douglas Jerrold*. 2 vols.   225–6
    MISCELLANEOUS ESSAYS, 1823–59; LAYS OF ANCIENT ROME, 1842; and MISCELLANEOUS POEMS, 1812–47. Introduction by *Prof. G. M. Trevelyan*, O.M.   439
    (*See also* History.)
Machiavelli, Niccolò (1469–1527).
    THE PRINCE, 1513. New Introduction by *Prof. H. Butterfield*, M.A., HON. D.LITT. Translated by *W. K. Marriott*.   280
Mazzini, Joseph (1805–72).
    THE DUTIES OF MAN (translated by *Miss E. Noyes*); and OTHER ESSAYS. New Introduction by *Dr Thomas Jones*, C.H., LL.D.   224
Milton, John (1608–74).
    PROSE WRITINGS. Introduction by *K. M. Burton*, M.A. The contents of this volume include 'Areopagitica,' 1644, and other important prose works.   795
    (*See also* Poetry, etc.)
Mitford, Mary Russell (1787–1855).
    OUR VILLAGE, 1824–32. Edited, with an Introduction, by *Sir John Squire*.   927
Modern Humour. An Anthology in Prose and Verse from over sixty authors.   957
Newman, John Henry (1801–90).
    ON THE SCOPE AND NATURE OF UNIVERSITY EDUCATION; and CHRISTIANITY AND SCIENTIFIC INVESTIGATION, 1852. Introduction by *Wilfrid Ward*.   723
    (*See also* Religion and Philosophy.)
Paine, Thomas (1737–1809).
    RIGHTS OF MAN, 1792. Introduction by *Arthur Seldon*.   718
Poe, Edgar Allan (1809–49).
    ESSAYS. (*See* Poetry.)
Quiller-Couch, Sir Arthur (1863–1944).
    CAMBRIDGE LECTURES, from 'Q.'s' well-known books *The Art of Reading*, 1920; *The Art of Writing*, 1916; *Studies in Literature*, 1918; and *Shakespeare's Workmanship*, 1918.   (*See also* Fiction.) 974
Rousseau, Jean Jacques (1712–78).
    ÉMILE; OR, EDUCATION. Translated by *Barbara Foxley*, M.A. Intro. (1955) by *Prof. Andre Boutet de Monvel*.   (*See also* Biography, Science.) 518
Ruskin, John (1819–1900).
    SESAME, AND LILIES, 1864: THE TWO PATHS, 1859; and THE KING OF THE GOLDEN RIVER; or THE BLACK BROTHERS, 1851.   219
    THE SEVEN LAMPS OF ARCHITECTURE, 1849. Illustrated with 14 plates of engravings.   207
Sévigné, Marie de Rabutin-Chantal, Marquise de (1626–96).
    SELECTED LETTERS. Selected and translated by *H. T. Barnwell*, M.A.   98

Spectator, The, 1711–14. By Joseph Addison (1672–1719), Sir Richard Steele (1672–1729) and Others. Edited by *Prof. Gregory Smith.* New Introduction by *P. Smithers,* D.PHIL., M.P., and a Biographical and General Index by *Prof. Gregory Smith.* Reset with minor revisions 1945. 4 vols.   *(See also* Essays *under* Steele.) 164–7

Spencer, Herbert (1820–1903).
ESSAYS ON EDUCATION, 1861. Introduction by *C. W. Eliot.*   504

Steele, Sir Richard (1672–1729).
THE TATLER, 1709–11.   993

Stevenson, Robert Louis (1850–94).
VIRGINIBUS PUERISQUE, 1881; and FAMILIAR STUDIES OF MEN AND BOOKS, 1882.
Introduction by *M. R. Ridley,* M.A.
       (See also Fiction, Travel.) 765

Swift, Jonathan (1667–1745).
A TALE OF A TUB, 1704; THE BATTLE OF THE BOOKS, 1704; and OTHER SATIRES.
       (See also Biography, Fiction.) 347

Swinnerton, Frank (*b.* 1884).
THE GEORGIAN LITERARY SCENE, 1935. A panorama, revised 1951, of English writers (novelists, essayists, dramatists, poets) from 1919.   943

Thackeray, William Makepeace (1811–63).
THE ENGLISH HUMOURISTS, 1851; CHARITY AND HUMOUR, 1853; and THE FOUR GEORGES, 1855. Introduction by *Walter Jerrold.*   *(See also* Fiction.) 610

Thoreau, Henry David (1817–62).
WALDEN, OR LIFE IN THE WOODS, 1854. Introduction by *Prof. Basil Willey.* 281

Trench, Richard Chenevix (1807–86).
ON THE STUDY OF WORDS, 1851; and ENGLISH PAST AND PRESENT, 1855. Introduction by *George Sampson.*   788

Walton, Izaak (1593–1683).
THE COMPLEAT ANGLER, 1653. Introduction by *Margaret Bottrall,* M.A.   70

FICTION

Ainsworth, William Harrison (1805–82).
ROOKWOOD, 1834. Introduction by *Frank Swinnerton.* Dick Turpin.   870
THE TOWER OF LONDON, 1840. Lady Jane Grey.   400
WINDSOR CASTLE, 1843. Henry VIII and Ann Boleyn.   709

American Short Stories of the Nineteenth Century. Edited, with an Introduction, by *John Cournos.* Twenty stories from representative writers.   840

Andersen, Hans Christian (1805–75).
FAIRY TALES AND STORIES. This represents a completely new selection and in the Reginald Spink Translation.   4

Austen, Jane (1775–1817).
EMMA, 1816.   24   PRIDE AND PREJUDICE, 1823.   22
MANSFIELD PARK, 1814.   23   SENSE AND SENSIBILITY, 1811.   21
NORTHANGER ABBEY, 1818; and PERSUASION, 1818.   25

Balzac, Honoré de (1799–1850).
AT THE SIGN OF THE CAT AND RACKET, 1830; and OTHER STORIES. Translated by *Clara Bell.* Introduction by *George Saintsbury.*   349
THE COUNTRY DOCTOR, 1833. Introduction by *Prof. Marcel Girard*   530
EUGÉNIE GRANDET, 1834. Translated by *Ellen Marriage.* New Introduction by *Prof. Marcel Girard.*   169
OLD GORIOT, 1835. Translated by *Ellen Marriage.* New Introduction by *Prof. Marcel Girard.*   170
THE WILD ASS'S SKIN, 1831. A youth makes a bargain with destiny. New Introduction by *Prof. Marcel Girard.*   26

Barbusse, Henri (1874–1935).
UNDER FIRE, THE STORY OF A SQUAD, 1916. Introduction by *Brian Rhys.*   798

Beaconsfield, Benjamin Disraeli, Earl of (1804–81).
CONINGSBY, 1844. Introduction and Notes (with a Key to the Characters) by *B. N. Langdon-Davies.*   535

Bennett, Arnold (1867–1931).
THE OLD WIVES' TALE, 1908. The most durable novel of Bennett's.   919

Blackmore, Richard Doddridge (1825–1900).
LORNA DOONE: A ROMANCE OF EXMOOR, 1869. Introduction by *Ernest Rhys.*   304

Boccaccio, Giovanni (1313–75).
DECAMERON, 1471. Translated by *J. M. Rigg,* 1903. Introduction by *Edward Hutton.* Unabridged. 2 vols.   845–6

Borrow, George (1803–81).
THE ROMANY RYE, 1857. Practically a sequel to *Lavengro.* (119) *(See also* Travel.) 120

Brontë, Anne (1820–49).
THE TENANT OF WILDFELL HALL and AGNES GREY.   685

Brontë, Charlotte (1816–55). For Mrs Gaskell's 'Life' *see* Biography.
JANE EYRE, 1847.   287
THE PROFESSOR, 1857.   417
SHIRLEY, 1849.   288
VILLETTE, 1853.   351
Each Charlotte Brontë novel is introduced by *Margaret Lane*.

Brontë, Emily (1818–48).
WUTHERING HEIGHTS, 1848; and POEMS. Introduction by *Margaret Lane*.   243

Bunyan, John (1628–88).
GRACE ABOUNDING, 1666; and THE LIFE AND DEATH OF MR BADMAN, 1658. Introduction by *Prof. G. B. Harrison*, M.A., PH.D.   815
PILGRIM'S PROGRESS, Parts I and II, 1678–84. Reset edition. Introduction by *Prof. G. B. Harrison*, M.A., PH.D.   204

Burney, Fanny (Madame Frances d'Arblay, 1753–1849).
EVELINA, 1778. Introduction by *Lewis Gibbs*.   352

Butler, Samuel (1835–1902).
EREWHON, 1872 (revised 1901); and EREWHON REVISITED, 1901. Introduction by *Desmond MacCarthy*.   881
THE WAY OF ALL FLESH, 1903. Introduction by *A. J. Hoppe*.   895

Cervantes, Saavedra Miguel de (1547–1616).
DON QUIXOTE DE LA MANCHA. Translated by *P. A. Motteux*. Notes by *J. G. Lockhart*. Introduction and supplementary Notes by *L. B. Walton*. M.A., B.LITT. 2 vols.   385–6

Collins, Wilkie (1824–89).
THE MOONSTONE, 1868. Introduction by *Dorothy L. Sayers*.   979
THE WOMAN IN WHITE, 1860. New Introduction by *Maurice Richardson*.   464

Conrad, Joseph (1857–1924).
LORD JIM, 1900. Characteristically set in the East Indies. Introduction by *R. B. Cunninghame Graham*.   925
THE NIGGER OF THE 'NARCISSUS,' 1897; TYPHOON, 1903; and THE SHADOW LINE, 1917. Three of Conrad's best-known sea stories.   980
NOSTROMO, 1904. Edition of Conrad's greatest novel with an Introduction by *Richard Curle*.   38
THE SECRET AGENT, 1907.   282

Cooper, James Fenimore (1789–1851).
THE LAST OF THE MOHICANS, 1826, A NARRATIVE OF 1757.   79

Craik, Mrs. *See* Mulock.

Daudet, Alphonse (1840–97).
TARTARIN OF TARASCON, 1872; and TARTARIN ON THE ALPS, 1885. Two light episodic novels, some of the funniest episodes ever written in French.   423

Defoe, Daniel (1661?–1731).
THE FORTUNES AND MISFORTUNES OF MOLL FLANDERS, 1722. Introduction by *G. A. Aitken*. One of Defoe's greatest books, famous for its picture of low life.   837
JOURNAL OF THE PLAGUE YEAR, 1722. Containing extracts from contemporary narratives of the Plague.   289
LIFE, ADVENTURES AND PIRACIES OF THE FAMOUS CAPTAIN SINGLETON, 1720. Introduction by *Prof. J. R. Sutherland*. A supposed record of a journey across Africa.   74
ROBINSON CRUSOE, 1719. Parts 1 and 2 complete.   (*See also* Travel.)   59

De Rojas, Fernando (15th century).
CELESTINA: OR THE TRAGI-COMEDY OF CALISTO AND MELIBEA, attributed to Fernando de Rojas. Translated, with an Introduction, by *Phyllis Hartnoll*, M.A., L. ÉS L. This is a new translation (1958).   100

Dickens, Charles (1812–70). Each of the following volumes of Dickens's works has an Introduction by *G. K. Chesterton*:
BARNABY RUDGE, 1841.   76
BLEAK HOUSE, 1852–3.   236
A CHRISTMAS CAROL AND OTHER CHRISTMAS BOOKS, 1843–8.   239
CHRISTMAS STORIES, 1850–67.   414
DAVID COPPERFIELD, 1849–50.   242
DOMBEY AND SON, 1846–8.   240
GREAT EXPECTATIONS, 1861.   234
HARD TIMES, 1854.   292
LITTLE DORRIT, 1857.   293
MARTIN CHUZZLEWIT, 1843–4.   241
NICHOLAS NICKLEBY, 1838–9.   238
OLD CURIOSITY SHOP, 1841.   173
OLIVER TWIST, 1838.   233
OUR MUTUAL FRIEND, 1864–5.   294
PICKWICK PAPERS, 1836–7.   235
A TALE OF TWO CITIES, 1859.   102
(*See also* Biography.)

Disraeli, Benjamin. *See* Beaconsfield.

Dostoyevsky, Fyodor (1821–81).
THE BROTHERS KARAMAZOV, 1879–80. Translated by *Constance Garnett*. Introduction by *Edward Garnett*. 2 vols.   802–3
CRIME AND PUNISHMENT, 1866. *Constance Garnett* translation.   501
THE IDIOT, 1873. Translated by *Eva M. Martin*. New Introduction by *Richard Curle*.   682

LETTERS FROM THE UNDERWORLD, 1864; and OTHER TALES (THE GENTLE MAIDEN; THE LANDLADY). Translated, with Introduction, by *C. J. Hogarth.* 654
POOR FOLK, 1845; and THE GAMBLER, 1867. Translated, with Introduction, by *C. J. Hogarth.* 711
THE POSSESSED, 1871. Translated by *Constance Garnett.* Introduction by *Nikolay Andreyev*, PH.D., M.A. 2 vols. 861–2

Dumas, Alexandre (1802–70).
THE BLACK TULIP, 1850. The brothers De Witt in Holland, 1672–5. New Introduction by *Prof. Marcel Girard.* 174
COUNT OF MONTE CRISTO, 1844. Napoleon's later phase. New Introduction by *Prof. Marcel Girard.* 2 vols. 393–4
MARGUERITE DE VALOIS, 1845. The Eve of St Bartholomew. 326
THE THREE MUSKETEERS, 1844. The France of Cardinal Richelieu. 81

Du Maurier, George Louis Palmella Busson (1834–96).
TRILBY, 1894. Illustrated by the author. Preface by *Sir Gerald Du Maurier. Trilby* breathes the air of Paris in the eighties and is drawn largely from the author's own experience. 863

Edgeworth, Maria (1767–1849).
CASTLE RACKRENT, 1800; and THE ABSENTEE, 1812. Introduction by *Prof. Brander Matthews.* 410

Eliot, George (pseudonym of Mary Ann Evans, 1819–80).
ADAM BEDE, 1859. Introduction by *Robert Speaight.* 27
MIDDLEMARCH, 1872. Introduction by *Gerald Bullett.* 2 vols. 854–5
THE MILL ON THE FLOSS, 1860. Introduction by *Sir W. Robertson Nicoll.* 325
ROMOLA, 1863. Intro. by *Rudolph Dircks.* The Florence of Savonarola. 231
SILAS MARNER, THE WEAVER OF RAVELOE, 1861. Introduction by *John Holloway*, PH.D., M.A. 12

English Short Stories. Thirty-six selected stories from Middle Ages to present time. Introduction by *Richard Wilson*, B.A., D.LITT. 743

Fielding, Henry (1707–54).
AMELIA, 1751. Amelia is drawn from Fielding's first wife. 2 vols. 852–3
JONATHAN WILD, 1743; and JOURNAL OF A VOYAGE TO LISBON, 1755. *Jonathan Wild* is a satire on false hero-worship; the *Journal* (published posthumously) narrates the incidents of Fielding's last voyage. 877
JOSEPH ANDREWS, 1742. A skit on Richardson's *Pamela.* 467
TOM JONES, 1749. The first great English novel of humour. New Introduction by *Prof. A. R. Humphreys.* 2 vols. 355–6

Flaubert, Gustave (1821–80).
MADAME BOVARY, 1857. Translated by *Eleanor Marx-Aveling.* Introduction by *George Saintsbury.* 808
SALAMMBO, 1862. Translated by *J. C. Chartres.* Introduction by *Prof. F. C. Green*, M.A., PH.D. The war of the Mercenaries against Carthage. 869
SENTIMENTAL EDUCATION, 1869. Modern translation, with Introduction and Notes by *Anthony Goldsmith.* 969

Forster, Edward Morgan (b. 1879).
A PASSAGE TO INDIA, 1924. With an Introduction by *Peter Burra.* 972

Galsworthy, John (1867–1933).
THE COUNTRY HOUSE. 917

Gaskell, Mrs Elizabeth (1810–65).
CRANFORD, 1853. Introduction by *Frank Swinnerton.* (See also Biography.) 83
GHOST STORIES. Introduction by *John Hampden.* Eighteen stories. 952

Gogol, Nikolay (1809–52).
DEAD SOULS, 1842. Introduction by *Nikolay Andreyev*, PH.D., M.A. 726

Goldsmith, Oliver (1728–74).
THE VICAR OF WAKEFIELD, 1766. Introduction by *J. M. Dent.* 295
(See also Poetry.)

Goncharov, Ivan (1812–91).
OBLOMOV, 1857. First complete English translation by *Natalie Duddington.* Introduction by *Nikolay Andreyev*, PH.D., M.A. 878

Gorky, Maxim (pseudonym of Alexei Maximovitch Pieshkov, 1868–1936).
THROUGH RUSSIA. Translated, with an Introduction, by *C. J. Hogarth.* 741

Grossmith, George (1847–1912), and **Weedon** (1853–1919).
THE DIARY OF A NOBODY, 1894. With Weedon Grossmith's illustrations. 63

Hawthorne, Nathaniel (1804–64).
THE HOUSE OF THE SEVEN GABLES, 1851. New Introduction by *Prof. Roy Harvey Pearce.* 176
THE SCARLET LETTER: A ROMANCE, 1850. With new Introduction by *Prof. Roy Harvey Pearce.* 122
TWICE-TOLD TALES, 1837–42. With a new Introduction by *Prof. Roy Harvey Pearce.* 531

Hugo, Victor Marie (1802–85).
LES MISÉRABLES, 1862. Introduction by *Denis Saurat.* 2 vols. 363–4
NOTRE DAME DE PARIS, 1831. Introduction by *Denis Saurat.* 422
TOILERS OF THE SEA, 1866. Introduction by *Prof. F. C. Green.* 509

Huxley, Aldous.
    STORIES, ESSAYS AND POEMS. (*See under* Essays.)

James, Henry (1843–1916).
    THE AMBASSADORS, 1903. Introduction by *Frank Swinnerton.*   987
    THE TURN OF THE SCREW, 1898; and THE ASPERN PAPERS, 1888. Two famous short novels. Introduction by *Prof. Kenneth B. Murdock*, A.M., PH.D.   912

Jefferies, Richard (1848–87).
    AFTER LONDON, 1884; and AMARYLLIS AT THE FAIR, 1886. Introduction by *Richard Garnett.*   951

Jerome, Jerome K. (1859–1927).
    THREE MEN IN A BOAT and THREE MEN ON THE BUMMEL. Introduction by *D. C. Browning*, M.A., B.LITT.   118

Kingsley, Charles (1819–75).
    HEREWARD THE WAKE, 1866.   296
    WESTWARD HO!, 1855. Introduction by *Dr J. A. Williamson*, M.A.   20
        (*See also* Poetry and Drama.)

Lamb, Charles (1775–1834), and **Mary** (1764–1847).
    TALES FROM SHAKESPEARE, 1807. Illustrated by *Arthur Rackham.*   8
        (*See also* Biography.)

Lawrence, David Herbert (1885–1930).
    THE WHITE PEACOCK, 1911.   (*See also* Essays.) 914

Loti, Pierre (1850–1923).
    ICELAND FISHERMAN, 1886. Translated by *W. P. Baines.*   920

Lover, Samuel (1797–1868).
    HANDY ANDY, 1842. Lover was a musician, portrait-painter, song-writer and actor who also wrote four novels of which this is generally accounted the best.   178

Lytton, Edward Bulwer, Baron (1803–73).
    THE LAST DAYS OF POMPEII, 1834. A romance of the first century A.D.   80

Mann, Thomas (1875–1955).
    STORIES AND EPISODES. Introduction by *Prof. Erich Heller*, PH.D.   962

Manzoni, Alessandro (1785–1873).
    THE BETROTHED (*I Promessi Sposi*, 1840, rev. ed.). Translated (1951) from the Italian by *Archibald Colquhoun*, who also adds a preface.   999

Marryat, Frederick (1792–1848).
    MR MIDSHIPMAN EASY. New Introduction by *Oliver Warner.*   82
    THE SETTLERS IN CANADA, 1844. Introduction by *Oliver Warner.*   370

Maugham, W. Somerset (*b.* 1874).
    CAKES AND ALE, 1930. The finest novel of the author's inter-war period.   932

Maupassant, Guy de (1850–93).
    SHORT STORIES. Translated by *Marjorie Laurie.* Intro. by *Gerald Gould.*   907

Melville, Herman (1819–91).
    MOBY DICK, 1851. Intro. by *Prof. Sherman Paul.*   179
    TYPEE, 1846; and BILLY BUDD (*published* 1924). South Seas adventures. Introduction by *Milton R. Stern.*   180

Meredith, George (1828–1909).
    THE ORDEAL OF RICHARD FEVEREL, 1859. Introduction by *Robert Sencourt.*   916

Mickiewicz, Adam (1798–1855).
    PAN TADEUSZ, 1834. Translated into English prose, with Introduction, by *Prof. G. R. Noyes.* Poland's epic of Napoleonic wars.   842

Modern Short Stories. Selected by *John Hadfield.* Twenty stories.   954

Moore, George (1852–1933).
    ESTHER WATERS, 1894. The story of Esther Waters, the servant girl who 'went wrong.' Introduction by *C. D. Medley.*   933

Mulock [Mrs Craik], Maria (1826–87).
    JOHN HALIFAX, GENTLEMAN, 1856. Introduction by *W. M. Parker*, M.A.   123

Pater, Walter (1839–94).
    MARIUS THE EPICUREAN, 1885. Introduction by *Osbert Burdett.*   903

Peacock, Thomas Love (1785–1866).
    HEADLONG HALL and NIGHTMARE ABBEY. New Intro. by *P. M. Yarker*, M.A.   327

Poe, Edgar Allan (1809–49).
    TALES OF MYSTERY AND IMAGINATION. Introduction by *Padraic Colum.*   336
        (*See also* Poetry and Drama.)

Priestley, J. B. (*b.* 1894).
    ANGEL PAVEMENT. 1931. A finely conceived novel of London.   938

Quiller-Couch, Sir Arthur (1863–1944).
    HETTY WESLEY, 1903. Introduction by the author.   (*See also* Essays.) 864

Rabelais, François (1494?–1553).
    THE HEROIC DEEDS OF GARGANTUA AND PANTAGRUEL, 1532–5. Introduction by *D. B. Wyndham Lewis.* A complete unabridged edition of Urquhart and Motteux's translation, 1653–94. 2 vols.   826–7

Radcliffe, Mrs Ann (1764–1823).
    THE MYSTERIES OF UDOLPHO, 1794. Intro. by *R. A. Freeman.* 2 vols.   865–6

Reade, Charles (1814–84).
    THE CLOISTER AND THE HEARTH, 1861. Introduction by *Swinburne.*   29

Richardson, Samuel (1689–1761).
    PAMELA, 1740. Introduction by *M. Kinkead-Weekes*. 2 vols.   683–4
    CLARISSA, 1747–8. Introduction by *Prof. John Butt*. 4 vols.   882–5
Russian Short Stories. Translated, with Introduction, by *Rochelle S. Townsend*. Stories by Pushkin, Gogol, Tolstoy, Korolenko, Chehov, Chirikov, Andreyev, Kuprin, Gorky, Sologub.   758
Scott, Sir Walter (1771–1832).
    THE ANTIQUARY, 1816. Introduction by *W. M. Parker*, M.A.   126
    THE BRIDE OF LAMMERMOOR, 1819. A romance of life in East Lothian, 1695. New Introduction by *W. M. Parker*, M.A.   129
    GUY MANNERING, 1815. A mystery story of the time of George III. New Introduction by *W. M. Parker*, M.A.   133
    THE HEART OF MIDLOTHIAN, 1818. Period of the Porteous Riots, 1736. New Introduction by *W. M. Parker*, M.A.   134
    IVANHOE, 1820. A romance of the days of Richard I.   16
    KENILWORTH, 1821. The tragic story of Amy Robsart, in Elizabeth I's time. New Preface and Glossary by *W. M. Parker*, M.A.   135
    OLD MORTALITY, 1817. Battle of Bothwell Bridge, 1679. New Introduction by *W. M. Parker*, M.A.   137
    QUENTIN DURWARD, 1823. A tale of adventures in fifteenth-century France. New Introduction by *W. M. Parker*, M.A.   140
    REDGAUNTLET, 1824. A tale of adventure in Cumberland, about 1763. New Introduction by *W. M. Parker*, M.A.   141
    ROB ROY, 1818. A romance of the Rebellion of 1715.   142
    THE TALISMAN, 1825. Richard Cœur-de-Lion and the Third Crusade, 1191. New Preface by *W. M. Parker*, M.A.   (*See also* Biography.) 144
Shchedrin (M. E. Saltykov, 1826–92).
    THE GOLOVLYOV FAMILY. Translated by *Natalie Duddington*. Introduction by *Edward Garnett*.   908
Shelley, Mary Wollstonecraft (1797–1851).
    FRANKENSTEIN, 1818. With Mary Shelley's own Preface. Introduction by *Dr. Dowse* and *D. A. Palmer*.   616
Shorter Novels.
    Vol. I: ELIZABETHAN. Introduction by *George Saintsbury* and Notes by *Philip Henderson*. Contains: Deloney's 'Jack of Newberie' and 'Thomas of Reading'; Nashe's 'The Unfortunate Traveller'; Green's 'Carde of Fancie'.   824
    VOL. II: SEVENTEENTH CENTURY. Edited, with Introduction, by *Philip Henderson*. Contains: Emanuel Ford's 'Ornatus and Artesia'; Aphra Behn's 'Oroonoko'; Neville's 'The Isle of Pines'; Congreve's 'Incognita'.   841
    Vol. III: EIGHTEENTH CENTURY. Edited, with Introduction, by *Philip Henderson*. Contains: Beckford's 'Vathek'; Horace Walpole's 'The Castle of Otranto'; Dr Johnson's 'Rasselas.'   856
Sienkiewicz, Henryk (1846–1916).
    QUO VADIS? 1896. Translated by *C. J. Hogarth*. Intro. by *Monica Gardner*.   970
    TALES. Edited, with Introduction, by *Monica Gardner*.   871
Smollett, Tobias (1721–71).
    THE EXPEDITION OF HUMPHRY CLINKER, 1771. Introduction by *Howard Mumford Jones*, and 36 pages of Notes by *Charles Lee*.   975
    PEREGRINE PICKLE, 1751. Introduction by *Walter Allen*. 2 vols.   838–9
    RODERICK RANDOM, 1742. Introduction by *H. W. Hodges*.   790
Somerville, E. Œ. (1858–1949), and **Ross, Martin** (pseudonym of Violet Florence Martin, 1862–1915).
    EXPERIENCES OF AN IRISH R.M. Contains the authors' two books, *Some Experiences of an Irish R.M.*, 1897, and *Further Experiences of an Irish R.M.*, 1908.   978
Stendhal (pseudonym of Henri Beyle, 1783–1842).
    SCARLET AND BLACK, 1831. Translated by *C. K. Scott Moncrieff*. Introduction by *Prof. F. C. Green*, M.A., DR.PHIL. 2 vols.   945–6
Sterne, Laurence (1713–68).
    A SENTIMENTAL JOURNEY THROUGH FRANCE AND ITALY, 1768; JOURNAL TO ELIZA, written in 1767; and LETTERS TO ELIZA, 1766–7. Introduction by *Daniel George*.   796
    TRISTRAM SHANDY, 1760–7. Intro. by *George Saintsbury*.   617
Stevenson, Robert Louis (1850–94).
    DR JEKYLL AND MR HYDE, 1886; THE MERRY MEN, 1887; WILL O' THE MILL, 1878; MARKHEIM, 1886; THRAWN JANET, 1881; OLALLA, 1885; THE TREASURE OF FRANCHARD. Introduction by *M. R. Ridley*, M.A.   767
    KIDNAPPED, 1886; and CATRONA, 1893, Introduction by *M. R. Ridley*, M.A.   762
    THE MASTER OF BALLANTRAE, 1869; WEIR OF HERMISTON, 1896. Introduction by *M. R. Ridley*, M.A.   764
    ST IVES, 1898. Completed by Sir Arthur Quiller-Couch. Introduction (1958) by *M. R. Ridley*, M.A.   904

Treasure Island, 1883; and New Arabian Nights, 1882. Introduction by
  M. R. Ridley, M.A.   (*See also* Essays, Travel.) 763
Story Book for Boys and Girls. Edited by *Guy Pocock* (1955).   934
Surtees, Robert Smith (1803–64).
  Jorrocks's Jaunts and Jollities, 1838.   817
Swift, Jonathan (1667–1745).
  Gulliver's Travels, 1726. An unabridged edition; with an Introduction by *Sir
  Harold Williams*, F.B.A., F.S.A., M.A.   (*See also* Biography, Essays.) 60
Tales of Detection. Introduction by *Dorothy L. Sayers*. Nineteen stories, tracing the
  development of the genuine detective story during the last hundred years. 928
Thackeray, William Makepeace (1811–63).
  Henry Esmond, 1852. Introduction by *M. R. Ridley*, M.A.   73
  The Newcomes, 1853–5. Introduction by *M. R. Ridley*, M.A. 2 vols.   465–6
  Pendennis, 1848–50. Introduction by *M. R. Ridley*, M.A. 2 vols.   425–6
  Vanity Fair, 1847–8. Introduction by *M. R. Ridley*, M.A.   298
  The Virginians, 1857–9. Introduction by *M. R. Ridley*, M.A. 2 vols.   507–8
                                             (*See also* Essays and Criticism.)
Tolstoy, Count Leo (1828–1910).
  Anna Karenina, 1873–7. Translated by *Rochelle S. Townsend*. With Introduction
  by *Nikolay Andreyev*, PH.D., M.A. 2 vols.   612–13
  Master and Man, 1895; and Other Parables and Tales. Introduction (1958)
  by *Nikolay Andreyev*, PH.D., M.A.   469
  War and Peace, 1864–9. Introduction by *Vicomte de Vogüé*. 3 vols.   525–7
Trollope, Anthony (1815–82).
  The Warden, 1855. The first of the 'Chronicles of Barset.' Introduction by
  Kathleen Tillotson, M.A., B.LITT.   182
  Barchester Towers, 1857. The second of the 'Chronicles of Barset.' Introduction
  (1956) on Anthony Trollope's 'Clergy' by *Michael Sadleir*.   30
  Doctor Thorne, 1858. The third of the 'Chronicles of Barset.'   360
  Framley Parsonage, 1861. The fourth of the 'Chronicles of Barset.' Introduction
  by *Kathleen Tillotson*.   181
  The Small House at Allington, 1864. The fifth of the 'Chronicles of Barset.' 361
  The Last Chronicle of Barset, 1867. 2 vols.   391–2
Turgenev, Ivan (1818–83).
  Fathers and Sons, 1862. Translated by *Dr Avril Pyman*.   742
  Smoke, 1867. A new translation, with Introduction, by *Natalie Duddington*. 988
  Virgin Soil, 1877. Translated by *Rochelle S. Townsend*.   528
Twain, Mark (pseudonym of Samuel Langhorne Clemens, 1835–1910).
  Tom Sawyer, 1876; and Huckleberry Finn, 1884. Introduction by *Christopher
  Morley*.   976
Verne, Jules (1828–1905).
  Five Weeks in a Balloon, 1862, translated by *Arthur Chambers*; and Around
  the World in Eighty Days, translated by *P. Desages*.   779
  Twenty Thousand Leagues under the Sea, 1869.   319
Voltaire, François Marie Arouet de (1694–1778).
  Candide, and other Tales. Smollett's translation, edited by *J. C. Thornton*. 936
                                                          (*See also* History.)
Walpole, Hugh Seymour (1884–1941).
  Mr Perrin and Mr Traill, 1911.   918
Wells, Herbert George (1866–1946).
  Ann Veronica, 1909. Introduction by *A. J. Hoppé*.   977
  The Wheels of Chance, 1896; and The Time Machine, 1895.   915
Wilde, Oscar.
  The Picture of Dorian Gray, 1891.   (*See* Poetry and Drama.)
Woolf, Virginia (1882–1941).
  To the Lighthouse, 1927. Introduction by *D. M. Hoare*, PH.D.   949
Zola, Émile (1840–1902).
  Germinal, 1885. Translated, with an Introduction, by *Havelock Ellis*.   897

HISTORY

Anglo-Saxon Chronicle. Translated and Edited by *G. N. Garmonsway*, F.R.HIST.SOC.
  Foreword by *Prof. Bruce Dickins*.   624
Bede, the Venerable (673–735).
  The Ecclesiastical History of the English Nation. Translated by *John
  Stevens*, revised by *J. A. Giles*, with notes by *L. C. Jane*. Introduction by *Prof.
  David Knowles*, O.S.B., M.A., LITT.D., F.B.A., F.S.A.   479
British Orations. The 1960 edition of this selection of British historical speeches con-
  tains selections from four of the most famous of Sir Winston Churchill's World War
  II speeches.   714
Burke, Edmund (1729–97).
  Speeches and Letters on American Affairs. New Introduction by the *Very Rev.
  Canon Peter McKevitt*, PH.D.   (*See also* Essays and Criticism.) 340

Caesar, Julius (102 ?–44 B.C.).
WAR COMMENTARIES. 'The Gallic Wars' and 'The Civil War.' Newly translated and edited by *John Warrington*. 70

Carlyle, Thomas (1795–1881).
THE FRENCH REVOLUTION, 1837. Introduction by *Hilaire Belloc*. 2 vols. 31–2
(See also Essays.)

Chesterton, Cecil (1879–1918). A HISTORY OF THE U.S.A., 1917. Edited by *Prof. D. W. Brogan*, M.A. 96

Creasy, Sir Edward (1812–78).
FIFTEEN DECISIVE BATTLES OF THE WORLD, FROM MARATHON TO WATERLOO, 1852. With Diagrams and Index. New Introduction by *Audrey Butler*, M.A. (OXON.). 300

Demosthenes (384–322 B.C.).
PUBLIC ORATIONS. Translated with Introduction by *A. W. Pickard-Cambridge*, M.A.

Gibbon, Edward (1737–94).
THE DECLINE AND FALL OF THE ROMAN EMPIRE, 1776–88. Notes by *Oliphant Smeaton*. Intro. by *Christopher Dawson*. Complete text in 6 vols. 434–6, 474–6

Green, John Richard (1837–83).
A SHORT HISTORY OF THE ENGLISH PEOPLE, 1874. Introduction by *L. C. Jane*. English history from 607 to 1873. Continued by: 'A Political and Social Survey from 1815 to 1915,' by *R. P. Farley*, and revised to 1950. 727–8

Herodotus (484 ?–425 ? B.C.).
HISTORY. The 'History' deals with the period covering the Persian invasion of Greece, 492–480 B.C. Rawlinson's Translation. Introduction by *John Warrington*. 2 vols. 405–6

Holinshed, Raphael (*d.* 1580 ?).
HOLINSHED'S CHRONICLE AS USED IN SHAKESPEARE'S PLAYS, 1578. Introduction by *Prof. Allardyce Nicoll* and *Josephine Nicoll*. 800

Joinville, Jean de. *See* Villehardouin.

Lincoln, Abraham (1809–65).
SPEECHES AND LETTERS, 1832–65. A new selection edited with an Introduction by *Paul M. Angle*. Chronology of Lincoln's life and index. 206

Lützow, Count Franz von (1849–1916).
BOHEMIA: AN HISTORICAL SKETCH, 1896. Introduction by *President T. G. Masaryk*. H. A. Piehler covers events from 1879 to 1938. 432

Macaulay, Thomas Babington, Baron (1800–59).
THE HISTORY OF ENGLAND. The complete text in four volumes, which together contain 2,450 pages. Introduction by *Douglas Jerrold*. 34–7
(See also Essays.)

Maine, Sir Henry (1822–88).
ANCIENT LAW, 1861. Introduction by *Prof. J. H. Morgan*. 734

Motley, John (1814–77).
THE RISE OF THE DUTCH REPUBLIC, 1856. Intro. by *V. R. Reynolds*. 3 vols. 86–8

Paston Letters, The, 1418–1506. 2 vols. A selection. 752–3

Prescott, William Hickling (1796–1859).
HISTORY OF THE CONQUEST OF MEXICO, 1843. 2 vols. 397–8
HISTORY OF THE CONQUEST OF PERU, 1847. The natural successor to *Mexico*. 301

Thucydides (*c.* 460–401 B.C.).
HISTORY OF THE PELOPONNESIAN WAR. Translation by *Richard Crawley*. Index and five plans. 455

Villehardouin, Geoffrey de (1160 ?–1213 ?), **and Joinville, Jean, Sire de** (1224–1317).
MEMOIRS OF THE CRUSADES. Translated, with an Introduction, by *Sir Frank T. Marzials*. 333

Voltaire, François Marie Arouet de (1694–1778).
THE AGE OF LOUIS XIV, 1751. Translation by *Martyn P. Pollack*. 780
(See also Fiction.)

LEGENDS AND SAGAS

Chrétien de Troyes (fl. 12th cent.).
ARTHURIAN ROMANCES ('Erec et Enide'; 'Cligés'; 'Yvain' and 'Lancelot'). Translated into prose, with Introduction, notes and bibliography, by *William Wistar Comfort*. 698

Kalevala, or The Land of Heroes. Translated from the Finnish by *W. F. Kirby*. 2 vols. 259–60

Mabinogion, The. Translated with Introduction by *Thomas Jones*, M.A., D.LITT., and *Gwyn Jones*, M.A. 97

Malory, Sir Thomas (fl. 1400 ?–70).
LE MORTE D'ARTHUR. Introduction by *Sir John Rhys*. 2 vols. 45–6

Marie de France (12th century), LAYS OF, AND OTHER FRENCH LEGENDS. Eight of Marie's 'Lais' and two of the anonymous French love stories of the same period translated with an Introduction by *Eugene Mason*. 557

Njal's Saga. THE STORY OF BURNT NJAL (written about 1280–90). Translated from the Icelandic by *Sir G. W. Dasent* (1861). Introduction (1957) and Index by *Prof. Edward Turville-Petre*, B.LITT., M.A. 558

10

POETRY AND DRAMA

Aeschylus (525–455 B.C.).
PLAYS. Translated into English Verse by *G. M. Cookson*. New Introduction by *John Warrington*, and notes on each play. 62

Anglo-Saxon Poetry. English poetry between A.D. 650 and 1000, from 'Widsith' and 'Beowulf' to the battle-pieces of 'Brunanburh' and 'Maldon.' Selected and translated by *Prof. R. K. Gordon*, M.A. Reset, and revised by the translator, 1954. 794

Aristophanes (450?–385? B.C.).
THE COMEDIES. Translated by *J. Hookham Frere*, etc. Edited, with Introduction, by *J. P. Maine* and *J. H. Frere*. 2 vols. (*Vol. 1 temporarily out of print*.) 516

Arnold, Matthew (1822–88).
COMPLETE POEMS. Introduction by *Kenneth Allott*. 334

Ballads, A Book of British. Introduction and Notes by *R. Brimley Johnson*. Ballads from the earliest times to those of Yeats and Kipling. 572

Beaumont, Francis (1584–1616), and **Fletcher, John** (1579–1625).
SELECT PLAYS. Introduction by *M. C. Bradbrook*. 'The Knight of the Burning Pestle,' 'The Maid's Tragedy,' 'A King and No King,' 'The Faithful Shepherdess.' 'The Wild Goose Chase,' 'Bonduca,' with a glossary. 506

Blake, William (1757–1827).
POEMS AND PROPHECIES. Edited, with special Introduction, by *Max Plowman*. 792

Brontë, Emily.
POEMS. (*See* Fiction.)

Browning, Robert (1812–89).
COMPLETE POETICAL WORKS. POEMS AND PLAYS (1833–64). Volumes I and II, with a new Introduction by *John Bryson*, M.A., dealing with the five-volume Everyman Browning set. 2 vols. (Nos. 41–2). Volume III, containing *The Ring and the Book*, Browning's long dramatic poem (No. 502), and Volumes IV and V, POEMS, 1871–90, with Introduction by *M. M. Bozman* (Nos. 964, 966).

Burns, Robert (1759–96).
POEMS AND SONGS. A very full selection and a very accurate text of Burns's copious lyrical output. Edited and introduced by *Prof. James Kinsley*, M.A., PH.D. 94

Byron, George Gordon Noel, Lord (1788–1824).
THE POETICAL AND DRAMATIC WORKS. Edited with new Introduction by *Professor V. de Sola Pinto*, M.A., D.PHIL.(OXON.). 3 vols. (*See also* Biography.) 486–8

Century. A CENTURY OF HUMOROUS VERSE, 1850–1950. Edited by *Roger Lancelyn Green*, M.A., B.LITT. 813

Chaucer, Geoffrey (*c.* 1343–1400).
CANTERBURY TALES. New standard text edited by *A. C. Cawley*, M.A., PH.D., based on the Ellesmere Manuscript, with an ingenious system of glosses, page by page. 307
TROILUS AND CRISEYDE. Prepared by *John Warrington* from the Campsall Manuscript. 992

Coleridge, Samuel Taylor (1772–1834).
POEMS. Edited by *John Beer*, M.A., PH.D. (*See also* Essays, etc.) 43

Cowper, William (1731–1800).
POEMS. Intro. by *Hugh I'Anson Fausset*. 872

Dante Alighieri (1265–1321).
THE DIVINE COMEDY, first printed 1472. H. F. Cary's Translation, 1805–14. Edited, with Notes and Index, by *Edmund Gardner*. Foreword by *Prof. Mario Praz*. 308

De la Mare, Walter (1873–1956). (*See* Essays.)

Donne, John (1573–1631).
COMPLETE POEMS. Edited, with a revised Intro., by *Hugh I'Anson Fausset*. 867

Dryden, John (1631–1700).
POEMS. Edited by *Bonamy Dobrée*, O.B.E., M.A. 910

Early Seventeenth Century Drama. Edited with Introduction by *R. G. Lawrence*. 390

Eighteenth-century Plays. Edited by *John Hampden*. Includes Gay's 'Beggar's Opera,' and plays by Addison, Rowe, Fielding, Lillo, Colman and Garrick, and Cumberland 818

English Galaxy of Shorter Poems, The. Chosen and Edited by *Gerald Bullett*. 959

English Religious Verse. Edited by *G. Lacey May*. An anthology from the Middle Ages to the present day, including some 300 poems by 150 authors. 937

Euripides (484?–407 B.C.).
PLAYS. Introduction by *John Warrington*. Trans. by *A. S. Way*, D.LITT. 2 vols. 63, 271

Everyman, and Medieval Miracle Plays. New edition edited by *A. C. Cawley*, M.A., PH.D. Forewords to individual plays. 381

Fitzgerald, Edward (1809–83). *See* 'Persian Poems.'

Fletcher, John (1579–1625). *See* Beaumont.

Ford, John (1586–1639). *See* Webster.

Goethe, Johann Wolfgang von (1749–1832).
FAUST. Both parts of the tragedy which are the core of Goethe's life-work, in the re-edited translation of *Sir Theodore Martin*. (*See also* Biography, Essays.) 335

11

Golden Book of Modern English Poetry, The. Edited by *Thomas Caldwell* and *Philip Henderson*, containing some 300 poems by 130 poets, from T. E. Brown to Stephen Spender and C. Day Lewis. 921

Golden Treasury of English Songs and Lyrics, The, 1861. Compiled by Francis Turner Palgrave (1824–97). Enlarged edition, containing 88-page supplement. 96

Golden Treasury of Longer Poems, The. Revised edition (1954) with new supplementary poems. An anthology ranging from Chaucer to Walter de la Mare. 746

Goldsmith, Oliver (1728–74).
POEMS AND PLAYS. Edited, with Introduction, by *Austin Dobson*. (*See also* Fiction.) 415

Gray, Thomas (1716–71).
POEMS: WITH A SELECTION OF LETTERS AND ESSAYS. Introduction by *John Drinkwater*, and biographical notes by *Lewis Gibbs*. 628

Heine, Heinrich (c. 1797–1856).
PROSE AND POETRY. 911

Homer (? ninth century B.C.).
ILIAD. New verse translation by *S. O. Andrew* and *Michael Oakley*. 453
ODYSSEY. The new verse translation (first published 1953) by *S. O. Andrew*. Introduction by *John Warrington*. 454

Ibsen, Henrik (1828–1906).
A DOLL'S HOUSE, 1879; THE WILD DUCK, 1884; and THE LADY FROM THE SEA, 1888. Translated by *R. Farquharson Sharp* and *Elanor Marx-Aveling*. 494
GHOSTS, 1881; THE WARRIORS AT HELGELAND, 1857; and AN ENEMY OF THE PEOPLE, 1882. Translated by *R. Farquharson Sharp*. 552
PEER GYNT, 1867. Translated by *R. Farquharson Sharp*. 747
THE PRETENDERS, 1864; PILLARS OF SOCIETY, 1877; and ROSMERSHOLM, 1887. Translated by *R. Farquharson Sharp*. 659

Ingoldsby Legends, or *Mirth and Marvels*, by 'Thomas Ingoldsby, Esq.' Edited by *D. C. Browning*, M.A., B.LITT. 185

International Modern Plays. August Strindberg's 'Lady Julie,' Gerhard Hauptmann's 'Hannele,' Brothers Čapek's 'The Life of the Insects,' Jean Cocteau's 'The Infernal Machine,' and Luigi Chiarelli's 'The Mask and the Face.' Introduction by *Anthony Dent*. 989

Jonson, Ben (1573–1637).
PLAYS. Introduction by *Prof. F. E. Schelling*. Complete collectiod. 2 vols. 489–90

Juvenal (c. A.D. 50–c. 130).
SATIRES; with THE SATIRES OF PERSIUS. Introduction by *Prof. H. J. Rose*, M.A., F.B.A. William Gifford Translation, 1802. Revised by *John Warrington*. 997

Keats, John (1795–1821).
POEMS. Revised, reset edition (1944). Edited by *Gerald Bullett*. 101
(*See also* Biography.)

Kingsley, Charles (1819–75).
POEMS. With Introduction by *Ernest Rhys*. (*See also* Fiction.) 793

La Fontaine, Jean de (1621–95).
FABLES, 1668. Presented complete in the renowned Sir Edward Marsh translation. 991

'Langland, William' (1330?–1400?).
PIERS PLOWMAN, 1362. Translation into modern English by *Donald* and *Rachel Attwater*. 571

Lawrence, David Herbert (1885–1930). (*See* Essays.)

Lessing, Gotthold Ephraim (1729–81).
LAOCOÖN, 1766, AND OTHER WRITINGS. Introduction by *W. A. Steel*. Contents: 'Laocoön'; 'Minna von Barnhelm,' 1767, a comedy in five acts; and 'Nathan the Wise,' 1779, his philosophical drama. 843

Longfellow, Henry Wadsworth (1807–82).
POEMS, 1823–66. 382

Marlowe, Christopher (1564–93).
PLAYS AND POEMS. New edition with an Introduction by *M. R. Ridley*, M.A. 383

Milton, John (1608–74).
POEMS. New edition by *Prof. B. A. Wright*, M.A., based on Milton's editions and manuscripts. With a new Introduction by *Prof. Wright*. (*See also* Essays.) 384

Minor Elizabethan Drama. 2 vols. Vol. I. Tragedy. Norton and Sackville's 'Gorboduc,' Kyd's 'Spanish Tragedy,' Peele's 'David and Bethsabe,' and 'Arden of Feversham.' Vol. II. Comedy. Udall's 'Ralph Roister Doister,' Lyly's 'Endimion,' Peele's 'Old Wives' Tale,' Greene's 'Friar Bacon and Friar Bungay,' etc. Introduction by *Prof. A. Thorndike*. Glossary. 491–2

Minor Poets of the Seventeenth Century. The Poems of Thomas Carew, Sir John Suckling, Lord Herbert, Richard Lovelace. Edited and revised by *R. G. Howarth*, B.A., B.LITT., F.R.S.L. 873

Modern Plays. R. C. Sherriff's 'Journey's End,' W. Somerset Maugham's 'For Services Rendered,' Noel Coward's 'Hay Fever,' A. A. Milne's 'The Dover Road,' Arnold Bennett and Edward Knoblock's 'Milestones.' Introduction by *John Hadfield*. 942.

Molière, Jean Baptiste de (1622–73).
COMEDIES. Introduction by *Prof. F. C. Green*. 2 vols. 830–1

New Golden Treasury, The. Introduction by *Ernest Rhys.* A companion to Palgrave (q.v.), giving earlier lyrics than he did, and also later. 695

Omar Khayyám (*d.* 1123?). (*See under* Persian Poems.)

Ovid (43 B.C.–A.D. 18).
SELECTED WORKS. Chosen by *J. C.* and *M. J. Thornton.* Selections from the *Metamorphoses, Heroical Epistles,* the *Festivals,* the *Ibis,* and his epistles written in exile: also his *Art of Love.* 955

Pearl and Sir Gawain and the Green Knight. 346

Persian Poems. Selected and edited by *Prof. A. J. Arberry,* M.A., LITT.D., F.B.A. 996

Poe, Edgar Allan (1809–49).
POEMS AND ESSAYS. Introduction by *Andrew Lang.* (*See also* Fiction.) 791

Poems of our Time. An Anthology edited by *Richard Church,* C.B.E., *M. M. Bozman* and *Edith Sitwell,* D.LITT., D.B.E. Nearly 400 poems by about 130 poets. 981

Pope, Alexander (1688–1744).
COLLECTED POEMS. Edited with Intro. (1956) by *Prof. Bonamy Dobrée,* O.B.E., M.A. 760

Ramayana and Mahabharata. Condensed into English verse by *Romesh Dutt,* C.I.E. 403

Restoration Plays. Introduction by *Edmund Gosse.* Includes Dryden's 'All for Love,' Wycherley's 'The Country Wife,' Congreve's 'The Way of the World,' Otway's 'Venice Preserved,' Farquhar's 'Beaux-Stratagem,' Vanbrugh's 'Provoked Wife,' Etherege's 'Man of Mode.' 604

Rossetti, Dante Gabriel (1828–82).
POEMS. Edited with Introduction by *Oswald Doughty,* B.LITT., M.A., F.R.S.L. 627

Shakespeare, William (1564–1616).
A Complete Edition, based on Clark and Wright's Cambridge text, and edited by *Oliphant Smeaton.* With biographical Introduction, Chronological Tables and full Glossary. 3 vols. Comedies, 153; Histories, Poems and Sonnets, 154; Tragedies, 155

Shelley, Percy Bysshe (1792–1822).
POETICAL WORKS. Introduction by *A. H. Koszul.* 2 vols. 257–8

Sheridan, Richard Brinsley (1751–1816).
COMPLETE PLAYS. Introduction and notes by *Lewis Gibbs.* 95

Silver Poets of the Sixteenth Century. Edited by *Gerald Bullett.* The works of Sir Thomas Wyatt (1503–42), Henry Howard, Earl of Surrey (1517?–47), Sir Philip Sidney (1554–86), Sir Walter Ralegh (1552–1618) and Sir John Davies (1569–1626.) 985

Sophocles (496?–406 B.C.).
DRAMAS. This volume contains the seven surviving dramas. 114

Spenser, Edmund (1552–99).
THE FAERIE QUEENE. Introduction by *Prof. J. W. Hales,* and Glossary. The reliable Morris text and glossary are used for this edition. 2 vols. 443–4
THE SHEPHERD'S CALENDAR, 1579; and OTHER POEMS. Introduction by *Philip Henderson.* 879

Synge, J. M. (1871–1909).
PLAYS, POEMS AND PROSE. Introduction by *Michaél Mac Liammóir.* 968

Tchekhov, Anton (1860–1904).
PLAYS AND STORIES. 'The Cherry Orchard,' 'The Seagull,' 'The Wood Demon,' 'Tatyana Riepin' and 'On the Harmfulness of Tobacco' are included, as well as 13 of his best stories. The translation is by *S. S. Koteliansky.* Introduction by *David Magarshack.* 941

Tennyson, Alfred, Lord (1809–92).
POEMS. A comprehensive edition (1950), with an Introduction by *Mildred Bozman.* 2 vols. 44, 626

Twenty-four One-Act Plays. Enlarged edition, new Introduction by *John Hampden.* Contains plays by T. S. Eliot, Sean O'Casey, Laurence Housman, W. B. Yeats, James Bridie, Noel Coward, Lord Dunsany, Wolf Mankowitz and others. 947

Virgil (70–19 B.C.).
AENEID. Verse translation by *Michael Oakley.* Introduction by *E. M. Forster.* 161
ECLOGUES AND GEORGICS. Verse Translation by *T. F. Royds.* The 'Eclogues' were inspired by Theocritus; the 'Georgics' describe a countryman's life. 222

Webster, John (1580?–1625?), and **Ford, John** (1586–1639).
SELECTED PLAYS. Introduction by *Prof. G. B. Harrison,* M.A., PH.D. In one volume: 'The White Devil,' 'The Duchess of Malfi,' 'The Broken Heart,' ''Tis Pity She's a Whore.' 899

Whitman, Walt (1819–92).
LEAVES OF GRASS, 1855–92. New edition (1947) by *Dr Emory Holloway.* 573

Wilde, Oscar (1854–1900).
PLAYS, PROSE WRITINGS, AND POEMS. Edited, with Introduction, by *Hesketh Pearson.* Including the two plays, 'The Importance of Being Earnest' and 'Lady Windermere's Fan'; his novel, 'The Picture of Dorian Gray'; the poem, 'The Ballad of Reading Gaol'; the essay, 'The Soul of Man,' etc. 858

Wordsworth, William (1770–1850).
POEMS. Edited, with Introductory study, notes, bibliography and full index, by *Philip Wayne,* M.A. 3 vols. 203, 311, 998

REFERENCE

Reader's Guide to Everyman's Library. Compiled by *A. J. Hoppé*. This volume is a new compilation and gives in one alphabetical sequence the names of all the authors, titles and subjects in Everyman's Library and its supplementary series, Everyman's Reference Library and the Children's Illustrated Classics. An Everyman Paperback.
                                                                                                                    1889

Many volumes formerly included in Everyman's Library reference section are now included in Everyman's Reference Library and are bound in larger format.

RELIGION AND PHILOSOPHY

Aquinas, Saint Thomas (1225–74).
   SELECTED WRITINGS. Selected and edited by *Father M. C. D'Arcy*.   953
Aristotle (384–322 B.C.).
   METAPHYSICS. Edited and translated by *John Warrington*. Introduction by *Sir David Ross*, K.B.E., M.A., D.LITT.   (*See also* Science.) 1000
Augustine, Saint (353–430).
   CONFESSIONS. Dr Pusey's Translation, 1838, with Introduction by *A. H. Armstrong*, M.A.   200
   THE CITY OF GOD. Complete text of John Healey's Elizabethan Translation, 1610. Edited by *R. V. G. Tasker*, M.A., B.D., with an Introduction by *Sir Ernest Barker*. 2 vols.   982–3
Bacon, Francis (1561–1626).
   THE ADVANCEMENT OF LEARNING, 1605. Introduction, Notes, Index and Glossary, by *G. W. Kitchin*.   (*See also* Essays.) 719
Berkeley, George (1685–1753).
   A NEW THEORY OF VISION, 1709. Introduction by *A. D. Lindsay*, C.B.E., LL.D. 483
Browne, Sir Thomas (1605–82).
   RELIGIO MEDICI, 1642. New Introduction by *Halliday Sutherland*, M.D., F.R.S.L.   92
Burton, Robert (1577–1640).
   THE ANATOMY OF MELANCHOLY. 1621. 3 vols.   886–8
Chinese Philosophy in Classical Times. Covering the period 1500 B.C.–A.D. 100. Edited and translated, with Introduction and Notes.   973
Cicero, Marcus Tullius (106–43 B.C.).
   THE OFFICES (translated by *Thomas Cockman*, 1699); LAELIUS, ON FRIENDSHIP; CATO, ON OLD AGE; AND SELECT LETTERS (translated by *W. Melmoth*, 1753). With Note on Cicero's Character by De Quincey. Introduction by *John Warrington*. 345
Descartes, René (1596–1650).
   A DISCOURSE ON METHOD, 1637; MEDITATIONS ON THE FIRST PHILOSOPHY, 1641; and PRINCIPLES OF PHILOSOPHY, 1644. Translated by *Prof. J. Veitch*. Introduction by *A. D. Lindsay*, C.B.E., LL.D.   570
Epictetus (*b. c.* A.D. 60).
   MORAL DISCOURSES. THE ENCHIRIDION AND FRAGMENTS. Translated by *Elizabeth Carter* (1717–1806). Edited by *W. H. D. Rouse*, M.A.   404
Francis, Saint (1182–1226).
   THE LITTLE FLOWERS; THE MIRROR OF PERFECTION (by Leo of Assisi); and THE LIFE OF ST FRANCIS (by St Bonaventura). Introduction by *Thomas Okey*.   485
Gore, Charles (1853–1932).
   THE PHILOSOPHY OF THE GOOD LIFE, 1930.   924
Gracián, Baltazer (1601–58).
   THE ORACLE: A Manual of Discretion. Translated and introduced by *E. B. Walton*.   401
Hindu Scriptures. Edited by *Nicol Macnicol*, M.A., D.LITT., D.D. Foreword by *Rabindranath Tagore*.   944
Hooker, Richard (1554–1600).
   OF THE LAWS OF ECCLESIASTICAL POLITY, 1597. Introduction by *G. C. Morris*, M.A.   201–2
Hume, David (1711–76).
   A TREATISE OF HUMAN NATURE, 1739. Intro. by *A. D. Lindsay*, C.B.E., LL.D. 2 vols.   548–9
James, William (1842–1910).
   PAPERS ON PHILOSOPHY. Introduction by *Prof. C. M. Bakewell*.   739
Kant, Immanuel (1724–1804).
   CRITIQUE OF PURE REASON, 1781. With an Introduction by *A. D. Lindsay*, C.B.E., LL.D. Translated by *J. M. D. Meiklejohn*.   909
Kempis, Thomas à (1380?–1471).
   THE IMITATION OF CHRIST, 1471.   484
Koran, The. Rodwell's Translation, 1861. Intro. by *Rev. G. Margoliouth*, M.A.   380
Law, William (1686–1761).
   A SERIOUS CALL TO A DEVOUT AND HOLY LIFE, 1728. Introduction by *Prof. Norman Sykes*, F.B.A., M.A., D.PHIL.   91

Leibniz, Gottfried Wilhelm (1646–1716).
PHILOSOPHICAL WRITINGS. Selected and translated by *Mary Morris*, with an Introduction by *C. R. Morris*, M.A.   905
Locke, John (1632–1704).
AN ESSAY CONCERNING HUMAN UNDERSTANDING, 1690. Complete edition, edited by *Prof. J. W. Yolton* (1961). 2 vols.   332, 984
(*See also* Science.)
More, Sir Thomas (1478–1535).
UTOPIA, 1516; and DIALOGUE OF COMFORT AGAINST TRIBULATION, 1553. Introduction by *John Warrington*. Revised edition (1951).   461
New Testament, The.   93
Newman, John Henry, Cardinal (1801–90).
APOLOGIA PRO VITA SUA, 1864. Introduction by *Sir John Shane Leslie*.   636
(*See also* Essays.)
Nietzsche, Friedrich Wilhelm (1844–1900).
THUS SPAKE ZARATHUSTRA, 1883–91. Translated by *Prof. A. Tille* and revised by *M. M. Bozman*. Introduction (1957) by *Prof. Roy Pascal*, M.A., D.LITT.   892
Pascal, Blaise (1623–62).
PENSÉES, 1670. Translated by *John Warrington*. Introduction by *Louis Lafuma*. This translation is from Lafuma's second edition.   874
Plato (427–347 B.C.).
THE REPUBLIC. Translated, with an Introduction, by *A. D. Lindsay*, C.B.E., LL.D. The greatest achievement of the Greek intellect in philosophy and statecraft.   64
THE TRIAL AND DEATH OF SOCRATES. Newly translated and introduced by *John Warrington*.   459
THE LAWS. The last of Plato's dialogues is here printed in the A. E. Taylor (1869–1945) Translation with translator's Introduction.   275
Prayer Books of King Edward VI. THE FIRST (1549) AND SECOND (1552) PRAYER BOOKS. Introduction by *Bishop Gibson*.   448
Saint Francis de Sales (1567–1622).
AN INTRODUCTION TO THE DEVOUT LIFE. 1609. Translated by *Father Michael Day*.   324
Spinoza, Benedictus de (1632–77).
ETHICS, 1677; and ON THE CORRECTION OF THE UNDERSTANDING, 1687. Translated by *Andrew Boyle*. New Introduction by *T. S. Gregory*.   481

SCIENCE

Aristotle (384–322 B.C.).
POLITICS and THE ATHENIAN CONSTITUTION. Edited and translated by *John Warrington*.   (*See also* Religion and Philosophy.) 605
Boyle, Robert (1627–91).
THE SCEPTICAL CHYMIST, 1661. Introduction by *E. A. Moelwyn-Hughes*.   559
Darwin, Charles (1809–82).
THE ORIGIN OF SPECIES, 1859. The sixth edition embodies Darwin's final additions and revisions. Introduction by *W. R. Thompson*, F.R.S.   811
(*See also* Travel and Topography.)
Eddington, Sir Arthur (1882–1944).
THE NATURE OF THE PHYSICAL WORLD, 1928. Introduction by *Sir Edmund Whittaker*, F.R.S., O.M. Explains Relativity and the Quantum Theory in 'Everyman' terms.   922
Euclid (fl. *c.* 330–*c.* 275 B.C.).
THE ELEMENTS OF EUCLID. Edited by *Isaac Todhunter*, with Introduction by *Sir Thomas L. Heath*, K.C.B., F.R.S.   891
Faraday, Michael (1791–1867).
EXPERIMENTAL RESEARCHES IN ELECTRICITY, 1839–55. With Plates and Diagrams, and an appreciation by *Prof. John Tyndall*.   576
Harvey, William (1578–1657).
THE CIRCULATION OF THE BLOOD. Translated and introduced by *Prof. Kenneth J. Franklin*, Emeritus Professor of Physiology, University of London.   262
Hobbes, Thomas (1588–1679).
LEVIATHAN, 1651. Introduction by *A. D. Lindsay*, C.B.E., LL.D.   691
Howard, John (1726?–90).
THE STATE OF THE PRISONS, 1777. Intro. and Notes by *Kenneth Ruck*.   835
Locke, John (1632–1704).
TWO TREATISES OF CIVIL GOVERNMENT, 1690. Introduction by *Prof. W. S. Carpenter*.   (*See also* Religion and Philosophy.) 751
Malthus, Thomas Robert (1766–1834).
AN ESSAY ON THE PRINCIPLE OF POPULATION, 1798. New Introduction by *Prof. Michael P. Fogarty*, M.A. 2 vols.   692–3
Marx, Karl (1818–83).
CAPITAL, 1867. Translated by *Eden* and *Cedar Paul*. Introduction by *Prof. G. D. H. Cole*. 2 vols.   848–9

Mill, John Stuart (1806–73). (*See also under* Wollstonecraft.)
    UTILITARIANISM, 1863; LIBERTY, 1859; and REPRESENTATIVE GOVERNMENT
    1861. Introduction by *A. D. Lindsay*, C.B.E., LL.D.   482
Owen, Robert (1771–1858).
    A NEW VIEW OF SOCIETY, 1813; and OTHER WRITINGS. Introduction by *G. D. H.*
    Cole.   799
Pearson, Karl (1857–1936).
    THE GRAMMAR OF SCIENCE, 1892.   939
Ricardo, David (1772–1823).
    THE PRINCIPLES OF POLITICAL ECONOMY AND TAXATION, 1817. Introduction by
    Prof. Michael P. Fogarty, M.A.   590
Rousseau, Jean Jacques (1712–78).
    THE SOCIAL CONTRACT, 1762; and OTHER ESSAYS. Introduction by *G. D. H. Cole*.
    (*See also* Biography, Essays.) 660
Smith, Adam (1723–90).
    THE WEALTH OF NATIONS, 1766. Intro. by *Prof. Edwin Seligman*. 2 vols. 412–13
White, Gilbert (1720–93).
    A NATURAL HISTORY OF SELBORNE, 1789. New edition (1949). Introduction and
    Notes by *R. M. Lockley*.   48
Wollstonecraft, Mary (1759–97), THE RIGHTS OF WOMAN, 1792; and **Mill, John Stuart**
    (1806–73), THE SUBJECTION OF WOMEN, 1869. New Introduction by *Pamela*
    Frankau.   825

TRAVEL AND TOPOGRAPHY

Borrow, George (1803–81).
    THE BIBLE IN SPAIN, 1842. Introduction by *Walter Starkie*. C.M.G., C.B.E., M.A.,
    D.LITT.   151
    WILD WALES: the People, Language and Scenery, 1862. Introduction by *David*
    Jones. C.B.E., the painter and Borrovian.   (*See also* Fiction.) 49
Boswell, James (1740–95).
    JOURNAL OF A TOUR TO THE HEBRIDES WITH SAMUEL JOHNSON, 1786. Edited, with
    a new Introduction, by *Lawrence F. Powell*, M.A., HON. D.LITT.   387
Calderón de la Barca, Mme (1804–82).
    ~~LIFE IN MEXICO, 1843. Introduction by *Manuel Romero De Terreros*.~~   664
Cobbett, William (1762–1835).
    RURAL RIDES, 1830. Introduction by *Asa Briggs*, M.A., B.SC. 2 vols.   638–9
Cook, Captain James (1728–79).
    VOYAGES OF DISCOVERY. Edited by *John Barrow*, F.R.S., F.S.A. Introduction by
    Guy Pocock, M.A.   99
Crèvecœur, St John de (1735–1813).
    LETTERS FROM AN AMERICAN FARMER, 1782. Intro. and Notes by *W. Barton Blake*.
    640
Darwin, Charles (1809–82).
    THE VOYAGE OF THE 'BEAGLE,' 1839.   (*See also* Science.) 104
Defoe, Daniel (1661?–1731).
    A TOUR THROUGH THE WHOLE ISLAND OF GREAT BRITAIN, 1724–6. Introduction by
    G. D. H. Cole. 2 vols. Includes the 'Scottish' Journey.   (*See also* Fiction.) 820–1
Hakluyt, Richard (1552–1616).
    VOYAGES. 8 vols.   264–5; 313–14; 338–9; 388–9
Kinglake, Alexander (1809–91).
    EOTHEN, 1844. Introduction by *Major-General Sir Edward Spears, Bart.*, K.B.E.,
    C.B.E., M.C., F.INST.D.   337
Lane, Edward William (1801–76).
    MANNERS AND CUSTOMS OF THE MODERN EGYPTIANS, 1836. With a new Introduction
    by *Moursi Saad el-Din*, of the Egyptian Ministry of Education.   315
Park, Mungo (1771–1806).
    TRAVELS. Introduction (1954) by *Prof. Ronald Miller*, M.A., PH.D.   205
Polo, Marco (1254–1324).
    TRAVELS. Introduction by *John Masefield*.   306
Portuguese Voyages, 1498–1663. Edited by *Charles David Ley*.   986
Stevenson, Robert Louis (1850–94).
    AN INLAND VOYAGE, 1878; TRAVELS WITH A DONKEY, 1879; and THE SILVERADO
    SQUATTERS, 1883. New Introduction by *M. R. Ridley*, M.A.   766
    (*See also* Essays, Fiction.)
Stow, John (1525?–1605).
    THE SURVEY OF LONDON. The fullest account of Elizabethan London.   589
Wakefield, Edward Gibbon (1796–1862).
    A LETTER FROM SYDNEY, AND OTHER WRITINGS ON COLONIZATION. Introduction
    by *Prof. R. C. Mills*.   828
Waterton, Charles (1782–1865).
    WANDERINGS IN SOUTH AMERICA, 1825. Introduction by *Edmund Selous*.   772